Rural Architecture

You are holding a reproduction of an original work that is in the public domain in the United States of America, and possibly other countries.You may freely copy and distribute this work as no entity (individual or corporate) has a copyright on the body of the work.This book may contain prior copyright references, and library stamps (as most of these works were scanned from library copies).These have been scanned and retained as part of the historical artifact.

This book may have occasional imperfections such as missing or blurred pages, poor pictures, errant marks, etc. that were either part of the original artifact, or were introduced by the scanning process. We believe this work is culturally important, and despite the imperfections, have elected to bring it back into print as part of our continuing commitment to the preservation of printed works worldwide. We appreciate your understanding of the imperfections in the preservation process, and hope you enjoy this valuable book.

FARM HOUSE.

RURAL ARCHITECTURE:

BEING A COMPLETE DESCRIPTION

OF

FARM HOUSES, COTTAGES,

AND

OUT BUILDINGS,

COMPRISING

WOOD HOUSES, WORKSHOPS, TOOL HOUSES, CARRIAGE AND WAGON HOUSES, STABLES, SMOKE AND ASH HOUSES, ICE HOUSES, APIARY OR BEE HOUSE, POULTRY HOUSES, RABBITRY, DOVECOTE, PIGGERY, BARNS, AND SHEDS FOR CATTLE, &c., &c., &c.

TOGETHER WITH

LAWNS, PLEASURE GROUNDS AND PARKS; THE FLOWER, FRUIT, AND VEGETABLE GARDENS; ALSO USEFUL AND ORNAMENTAL DOMESTIC ANIMALS FOR THE COUNTRY RESIDENT, &c., &c.

ALSO,

THE BEST METHOD OF

CONDUCTING WATER INTO CATTLE YARDS AND HOUSES.

BY LEWIS F. ALLEN.

BEAUTIFULLY ILLUSTRATED.

NEW YORK:
ORANGE JUDD, PUBLISHER,
41 PARK ROW.
1865.

RURAL ARCHITECTURE.

BEING A COMPLETE DESCRIPTION

OF

FARM HOUSES, COTTAGES,

AND

OUT BUILDINGS,

COMPRISING

WOOD HOUSES, WORKSHOPS, TOOL HOUSES, CARRIAGE AND WAGON HOUSES, STABLES, SMOKE AND ASH HOUSES, ICE HOUSES, APIARY OR BEE HOUSE, POULTRY HOUSES, RABBITRY, DOVECOTE, PIGGERY, BARNS AND SHEDS FOR CATTLE, &c., &c., &c.

TOGETHER WITH

LAWNS, PLEASURE GROUNDS AND PARKS; THE FLOWER, FRUIT AND VEGETABLE GARDEN. ALSO, USEFUL AND ORNAMENTAL DOMESTIC ANIMALS FOR THE COUNTRY RESIDENT, &C., &C., &C.

ALSO,

THE BEST METHOD OF

CONDUCTING WATER INTO CATTLE YARDS AND HOUSES.

BY LEWIS F. ALLEN.

BEAUTIFULLY ILLUSTRATED.

NEW YORK:
ORANGE JUDD, PUBLISHER,
41 PARK ROW.
1865.

Entered according to Act of Congress, in the year 1852.

By LEWIS F. ALLEN,

In the Clerk's Office of the District Court of the United States for the Southern District of New York.

ADVERTISEMENT.

The writer of these pages ought, perhaps, to apologize for attempting a work on a subject, of which he is not a *professional* master, either in design or execution. In the science of Farm buildings he claims no better knowledge than a long practical observation has given him. The thoughts herein submitted for the consideration of those interested in the subject of Farm buildings are the result of that observation, added to his experience in the use of such buildings, and a conviction of the inconveniences attending many of those already planned and erected.

Nor is it intended, in the production of this work, to interfere with the labors of the professional builder. To such builder all who may be disposed to adopt any model or suggestion here presented, are referred, for the various details, in their specifications, and estimates, that may be required; presuming that the designs and descriptions of this work will be sufficient for the guidance of any master builder, in their erection and completion.

ADVERTISEMENT.

But for the solicitation of those who believe that the undersigned could offer some improvements in the construction of Farm buildings for the benefit of our landholders and practical farmers, these pages would probably never have appeared. They are offered in the hope that they may be useful in assisting to form the taste, and add to the comfort of those who are the main instruments in embellishing the face of our country in its most pleasing and agreeable features — the American Farmer.

LEWIS F. ALLEN.

BLACK ROCK, N. Y. 1851.

NOTE.—For throwing the Designs embraced in these pages into their present artistic form, the writer is indebted to Messrs. Otis & Brown, architects, of Buffalo, to whose skill and experience he takes a pleasure in recommending such as may wish instruction in the plans, drawings, specifications, or estimates relating to either of the designs here submitted, or for others of any kind that may be adapted to their purposes.

L. F. A.

CONTENTS.

	Page
PREFATORY,	9
INTRODUCTORY,	13
General Suggestions,	19
Style of Building — Miscellaneous,	23
Position of Farm Houses,	29
Home Embellishments,	32
Material for Farm Buildings,	37
Outside Color of Houses,	42
A Short Chapter on Taste,	48
The Construction of Cellars,	54
Ventilation of Houses,	56
Interior Accommodation of Houses,	65
Chimney Tops,	68
Preliminary to our Designs,	69
DESIGN I. A Farm House,	72
Interior Arrangement,	75
Ground Plan,	76
Chamber Plan,	77
Miscellaneous,	80
As a Tenant House,	81
DESIGN II. Description,	84
Ground and Chamber Plans,	89
Interior Arrangement,	90
Miscellaneous Details,	95
DESIGN III. Description,	101
Ground and Chamber Plans,	105
Interior Arrangement,	106
Miscellaneous,	111

CONTENTS.

	Page
DESIGN IV. Description,	114
Interior Arrangement,	118
Ground Plan,	119
Chamber Plan,	120
Surrounding Plantations, Shrubbery, Walks, &c.	125
Tree Planting in the Highway,	129
DESIGN V. Description,	133
Interior Arrangement,	135
Ground Plan,	136
Chamber Plan,	142
Construction, Cost of Building, &c.,	147
Grounds, Plantations, and Surroundings,	149
DESIGN VI. A Southern, or Plantation House,	154
Interior Arrangement,	159
Chamber Plan,	162
Carriage House,	163
Miscellaneous,	163
Lawn and Park Surroundings,	166
An Ancient New England Family,	168
An American Homestead of the Last Century,	169
Estimate of Cost of Design VI,	172
DESIGN VII. A Plantation House,	175
Interior Arrangement,	176
Ground Plan,	177
Chamber Plan,	178
MISCELLANEOUS,	179
Lawns, Grounds, Parks, and Woods,	181
The Forest Trees of America,	183
Influence of Trees and Forests on the Character of men,	184
Hillhouse and Walter Scott as Tree Planters,	187
Doctor Johnson, no Rural Taste,	188
Fruit Garden — Orchard,	194
How to lay out a Kitchen Garden,	197
Flowers,	202
Wild Flowers of America,	20
Succession of Home Flowers,	206
FARM COTTAGES,	206
DESIGN I, and Ground Plan,	213
Interior Arrangement,	214

CONTENTS.

	Page
Design II, and Ground Plan,	216
Interior Arrangement,	216
Design III, and Ground Plan,	220
Interior Arrangement,	220
Design IV, and Ground Plan,	226
Interior Arrangement,	229
Cottage Outside Decoration,	231
Cottages on the Skirts of Estates,	233
House and Cottage Furniture,	235
Apiary, or Bee House,	241
View of Apiary and Ground Plan, and description,	242
Mode of Taking the Honey,	252
An Ice House,	258
Elevation and Ground Plan,	260
An Ash House and Smoke House,	264
Elevation and Ground Plan,	265
The Poultry House,	267
Elevation and Ground Plan,	269
Interior Arrangement,	271
The Dovecote,	275
Different Varieties of Pigeons,	278
A Piggery,	279
Elevation and Ground Plan,	281
Interior Arrangement,	282
Construction of Piggery — Cost,	283
Farm Barns,	286
Design I. Description,	291
Interior Arrangement, and Main Floor Plan,	293
Underground Plan, and Yard,	295
Design II. Description,	300
Interior Arrangement,	303
Floor Plan,	304
Barn Attachments,	308
Rabbits,	311
Mr. Rotch's Description of his Rabbits,	313
Rabbits and Hutch,	315
Dutch, and English Rabbits,	318
Mode of Feeding,	319
Mr. Rodman's Rabbitry, Elevation, and Floor Plan,	322

CONTENTS.

	Page
Explanations,	323
Loft or Garret, Explanation,	324
Cellar plan, Explanation,	325
Front and Back of Hutches, and Explanation,	326
Dairy Buildings,	330
Cheese Dairy House,	330
Elevation of Dairy House and Ground Plan,	331
Interior Arrangement,	333
The Butter Dairy,	335
The Water Ram,	237
Figure and Description,	338
Granary — Rat-proof,	343
Improved Domestic Animals,	345
Remarks,	353
Waterfowls,	358
The African Goose,	358
China Goose,	359
Bremen Goose,	360
A Word About Dogs,	362
Smooth Terrier,	365
Shepherd Dog,	369
Fish-Ponds,	372

PREFATORY.

This work owes its appearance to the absence of any cheap and popular book on the subject of Rural Architecture, exclusively intended for the farming or agricultural interest of the United States. Why it is, that nothing of the kind has been heretofore attempted for the chief benefit of so large and important a class of our community as our farmers comprise, is not easy to say, unless it be that they themselves have indicated but little wish for instruction in a branch of domestic economy which is, in reality, one of great importance, not only to their domestic enjoyment, but their pecuniary welfare. It is, too, perhaps, among the category of neglects, and in the lack of fidelity to their own interests which pervades the agricultural community of this country, beyond those of any other profession — for we insist that agriculture, in its true and extended sense, is as much a profession as any other pursuit whatever. To the reality of such neglects they have but of late awaked, and indeed are now far too slowly wheeling into line for more active progress in the knowledge pertaining to their own advancement. As an accessory to their labors in such advancement, the present work is intended.

It is an opinion far too prevalent among those engaged in the more active occupations of our people,— fortified indeed in such opinion, by the too frequent example of the farmer himself — that everything connected with agriculture and agricultural life is of a rustic and uncouth character; that it is a profession in which ignorance, as they understand the term, is entirely consistent, and one with which no aspirations of a high or an elevated character should, or at least need be connected. It is a reflection upon the integrity of the great agricultural interest of the country, that any such opinion should prevail; and discreditable to that interest, that its condition or example should for a moment justify, or even tolerate it.

Without going into any extended course of remark, we shall find ample reason for the indifference which has prevailed among our rural population, on the subject of their own domestic architecture, in the absence of familiar and practical works on the subject, by such as have given any considerable degree of thought to it; and, what little thought has been devoted to this branch of building, has been incidentally rather than directly thrown off by those professionally engaged in the finer architectural studies appertaining to luxury and taste, instead of the every-day wants of a strictly agricultural population, and, of consequence, understanding but imperfectly the wants and conveniences of the farm house in its connection with the every-day labors and necessities of farm life.

It is not intended, in these remarks, to depreciate the efforts of those who have attempted to instruct our farmers in this interesting branch of agricultural economy. We owe them a debt of gratitude for what they have accomplished in the introduction of their designs to our notice; and when it is remarked that they are insufficient for the purposes intended, it may be also taken as an admission of our own neglect, that we have so far disregarded the subject ourselves, as to force upon others the duty of essaying to instruct us in a work of which we ourselves should long ago have been the masters.

Why should a farmer, because he *is* a farmer, only occupy an uncouth, outlandish house, any more than a professional man, a merchant, or a mechanic? Is it because he himself is so uncouth and outlandish in his thoughts and manners, that he deserves no better? Is it because his occupation is degrading, his intellect ignorant, his position in life low, and his associations debasing? Surely not. Yet, in many of the plans and designs got up for his accommodation, in the books and publications of the day, all due convenience, to say nothing of the respectability or the elegance of domestic life, is as entirely disregarded as if such qualities had no connection with the farmer or his occupation. We hold, that although many of the practical operations of the farm may be rough, laborious, and untidy, yet they are not, and need not be inconsistent with the knowledge and practice of neatness, order, and even elegance and refinement within doors; and, that the due accommodation of the various things appertaining to farm stock, farm labor, and farm life, should have a tendency to elevate the social position, the associations, thoughts, and entire condition of the farmer. As the man himself — no matter what his occupation — be lodged and fed, so influenced, in a degree, will be his practice in the daily duties of his life. A squalid, miserable tenement, with which they who inhabit it are content, can lead to no elevation of character, no improvement in condition, either social or moral, of its occupants. But, the family comfortably and tidily, although humbly provided in their habitation and domestic arrangements, have usually a corresponding character in their personal relations. A log cabin, even,— and I speak of this primitive American structure with profound affection and regard, as the shelter from which we have achieved the most of our prodigious and rapid agricultural conquests,— may be so constructed as to speak an air of neatness, intelligence, and even refinement in those who inhabit it.

Admitting, then, without further argument, that well conditioned household accommodations are as important to the farmer, even to the indulgence of luxury itself, when it can be afforded, as for those who occupy other and more active pursuits, it is quite important that he be equally well instructed in the art of planning and arranging these accommodations, and in designing, also, the various other structures which are necessary to his wants in their fullest extent. As a question of economy, both in saving and accumulating, good and sufficient buildings are of the first consequence, in a pecuniary light, and when to this are added other considerations touching our social enjoyment, our advancement in temporal condition, our associations, our position and influence in life, and, not least, the decided item of national good taste which the introduction of good buildings throughout our extended agricultural country will give, we find abundant cause for effort in improvement.

It is not intended in our remarks to convey the impression that we Americans, as a people, are destitute of comfortable, and, in many cases, quite convenient household and farm arrangements. Numerous farmeries in every section of the United States, particularly in the older ones, demonstrate most fully, that where our farmers have taken the trouble *to think* on the subject, their ingenuity has been equal, in the items of convenient and economical arrangement of their dwellings and out-buildings, to their demands. But, we are forced to say, that such buildings have been executed, in most cases, with great neglect of *architectural* system, taste, or effect; and, in many instances, to the utter violation of all *propriety* in appearance, or character, as appertaining to the uses for which they are applied.

The character of the farm should be carried out so as to *express* itself in everything which it contains. All should bear a consistent relation with each other. The farmer himself is a plain man. His family are plain people, although none the less worthy, useful, or exalted, on that account. His structures, of every kind, should be plain, also, yet substantial, where substance is required. All these detract nothing from his respectability or his influence in the neighborhood, the town, the county, or the state. A farmer has quite as much business in the field, or about his ordinary occupations, with ragged garments, out at elbows and a crownless hat, as he has to occupy a leaky, wind-broken, and dilapidated house. Neither is he any nearer the mark, with a ruffled shirt, a fancy dress, or gloved hands, when following his plough behind a pair of *fancy* horses, than in living in a finical, pretending house, such as we see stuck up in conspicuous places in many parts of the country. All these are out of place in each extreme, and the one is as absurd, so far as true propriety is concerned, as the other. A fitness of things, or a correspondence of one thing with another, should always be preserved upon the farm, as elsewhere; and there is not a single reason why propriety and good keeping should not as well distinguish it. Nor is there any good cause why the farmer himself should not be a man of taste, in the arrangement and architecture of every building on his place, as well as other men. It is only necessary that he devote a little time to study, in order to give his mind a right direction in all that appertains to this department. Or, if he prefer to employ the ingenuity of others to do his planning,— which, by the way, is, in most cases, the more natural and better course,— he certainly should possess sufficient judgment to see that such plans be correct and will answer his purposes.

The plans and directions submitted in this work are intended to be of the most practical kind; plain, substantial, and applicable, throughout, to the purposes intended, and such as are within the reach — each in their kind — of every farmer in our country. These plans are chiefly original; that is, they are not copied from any in the books, or from any structures with which the writer is familiar. Yet they will doubtless, on examination, be found in several cases to resemble buildings, both in outward appearance and interior arrangement, with which numerous readers may be acquainted. The object, in addition to our own designs, has been to apply practical hints, gathered from other structures in use, which have seemed appropriate for a work of the limited extent here offered, and that may serve to improve the taste of all such as, in building useful structures, desire to embellish their farms and estates in an agreeable style of home architecture, at once pleasant to the eye, and convenient in their arrangement.

INTRODUCTORY.

The lover of country life who looks upon rural objects in the true spirit, and, for the first time surveys the cultivated portions of the United States, will be struck with the incongruous appearance and style of our farm houses and their contiguous buildings; and, although, on examination, he will find many, that in their interior accommodation, and perhaps relative arrangement to each other, are tolerably suited to the business and convenience of the husbandman, still, the feeling will prevail that there is an absence of method, congruity, and correct taste in the architectural structure of his buildings generally, by the American farmer.

We may, in truth, be said to have no architecture at all, as exhibited in our agricultural districts, so far as any correct system, or plan is concerned, as the better taste in building, which a few years past has introduced among us, has been chiefly confined to our cities and towns of rapid growth. Even in the comparatively few buildings in the modern style to be seen in our farming districts, from the various requirements of those buildings being partially unknown to the architect and builder, who had their planning—and upon whom, owing to their own inexperience in such matters, their employers have relied—a majority of such dwellings have turned out, if not absolute failures, certainly not what the necessities of the farmer has demanded. Consequently, save in the mere item of outward appearance—and that, not always—the farmer and cottager have gained nothing, owing to the absurdity in style or arrangement, and want of fitness to circumstances adopted for the occasion.

We have stated that our prevailing rural architecture is discordant in appearance; it may be added, that it is also uncouth, out of keeping with correct rules, and, ofttimes offensive to the eye of any lover of rural harmony. Why it is so, no matter, beyond the apology already given—that of an absence of cultivation, and thought upon the subject. It may be asked, of what consequence is it that the farmer or small propertyholder should conform to given rules, or mode, in the style and arrangement of his dwelling, or out-buildings, so that they be reasonably convenient, and answer his purposes? For the same reason that he requires symmetry, excellence of form or style, in his horses, his cattle, or other farm stock, household furniture, or personal dress. It is an arrangement of artificial objects, in harmony with natural objects; a cultivation of the sympathies which every rational being should have, more or less, with true taste; that costs little or nothing in the attainment, and, when attained, is a source of gratification through life. Every human being is bound, under ordinary circumstances, to leave the world somewhat better, so far as his own acts or exertions are concerned, than he found it, in the exercise of such faculties as have been given him. Such duty, among thinking men, is conceded, so far as the moral world is concerned; and why not in the artificial? So far as the influence for good goes, in all practical use, from the building of a temple, to the knocking together of a pig-stye—a labor of years, or the work of a day—the exercise of a correct taste is important, in a degree.

In the available physical features of a country, no land upon earth exceeds North America. From scenery the most sublime, through the several gradations of magnificence and grandeur, down to the simply picturesque and beautiful, in all variety and shade; in compass vast, or in area limited, we have an endless variety, and, with a pouring out of God's harmonies in the creation, without a parallel, inviting every intelligent mind to study their features and character, in adapting them to his own uses, and, in so doing, to even embellish—if such a thing be possible—such exquisite objects with his own most ingenious handiwork. Indeed, it is a profanation to do otherwise; and when so to improve them requires no extraordinary application of skill, or any extravagant outlay in expense, not to plan and to build in conformity with good taste, is an absolute barbarism, inexcusable in a land like ours, and among a population claiming the intelligence we do, or making but a share of the general progress which we exhibit.

It is the idea of some, that a house or building which the farmer or planter occupies, should, in shape, style, and character, be like some of the stored-up commodities of his farm or plantation. We cannot subscribe to this suggestion. We know of no good reason why the walls of a farm house should appear like a hay rick, or its roof like the thatched covering to his wheat stacks, because such are the shapes best adapted to preserve his crops, any more than the grocer's habitation should be made to imitate a tea chest, or the shipping merchant's a rum puncheon, or cotton bale. We have an idea that the farmer, or the planter, according to his means and requirements, should be as well housed and accommodated, and in as agreeable style, too, as any other class of community; not in like character, in all things, to be sure, but in his own proper way and manner. Nor do we know why a farm house should assume a peculiarly primitive or uncultivated style of architecture, from other sensible houses. That it be a *farm* house, is sufficiently apparent from its locality upon the farm itself; that its interior arrangement be for the convenience of the in-door farm work, and the proper accommodation of the farmer's family, should be quite as apparent; but, that it should assume an uncouth or clownish aspect, is as unnecessary as that the farmer himself should be a boor in his manners, or a dolt in his intellect.

The farm, in its proper cultivation, is the foundation of all human prosperity, and from it is derived the main wealth of the community. From the farm chiefly springs that energetic class of men, who replace the enervated and physically decaying multitude continually thrown off in the waste-weir of our great commercial and manufacturing cities and towns, whose population, without the infusion — and that continually — of the strong, substantial, and vigorous life blood of the country, would soon dwindle into insignificance and decrepitude. Why then should not this first, primitive, health-enjoying and life-sustaining class of our people be equally accommodated in all that gives to social and substantial life, its due development? It is absurd to deny them by others, or that they deny themselves, the least of such advantages, or that any mark of *caste* be attempted to separate them from any other class or profession of equal wealth, means, or necessity. It is quite as well to say that the farmer should worship on the Sabbath in a *meeting-house*, built after the fashion of his barn, or that his district school house should look like a stable, as that his dwelling should not exhibit all that cheerfulness and respectability in form and feature which belongs to the houses of any class of our population whatever. Not that the farm house should be like the town or the village house, in character, style, or architecture, but that it should, in its own proper character, express all the comfort, repose, and quietude which belong to the retired and thoughtful occupation of him who inhabits it. Sheltered in its own secluded, yet independent domain, with a cheerful, *intelligent* exterior, it should exhibit all the pains-taking in home embellishment and rural decoration that becomes its position, and which would make it an object of attraction and regard.

RURAL ARCHITECTURE.

GENERAL SUGGESTIONS.

In ascertaining what is desirable to the conveniences, or the necessities in our household arrangement, it may be not unprofitable to look about us, and consider somewhat, the existing condition of the structures too many of us now inhabit, and which, in the light of true fitness for the objects designed, are inconvenient, absurd, and out of all harmony of purpose; yet, under the guidance of a better skill, and a moderate outlay, might be well adapted, in most cases, to our convenience and comfort, and quite well, to a reasonable standard of taste in architectural appearance.

At the threshold — not of the house, but of this treatise — it may be well to remark that it is not here assumed that there has been neither skill, ingenuity, nor occasional good taste exhibited, for many generations back, in the United States, in the construction of farm and country houses. On the contrary, there are found in the older states many farm and country houses that are almost models, in their way, for convenience in the main purposes required of structures of their kind, and such as can hardly be altered for the better. Such, however, form the exception, not the rule; yet instead of standing as objects for imitation, they have been ruled out as antiquated, and unfit for modern builders to consult, who have in the introduction of some real improvements, also left out, or discarded much that is valuable, and, where true comfort is concerned, indispensable to perfect housekeeping. Alteration is not always improvement, and in the rage for innovation of all kinds, among much that is valuable, a great deal in house-building has been introduced that is absolutely pernicious. Take, for instance, some of our ancient-looking country houses of the last century, which, in America, we call old. See their ample dimensions; their heavy, massive walls; their low, comfortable ceilings; their high gables; sharp roofs; deep porches, and spreading eaves, and contrast them with the ambitious, tall, proportionless, and card-sided things of a modern date, and draw the comparison in true comfort, which the ancient mansion really affords, by the side of the other. Bating its huge chimneys, its wide fire-places, its heavy beams dropping below the ceiling overhead, and the lack of some modern conveniences, which, to be added, would give all that is desired, and every man possessed of a proper judgment will concede the superiority to the house of the last century.

That American house-building of the last fifty years is out of joint, requires no better proof than that the main improvements which have been applied to our rural architecture, are in the English style of farm and country houses of two or three centuries ago; so, in that particular, we acknowledge the better taste and judgment of our ancestors. True, modern luxury, and in some particulars, modern improvement has made obsolete, if not absurd, many things considered indispensable in a ruder age. The wide, rambling halls and rooms; the huge, deep fire-places in the chimneys; the proximity of out-buildings, and the contiguity of stables, ricks, and cattle-yards — all these are wisely contracted, dispensed with, or thrown off to a proper distance; but instead of such style being abandoned altogether, as has too often been done, the house itself might better have been partially reformed, and the interior arrangement adapted to modern convenience. Such changes have in some instances been made; and when so, how often does the old mansion, with outward features in good preservation, outspeak, in all the expression of home-bred comforts, the flashy, gimcrack neighbor, which in its plenitude of modern pretension looks so flauntingly down upon it!

We cannot, in the United States, consistently adopt the domestic architecture of any other country, throughout, to our use. We are different in our institutions, our habits, our agriculture, our climates. Utility is our chief object, and coupled with that, the indulgence of an agreeable taste may be permitted to every one who creates a home for himself, or founds one for his family. The frequent changes of estates incident to our laws, and the many inducements held out to our people to change their locality or residence, in the hope of bettering their condition, is a strong hindrance to the adoption of a universally correct system in the construction of our buildings; deadening, as the effect of such changes that home feeling which should be a prominent trait of agricultural character. An attachment to locality is not a conspicuous trait of American character; and if there be a people on earth boasting a high civilization and intelligence, who are at the same time a roving race, the Americans are that people; and we acknowledge it a blemish in our domestic and social constitution.

Such remark is not dropped invidiously, but as a reason why we have thus far made so little progress in the arts of home embellishment, and in clustering about our habitations those innumerable attractions which win us to them sufficiently to repel the temptation so often presented to our enterprise, our ambition, or love of gain — and these not always successful — in seeking other and distant places of abode. If, then, this tendency to change — a want of attachment to any one spot — is a reason why we have been so indifferent to domestic architecture; and if the study and practice of a better system of building tends to cultivate a home feeling, why should it not be encouraged? Home attachment is a virtue. Therefore let that virtue be cherished. And if any one study tend to exalt our taste, and promote our enjoyment, let us cultivate that study to the highest extent within our reach.

STYLE OF BUILDING.--MISCELLANEOUS

Diversified as are the features of our country in climate, soil, surface, and position, no one style of rural architecture is properly adapted to the whole; and it is a gratifying incident to the indulgence in a variety of taste, that we possess the opportunity which we desire in its display to almost any extent in mode and effect. The Swiss chalêt may hang in the mountain pass; the pointed Gothic may shoot up among the evergreens of the rugged hill-side; the Italian roof, with its overlooking campanile, may command the wooded slope or the open plain; or the quaint and shadowy style of the old English mansion, embosomed in its vines and shrubbery, may nestle in the quiet, shaded valley, all suited to their respective positions, and each in harmony with the natural features by which it is surrounded. Nor does the effect which such structures give to the landscape in an ornamental point of view, require that they be more imposing in character than the necessities of the occasion may demand. True economy demands a structure sufficiently spacious to accommodate its occupants in the best manner, so far as convenience and comfort are concerned in a dwelling; and its conformity to just rules in architecture need not be additionally expensive or troublesome. He who builds at all, if it be anything beyond a rude or temporary shelter, may as easily and cheaply build in accordance with correct rules of architecture, as against such rules; and it no more requires an extravagance in cost or a wasteful occupation of room to produce a given effect in a house suited to humble means, than in one of profuse accommodation. Magnificence, or the attempt at magnificence in building, is the great fault with Americans who aim to build out of the common line; and the consequence of such attempt is too often a failure, apparent, always, at a glance, and of course a perfect condemnation in itself of the judgment as well as taste of him who undertakes it.

Holding our tenures as we do, with no privilege of entail to our posterity, an eye to his own interest, or to that of his family who is to succeed to his estate, should admonish the builder of a house to the adoption of a plan which will, in case of the sale of the estate, involve no serious loss. He should build such a house as will be no detriment, in its expense, to the selling value of the land on which it stands, and always fitted for the spot it occupies. Hence, an imitation of the high, extended, castellated mansions of England, or the Continent, although in miniature, are altogether unsuited to the American farmer or planter, whose lands, instead of increasing in his family, are continually subject to division, or to sale in mass, on his own demise; and when the estate is encumbered with unnecessarily large and expensive buildings, they become an absolute drawback to its value in either event. An expensive house requires a corresponding expense to maintain it, otherwise its effect is lost, and many a worthy owner of a costly mansion has been driven to sell and abandon his estate altogether, from his unwillingness or inability to support "the establishment" which it entailed; when, if the dwelling were only such as the estate required and could reasonably maintain, a contented and happy home would have remained to himself and family. It behooves, therefore, the American builder to examine well his premises, to ascertain the actual requirements of his farm or plantation, in convenience and accommodation, and build only to such extent, and at such cost as shall not impoverish his means, nor cause him future disquietude.

Another difficulty with us is, that we oftener build to gratify the eyes of the public than our own, and fit up our dwellings to accommodate "company" or visitors, rather than our own families; and in the indulgence of this false notion, subject ourselves to perpetual inconvenience for the gratification of occasional hospitality or ostentation. This is all wrong. A house should be planned and constructed for the use of the household, with *incidental* accommodation for our immediate friends or guests — which can always be done without sacrifice to the comfort or convenience of the regular inmates. In this remark, a stinted and parsimonious spirit is not suggested. A liberal appropriation of rooms in every department; a spare chamber or two, or an additional room on the ground floor, looking to a possible increase of family, and the indulgence of an easy hospitality, should always govern the resident of the country in erecting his dwelling. The enjoyments of society and the intercourse of friends, sharing for the time, our own table and fireside, is a crowning pleasure of country life; and all this may be done without extraordinary expense, in a wise construction of the dwelling.

The farm house too, should comport in character and area with the extent and capacity of the farm itself, and the main design for which it is erected. To the farmer proper — he who lives from the income which the farm produces — it is important to know the extent of accommodation required for the economical management of his estate, and then to build in accordance with it, as well as to suit his own position in life, and the station which he and his family hold in society. The owner of a hundred acre farm, living upon the income he receives from it, will require less house room than he who tills equally well his farm of three, six, or ten hundred acres. Yet the numbers in their respective families, the relative position of each in society, or their taste for social intercourse may demand a larger or smaller household arrangement, regardless of the size of their estates; still, the dwellings on each should bear, in extent and expense, a consistent relation to the land itself, and the means of its owner. For instance: a farm of one hundred acres may safely and economically erect and maintain a house costing eight hundred to two thousand dollars, while one of five hundred to a thousand acres may range in an expenditure of twenty-five hundred to five thousand dollars in its dwelling, and all be consistent with a proper economy in farm management.

Let it be understood, that the above sums are named as simply comporting with a financial view of the subject, and such as the economical management of the estate may warrant. To one who has no regard to such consideration, this rule of expenditure will not apply. He may invest any amount he so chooses in building beyond, if he only be content to pocket the loss which he can never expect to be returned in an increased value to the property, over-and above the price of cheaper buildings. On the other hand, he would do well to consider that a farm is frequently worth less to an ordinary purchaser, with an extravagant house upon it, than with an economical one, and in many cases will bring even less in market, in proportion as the dwelling is expensive. *Fancy* purchasers are few, and fastidious, while he who buys only for a home and an occupation, is governed solely by the profitable returns the estate will afford upon the capital invested.

There is again a grand error which many fall into in building, looking as they do only at the extent of wood and timber, or stone and mortar in the structure, and paying no attention to the surroundings, which in most cases contribute more to the effect of the establishment than the structure itself, and which, if uncultivated or neglected, any amount of expenditure in building will fail to give that completeness and perfection of character which every homestead should command. Thus the tawdry erections in imitation of a cast-off feudalism in Europe, or a copying of the massive piles of more recent date abroad, although in miniature, both in extent and cost, is the sheerest affectation, in which no sensible man should ever indulge. It is out of all keeping, or propriety with other things, as we in this country have them, and the indulgence of all such fancies is sooner or later regretted. Substance, convenience, purpose, harmony—all, perhaps, better summed up in the term EXPRESSION—these are the objects which should govern the construction of our dwellings and out-buildings, and in their observance we can hardly err in the acquisition of what will promote the highest enjoyment which a dwelling can bestow.

POSITION.

The site of a dwelling should be an important study with every country builder; for on this depends much of its utility, and in addition to that, a large share of the enjoyment which its occupation will afford. Custom, in many parts of the United States, in the location of the farm buildings, gives advantages which are denied in others. In the south, and in the slave states generally, the planter builds, regardless of roads, on the most convenient site his plantation presents; the farmer of German descent, in Pennsylvania and some other states, does the same: while the Yankee, be he settled where he will, either in the east, north, or west, inexorably huddles himself immediately upon the highway, whether his possessions embrace both sides of it or not, disregarding the facilities of access to his fields, the convenience of tilling his crops, or the character of the ground which his buildings may occupy, seeming to have no other object than proximity to the road — as if his chief business was upon that, instead of its being simply a convenience to his occupation. To the last, but little choice is left; and so long as a close connection with the thoroughfare is to control, he is obliged to conform to accident in what should be a matter of deliberate choice and judgment. Still, there are right and wrong positions for a house, which it is necessary to discuss, regardless of conventional rules, and they should be considered in the light of propriety alone.

A fitness to the purposes for which the dwelling is constructed should, unquestionably, be the governing point in determining its position. The site should be dry, and slightly declining, if possible, on every side; but if the surface be level, or where water occasionally flows from contiguous grounds, or on a soil naturally damp, it should be thoroughly drained of all superfluous moisture. That is indispensable to the preservation of the house itself, and the health of its inmates. The house should so stand as to present an agreeable aspect from the main points at which it is seen, or the thoroughfares by which it is approached. It should be so arranged as to afford protection from wind and storm, to that part most usually occupied, as well as be easy of access to the out-buildings appended to it. It should have an unmistakable front, sides, and rear; and the uses to which its various parts are applied, should distinctly appear in its outward character. It should combine all the advantages of soil, cultivation, water, shade, and shelter, which the most liberal gratification, consistent with the circumstances of the owner, may demand. If a site on the estate command a prospect of singular beauty, other things equal, the dwelling should embrace it; if the luxury of a stream, or a sheet of water in repose, present itself, it should, if possible, be enjoyed; if the shade and protection of a grove be near, its benefits should be included; in fine, any object in itself desirable, and not embarrassing to the main purposes of the dwelling and its appendages, should be turned to the best account, and appropriated in such manner as to combine all that is desirable both in beauty and effect, as well as in utility, to make up a perfect whole in the family residence.

Attached to the building site should be considered the quality of the soil, as affording cultivation and growth to shrubbery and trees,— at once the ornament most effective to all domestic buildings, grateful to the eye always, as objects of admiration and beauty— delightful in the repose they offer in hours of lassitude or weariness; and to them, that indispensable feature in a perfect arrangement, the garden, both fruit and vegetable, should be added. Happily for the American, our soils are so universally adapted to the growth of vegetation in all its varieties, that hardly a farm of considerable size can be found which does not afford tolerable facilities for the exercise of all the taste which one may indulge in the cultivation of the garden as well as in the planting and growth of trees and shrubbery; and a due appropriation of these to an agreeable residence is equal in importance to the style and arrangement of the house itself.

The site selected for the dwelling, and the character of the scenery and objects immediately surrounding it, should have a controlling influence upon the style in which the house is to be constructed. A fitness and harmony in all these is indispensable to both expression and effect. And in their determination, a single object should not control, but the entire picture, as completed, should be embraced in the view; and that style of building constituting the most agreeable whole, as filling the eye with the most grateful sensations, should be the one selected with which to fill up and complete the design.

HOME EMBELLISHMENTS.

A discussion of the objects by way of embellishment, which may be required to give character and effect to a country residence, would embrace a range too wide, in all its parts, for a simply practical treatise like this; and general hints on the subject are all indeed, that will be required, as no specific rules or directions can be given which would be applicable, indiscriminately, to guide the builder in the execution of his work. A dwelling house, no matter what the style, standing alone, either on hill or plain, apart from other objects, would hardly be an attractive sight. As a mere representation of a particular style of architecture, or as a model of imitation, it might excite our admiration, but it would not be an object on which the eye and the imagination could repose with satisfaction. It would be incomplete unless accompanied by such associates as the eye is accustomed to embrace in the full gratification of the sensations to which that organ is the conductor. But assemble around that dwelling subordinate structures, trees, and shrubbery properly disposed, and it becomes an object of exceeding interest and pleasure in the contemplation. It is therefore, that the particular style or outward arrangement of the house is but a part of what should constitute the general effect, and such style is to be consulted only so far as it may in itself please the taste, and give benefit or utility in the purposes for which it is intended. Still, the architectural design should be in harmony with the features of the surrounding scenery, and is thus important in completing the effect sought, and which cannot be accomplished without it.

A farm with its buildings, or a simple country residence with the grounds which enclose it, or a cottage with its door-yard and garden, should be finished sections of the landscape of which it forms a part, or attractive points within it; and of consequence, complete each within itself, and not dependent upon distant accessories to support it — an *imperium in imperio*, in classic phrase. A tower, a monument, a steeple, or the indistinct outline of a distant town may form a striking feature in a pictorial design and the associations connected with them, or, the character in which they are contemplated may allow them to stand naked and unadorned by other objects, and still permit them to fill up in perfect harmony the picture. This idea will illustrate the importance of embellishment, not only in the substitution of trees as necessary appendages to a complete rural establishment, but in the erection of all the buildings necessary for occupation in any manner, in form and position, to give effect from any point of view in which the homestead may be seen. General appearance should not be confined to one quarter alone, but the house and its surroundings on every side should show completeness in design and harmony in execution; and although humble, and devoted to the meanest purposes, a portion of these erections may be, yet the character of utility or necessity which they maintain, gives them an air of dignity, if not of grace. Thus, a house and out-buildings flanked with orchards, or a wood, on which they apparently fall back for support, fills the eye at once with not only a beautiful group, in themselves combined, but associate the idea of repose, of comfort, and abundance — indispensable requisites to a perfect farm residence. They also seem to connect the house and out-buildings with the fields beyond, which are of necessity naked of trees, and gradually spread the view abroad over the farm until it mingles with, or is lost in the general landscape.

These remarks may seem too refined, and as out of place here, and trenching upon the subject of Landscape Gardening, which is not designed to be a part, or but an incidental one of the present work, yet they are important in connection with the subject under discussion. The proper disposition of trees and shrubbery around, or in the vicinity of buildings, is far too little understood, although tree planting about our dwellings is a practice pretty general throughout our country. Nothing is more common than to see a man build a house, perhaps in most elaborate and expensive style, and then plant a row of trees close upon the front, which when grown will shut it almost entirely out of view; while he leaves the rear as bald and unprotected as if it were a barn or a horse-shed — as if in utter ignorance, as he probably is, that his house is more effectively set off by a *flanking* and *background* of tree and shrubbery, than in front. And this is called good taste! Let us examine it. Trees near a dwelling are desirable for shade; *shelter* they do not afford except in masses, which last is always better given to the house itself by a veranda. Immediately adjoining, or within touching distance of a house, trees create dampness, more or less litter, and frequently vermin. They injure the walls and roofs by their continual shade and dampness. They exclude the rays of the sun, and prevent a free circulation of air. Therefore, *close* to the house, trees are absolutely pernicious, to say nothing of excluding all its architectural effect from observation; when, if planted at proper distances, they compose its finest ornaments.

If it be necessary to build in good taste at all, it is quite as necessary that such good taste be kept in view throughout. A country dwelling should always be a conspicuous object in its full character and outline, from one or more prominent points of observation; consequently all plantations of tree or shrubbery in its immediate vicinity should be considered as aids to show off the house and its appendages, instead of becoming the principal objects of attraction in themselves. Their disposition should be such as to create a perfect and agreeable whole, when seen in connection with the house itself. They should also be so placed as to open the surrounding landscape to view in its most attractive features, from the various parts of the dwelling. Much in the effective disposition of trees around the dwelling will thus depend upon the character of the country seen from it, and which should control to a great extent their position. A single tree, of grand and stately dimensions, will frequently give greater effect than the most studied plantations. A ledge of rock, in the clefts of which wild vines may nestle, or around which a mass of shrubbery may cluster, will add a charm to the dwelling which an elaborate cultivation would fail to bestow; and the most negligent apparel of nature in a thousand ways may give a character which we might strive in vain to accomplish by our own invention. In the efforts to embellish our dwellings or grounds, the strong natural objects with which they are associated should be consulted, always keeping in view an *expression* of the chief character to which the whole is applied.

MATERIAL FOR FARM BUILDINGS.

In a country like ours, containing within its soils and upon its surface such an abundance and variety of building material, the composition of our farm erections must depend in most cases upon the ability or the choice of the builder himself.

Stone is the most durable, in the long run the cheapest, and as a consequence, the *best* material which can be furnished for the walls of a dwelling. With other farm buildings circumstances may govern differently; still, in many sections of the United States, even stone cannot be obtained, except at an expense and inconvenience altogether forbidding its use. Yet it is a happy relief that where stone is difficult, or not at all to be obtained, the best of clay for bricks, is abundant; and in almost all parts of our country, even where building timber is scarce, its transportation is so comparatively light, and the facilities of removing it are so cheap, that wood is accessible to every one. Hence we may indulge in almost every fitting style of architecture and arrangement, to which either kind of these materials are best adapted. We shall slightly discuss them as applicable to our purposes.

Stone is found either on the surface, or in quarries under ground. On the surface they lie chiefly as bowlders of less or greater size, usually of hard and durable kinds. Large bowlders may be either blasted, or split with wedges into sufficiently available shapes to lay in walls with mortar; or if small, they may with a little extra labor, be fitted by the aid of good mortar into equally substantial wall as the larger masses. In quarries they are thrown out, either by blasting or splitting in layers, so as to form regular courses when laid up; and all their varieties may, *unhammered*, except to strike off projecting points or angles, be laid up with a sufficiently smooth face to give fine effect to a building. Thus, when easily obtained, aside from the greater advantages of their durability, stone is as cheap in the first instance as lumber, excepting in new districts of country where good building lumber is the chief article of production, and cheaper than brick in any event. Stone requires no paint. Its color is a natural, therefore an agreeable one, be it usually what it may, although some shades are more grateful to the eye than others; yet it is always in harmony with natural objects, and particularly so on the farm where everything ought to wear the most substantial appearance. The outer walls of a stone house should always be *firred* off inside for *lathing* and plastering, to keep them thoroughly dry. Without that, the rooms are liable to dampness, which would penetrate through the stone into the inside plastering unless cut off by an open space of air between.

Bricks, where stone is not found, supply its place

tolerably well. When made of good clay, rightly tempered with sand, and well burned, they will in a wall remain for centuries, and as far as material is concerned, answer all purposes. Brick walls may be thinner than stone walls, but they equally require "firring off" for inside plastering, and in addition, they need the aid of paint quite as often as wood, to give them an agreeable color—bricks themselves not usually being in the category of desirable colors or shades.

Wood, when abundant and easily obtained, is worked with the greatest facility, and on many accounts, is the cheapest material, *for the time*, of which a building can be constructed. But it is perishable. It requires every few years a coat of paint, and is always associated with the idea of decay. Yet wood may be moulded into an infinite variety of form to please the eye, in the indulgence of any peculiar taste or fancy.

We cannot, in the consideration of material for house-building therefore, urge upon the farmer the adoption of either of the above named materials to the preference of another, in any particular structure he may require; but leave him to consult his own circumstances in regard to them, as best he may. But this we will say: *If it be possible*, never lay a *cellar* or underground wall of perishable material, such as wood or soft bricks; nor build with soft or *unburnt* bricks in a wall exposed to the weather *anywhere;* nor with stone which is liable to crumble or disintegrate by the action of frost or water upon it. We are aware that unburnt bricks have been strongly recommended for house-building in America; but from observation, we are fully persuaded that they are worthless for any *permanent* structure, and if used, will in the end prove a dead loss in their application. Cottages, outbuildings, and other cheap erections on the farm, for the accommodation of laborers, stock, or crops, may be made of wood, where wood is the cheapest and most easily obtained; and, even taking its perishable nature into account, it may be the most economical. In their construction, it may be simply a matter of calculation with him who needs them, to calculate the first cost of any material he has at hand, or may obtain, and to that add the interest upon it, the annual wear and tear, the insurance, and the period it may last, to determine this matter to his entire satisfaction — always provided he have the means at hand to do either. But other considerations generally control the American farmer. His pocket is apt more often to be pinched, than his choice is to be at fault; and this weighty argument compels him into the "make shift" system, which perhaps in its results, provided the main chance be attained, is quite as advantageous to his interests as the other.

As a general remark, all buildings should show for themselves, what they are built of. Let stone be stone; bricks show on their own account; and of all things, put no counterfeit by way of plaster, stucco, or other false pretence other than paint, or a durable wash upon wood: it is a miserable affectation always, and of no possible use whatever. All counterfeit of any kind as little becomes the buildings of the farmer, as the gilded *pinchbeck* watch would fit the finished attire of a gentleman.

Before submitting the several designs proposed for this work, it may be remarked, that in addressing them to a climate strictly American, we have in every instance adopted the wide, steeply-pitched roof, with broad eaves, gables and cornices, as giving protection, shade, and shelter to the walls; thus keeping them dry and in good preservation, and giving that well housed, and comfortable expression, so different from the stiff, pinched, and tucked-up look in which so many of the haberdasher-built houses of the present day exult.

We give some examples of the hipped roof, because they are convenient and cheap in their construction; and we also throw into the designs a lateral direction to the roofs of the wings, or connecting parts of the building. This is sometimes done for effect in architectural appearance, and sometimes for the economy and advantage of the building itself. Where roofs thus intersect or connect with a side wall, the connecting gutters should be made of copper, zinc, lead, galvanized iron, or tin, into which the shingles, if they be covered with that material, should be laid so as to effectually prevent leakage. The *eave gutters* should be of copper, zinc, lead, galvanized iron or tin, also, and placed *at least* one foot back from the edge of the roof, and lead the water into conductors down the wall into the cistern or elsewhere, as may be required. If the water be not needed, and the roof be wide over the walls, there is no objection to let it pass off naturally, if it be no inconvenience to the ground below, and can run off, or be absorbed into the ground without detriment to the cellar walls. All this must be subject to the judgment of the proprietor himself.

OUTSIDE COLOR.

We are not among those who cast off, and on a sudden condemn, as out of all good taste, the time-honored white house with its green blinds, often so tastefully gleaming out from beneath the shade of summer trees; nor do we doggedly adhere to it, except when in keeping, by contrast or otherwise, with everything around it. For a century past white has been the chief color of our wooden houses, and often so of brick ones, in the United States. This color has been supposed to be strong and durable, being composed chiefly of white lead; and as it *reflected* the rays of the sun instead of *absorbing* them, as some of the darker colors do, it was thus considered a better preserver of the weather-boarding from the cracks which the fervid heat of the sun is apt to make upon it, than the darker colors. White, consequently, has always been considered, until within a few years past, as a fitting and *tasteful* color for dwellings, both in town and country. A new school of *taste* in colors has risen, however, within a few years past, among us; about the same time, too, that the recent gingerbread and beadwork style of country building was introduced. And these were both, as all *new* things are apt to be, carried to extremes. Instead of *toning* down the glare of the white into some quiet, neutral shade, as a straw color; a drab of different hues — always an agreeable and appropriate color for a dwelling, particularly when the door and window casings are dressed with a deeper or lighter shade, as those shades predominate in the main body of the house; or a natural and soft *wood* color, which also may be of various shades; or even the warm russet hue of some of our rich stones — quite appropriate, too, as applied to wood, or bricks — the *fashion* must be followed without either rhyme or reason, and hundreds of our otherwise pretty and imposing country houses have been daubed over with the dirtiest, gloomiest pigment imaginable, making every habitation which it touched look more like a funeral appendage than a cheerful, life-enjoying home We candidly say that we have no sort of affection for such sooty daubs. The fashion which dictates them is a barbarous, false, and arbitrary fashion; void of all natural taste in its inception; and to one who has a cheerful, life-loving spirit about him, such colors have no more fitness on his dwelling or out-buildings, than a tomb would have in his lawn or dooryard.

Locality, amplitude of the buildings, the purpose to which they are applied — every consideration connected with them, in fact, should be consulted, as to color. Stone will give its own color; which, by the way, some prodigiously smart folks *paint* — quite as decorous or essential, as to "paint the lily." Brick sometimes must be painted, but it should be of a color in keeping with its character,— of substance and dignity; not a counterfeit of stone, or to cheat him who looks upon it into a belief that it may be marble, or other unfounded pretension. A *warm* russet is most appropriate for brick-work of any kind of color — the color of a russet apple, or undressed leather — shades that comport with Milton's beautiful idea of

"*Russet* lawns and fallows *gray.*"

Red and yellow are both too glaring, and slate, or lead colors too somber and cold. It is, in fact, a strong argument in favor of bricks in building, where they can be had as cheap as stone or wood, that any color can be given to them which the good taste of the builder may require, in addition to their durability, which, when made of good material, and properly burned, is quite equal to stone. In a wooden structure one may play with his fancy in the way of color, minding in the operation, that he does not play the mountebank, and like the clown in the circus, make his tattooed tenement the derision of men of correct taste, as the other does his burlesque visage the ridicule of his auditors.

A *wooden* country house, together with its out-buildings, should always be of a cheerful and softly-toned color — a color giving a feeling of warmth and comfort; nothing glaring or flashy about it. And yet, such buildings should not, in their color, any more than in their architecture, appear as if *imitating* either stone or brick. Wood, of itself, is light. One cannot build a *heavy* house of wood, as compared with brick or stone. Therefore all imitation or device which may lead to a belief that it may be other than what it really is, is nothing less than a fraud—not criminal, we admit, but none the less a fraud upon good taste and architectural truth.

It is true that in this country we cannot afford to place in stone and brick buildings those ornate trimmings and appendages which, perhaps, if economy were not to be consulted, might be more durably constructed of stone, but at an expense too great to be borne by those of moderate means. Yet it is not essential that such appendages should be of so expensive material. The very purposes to which they are applied, as a parapet, a railing, a balustrade, a portico, piazza, or porch; all these may be of wood, even when the material of the house *proper* is of the most durable kind; and by being painted in keeping with the building itself, produce a fine effect, and do no violence to good taste or the most fastidious propriety. They may be even sanded to a color, and grained, stained, or otherwise brought to an identity, almost, with the material of the house, and be quite proper, because they simply are *appendages* of convenience, necessity, or luxury, to the building itself, and may be taken away without injuring or without defacing the main structure. They are not a *material* part of the building itself, but reared for purposes which may be dispensed with. It is a matter of taste or preference, that they were either built there, or that they remain permanently afterward, and of consequence, proper that they be of wood. Yet they should not *imitate* stone or brick. They should still show that they *are* of wood, but in color and outside preservation denote that they are appendages to a *stone* or *brick* house, by complying with the proper shades in color which predominate in the building itself, and become their own subordinate character.

Not being a professional painter, or compounder of colors, we shall offer no receipts or specifics for painting or washing buildings. Climate affects the composition of both paints and washes, and those who are competent in this line, are the proper persons to dictate their various compositions; and we do but common justice to the skill and intelligence of our numerous mechanics, when we recommend to those who contemplate building, to apply forthwith to such as are masters of their trade for all the information they require on the various subjects connected with it. One who sets out to be his own architect, builder, and painter, is akin to the lawyer in the proverb, who has a fool for his client, when pleading his own case, and quite as apt to have quack in them all. Hints, general outlines, and oftentimes matters of detail in interior convenience, and many other minor affairs may be given by the proprietor, when he is neither a professional architect, mechanic, or even an amateur; but in all things affecting the *substantial* and important parts of his buildings, he should consult those who are proficient and experienced in the department on which he consults them. And it may perhaps be added that none *professing* to be such, are competent, unless well instructed, and whose labors have met the approbation of those competent to judge.

There is one kind of color, prevailing to a great extent in many parts of our country, particularly the northern and eastern, which, in its effect upon any one having an eye to a fitness of things in country buildings, is a monstrous perversion of good taste. That is the glaring red, made up of Venetian red, ochre, or Spanish brown, with doors and windows touched off with white. The only apology we have ever heard given for such a barbarism was, that it is a good, strong, and lasting color. We shall not go into an examination as to that fact, but simply answer, that if it be so, there are other colors, not more expensive, which are equally strong and durable, and infinitely more tasteful and fitting. There can be nothing less comporting with the simplicity of rural scenery, than a glaring red color on a building. It *connects* with nothing natural about it; it neither *fades* into any surrounding shade of soil or vegetation, and must of necessity, stand out in its own bold and unshrouded impudence, a perfect Ishmaelite in color, and a perversion of every thing harmonious in the design. We eschew *red*, therefore, from every thing in rural architecture.

A SHORT CHAPTER ON TASTE.

The compound words, or terms *good-taste* and *bad-taste* have been used in the preceding pages without, perhaps, sufficiently explaining what is meant by the word *taste*, other than as giving vague and unsatisfactory terms to the reader in measuring the subject in hand. *Taste* is a term universally applied in criticism of the fine-arts, such as painting, sculpture, architecture, &c., &c., of which there are many schools — of *taste*, we mean — some of them, perhaps natural, but chiefly conventional, and all more or less arbitrary. The proverb, "there is no accounting for taste," is as old as the aforesaid schools themselves, and defines perfectly our own estimate of the common usage of the term.

As we have intended to use it, Webster defines the word *taste* to be "the faculty of discerning beauty, order, congruity, proportion, symmetry, or whatever constitutes excellence; style; manner with respect to what is pleasing." With this understanding, therefore; a fitness to the purpose for which a thing is intended — got up in a manner agreeable to the eye and the mind —

preserving also a harmony between its various parts and uses; pleasing to the eye, as addressed to the sense, and satisfactory to the mind, as appropriate to the object for which it is required;—these constitute *good-taste*, as the term is here understood.

The term *style*, also, is "the *manner* or *form* of a thing." When we say, "that is a stylish house," it should mean that it is in, or approaches some particular style of building recognized by the schools. It may or may not be in accordance with good taste, and is, consequently, subject to the same capricious test in its government. Yet *styles* are subject to arrangement, and are classified in the several schools of architecture, either as distinct specimens of acknowledged orders, as the Doric, the Ionic, the Corinthian, in Grecian architecture, or, the Tuscan and Composite, which are, more distinctly, styles of Roman architecture. To these may be added the Egyptian, the most massive of all; and either of them, in their proper character, grand and imposing when applied to public buildings or extensive structures, but altogether inapplicable, from their want of lightness and convenience, to country or even city dwellings. Other styles — not exactly orders — of architecture, such as the Italian, the Romanesque, the Gothic, the Swiss, with their modifications — all of which admit of a variety of departures from fixed rules, not allowed in the more rigid orders — may be adapted in a variety of ways, to the most agreeable and harmonious arrangement in architectural effect, for **dwellings and structures appurtenant to them.**

The Italian style of architecture, modified somewhat in pretension and extent, is admirably adapted to most parts of the United States. Its general lightness, openness, anc. freedom gives a wide range of choice; and its wings, verandas, and terraces, stretching off in any and almost every direction desired, from the main building, make it exceedingly appropriate for general use. The modern, or rural Gothic, branching off sometimes into what is termed the English cottage style, and in many instances blending so intimately with the Italian, as hardly to mark the line of division, is also a beautiful *arrangement* of building for country dwellings. These, in ruder structures, may also be carried into the Rustic — not a style proper, in itself — but so termed as approximating in execution or pretension to either of the above; while the Swiss, with its hanging roofs, and sheltering eaves may be frequently brought in aid to show out the rustic form in more completeness, and in greater harmony with surrounding objects, than either of the others.

For farm houses, either of these *arrangements* or departures from a *set* and *positive* style, are better fitted than any which we have noticed; and in some one or other of the modifications named, we have applied them in the examples submitted in this work. They may not therefore be viewed as *distinct* delineations of an *order* of architecture, or style *proper*, even; but as a *mode* appropriate to the object required. And so long as they do not absolutely conflict with true taste, or in their construction commit a barbarism upon any acknowledged system of architecture, in any of its modifications, we hazard no impropriety in introducing them for the imitation of country builders. Congruity with the objects to which it is applied should be the chief merit of any structure whatever; and so long as that object be attained, good taste is not violated, and utility is fully subserved.

Intimately connected with this subject, in rural build ings, is the *shape* of the structure. Many of the designs recently introduced for the imitation of build- ers, are full of angles and all sorts of zig-zag lines, which, although they may add to the variety of style, or relieve the monotony of straight and continuous lines, are carried to a needless excess, expensive in their construction, and entail infinite trouble upon the owner or occupant, in the repairs they subject him to, in the leakages continually occurring, against which last, either of wind or rain, it is almost impossible to guard. And what, let us ask, are the benefits of a parcel of needless gables and peaked windows, running up like owl's ears, above the eaves of a house, except to create expense, and invite leakage and decay? If in appearance, they provoke an association of that kind, they certainly are not in good taste; and a foot or two of increased height in a wall, or a low window sufficient for the purpose intended, would give a tone of dignity, of comfort, and real utility, which a whole covey of such pretentious things could not. All such trumpery should be scouted from the dwelling house of the farmer, and left to the special indulgence of the town builder.

A *square* form of house will afford more area within

a given line of wall than any other *sensible* form which may be adopted. Yet a square house is not so agreeable to the eye as an oblong. Thus, a house should stand somewhat broader on one front than on another. It should also be relieved from an appearance of monotony and tameness, by one or more wings; and such wings should, at their junction with the main building, retreat or advance a sufficient distance from a continuous line, as to relieve it effectually from an appearance of stiffness, and show a different character of occupation from that of the main structure. The front of a house should be the most imposing and finished in its architecture of any one of its parts; and unless some motive of greater convenience control otherwise, its entrance the most highly wrought, as indicating the luxury of the establishment — for even the humblest habitations have their luxuries. The side rooms, or more usually occupied apartments, require less pretension in both architectural effect and finish, and should wear a more subdued appearance; while the kitchen section, and from that, the several grades of apartments stretching beyond it, should distinctly show that they are subservient in their character, and wear a style and finish accordingly. Thus, each part of the house speaks for itself. It is its own finger-board, pointing the stranger to its various accommodation, as plainly as if written on its walls, and saying as significantly as dumb walls can do, that here dwells a well regulated family, who have a parlor for their friends; a library, or sitting-room for their own leisure and comfort; an ample bedroom and nursery, for the parents and the little ones; a kitchen for the cooking; and a scullery and closets, and all the other etceteras which belong to a perfect family homestead.

And so with the grounds. The lawn or " dooryard," should be the best kept ground on the place. The most conspicuous part of the garden should show its shrubbery and its flowers. The side or rear approach should be separated from the lawn, and show its constant *business* occupation, and openly lead off to where men and farm stock meet on common ground, devoted to every purpose which the farm requires. Such arrangement would be complete in all its parts, satisfactory, and lasting. Tinsel ornament, or gewgaw decoration should never be permitted on any building where the sober enjoyment of agricultural life is designed. It can never add consideration or dignity to the retired gentleman even, and least of all should it be indulged in by the farmer, dwelling on his own cultivated acres.

THE CONSTRUCTION OF CELLARS.

Every farm house and farm cottage, where a family of any size occupy the latter, should have a good, substantial *stone*-walled cellar beneath it. No room attached to the farm house is more profitable, in its occupation, than the cellar. It is useful for storing numberless articles which are necessary to be kept warm and dry in winter, as well as cool in summer, of which the farmer is well aware. The walls of a cellar should rise at least one, to two, or even three feet above the level of the ground surrounding it, according to circumstances, and the rooms in it well ventilated by *two* or more sliding sash windows in each, according to size, position, and the particular kind of storage for which it is required, so that a draft of pure air can pass through, and give it thorough ventilation at all times. It should also be at least seven and a half feet high in the clear; and if it be even nine feet, that is not too much. If the soil be compact, or such as will hold water, it should be thoroughly drained from the lowest point or corner, and the drain always kept open; (a stone drain is the best and most durable,) and if floored with a coat of flat, or rubble stones, well set in good hydraulic cement — or cement alone, when the stone cannot be obtained — all the better. This last will make it *rat proof*. For the purpose of avoiding these destructive creatures, the *foundation* stones in the wall should be brought to a joint, and project at least six inches on each side, from the wall itself, when laid upon this bottom course; as the usual manner of rats is to burrow in a nearly perpendicular direction from the surface, by the side of the wall, when intending to undermine it. On arriving at the bottom, if circumvented by the projecting stones, they will usually abandon their work. Plank of hard wood, or hard burnt bricks, may answer this purpose when stone cannot be had.

All cellar walls should be laid in good lime mortar, or if that be not practicable, they should be well pointed with it. This keeps them in place, and renders them less liable to the ingress of water and vermin. The thickness of wall should not be less than fifteen to eighteen inches, in any event, when of stone; and if the house walls above be built of stone or brick, two feet is better; and in all cases the cellar wall should be full three inches thicker than the wall resting upon it.

In the cellar of every farm house there should be an outside door, with a flight of steps by which to pass roots and other bulky or heavy articles, to which a wagon or cart may approach, either to receive or discharge them. This is indispensable.

Every out-building upon the farm, let it be devoted to what purpose it may, having a wooden floor on the ground story, should be set up sufficiently high from the surface to admit a cat or small terrier dog beneath such floor, with openings for them to pass in and out, or these hiding places will become so many rat warrens upon the premises, and prove most destructive to the grain and poultry. Nothing can be more annoying to the farmer than these vermin, and a trifling outlay in the beginning, will exclude them from the foundations and walls of all buildings. Care, therefore, should be taken to leave no haunt for their convenience.

With these suggestions the ingenuity of every builder will provide sufficient guards against the protection of vermin beneath his buildings.

VENTILATION OF HOUSES.

Pure air, and enough of it, is the cheapest blessing one can enjoy; and to deny one's self so indispensable an element of good health, is little short of criminal neglect, or the sheerest folly. Yet thousands who build at much needless expense, for the protection of their health and that of their families, as they allege, and no doubt suppose, by neglecting the simplest of all contrivances, in the work of ventilation, invite disease and infirmity, from the very pains they so unwittingly take to ward off such afflictions.

A man, be he farmer or of other profession, finding himself prosperous in life, sets about the very sensible business of building a house for his own accommodation. Looking back, perhaps, to the days of his boyhood, in a severe climate, he remembers the not very highly-finished tenement of his father, and the wide, open fireplace which, with its well piled logs, was scarcely able to warm the large living-room, where the family were wont to huddle in winter. He possibly remembers, with shivering sympathy, the sprinkling of snow which he was accustomed to find upon his bed as he awaked in the morning, that had found its way through the frail casing of his chamber window — but in the midst of all which he grew up with a vigorous constitution, a strong arm, and a determined spirit. He is resolved that *his* children shall encounter no such hardships, and that himself and his excellent helpmate shall suffer no such inconvenience as his own parents had done, who now perhaps, are enjoying a strong and serene old age, in their old-fashioned, yet to them not uncomfortable tenement. He therefore determines to have a snug, *close* house, where the cold cannot penetrate. He employs all his ingenuity to make every joint an air-tight fit; the doors must swing to an air-tight joint; the windows set into air-tight frames; and to perfect the catalogue of his comforts, an air-tight stove is introduced into every occupied room which, perchance, if he can afford it, are further warmed and poisoned by the heated flues of an air-tight furnace in his air-tight cellar. In short, it is an air-tight concern throughout. His family breathe an air-tight atmosphere; they eat their food cooked in an "air-tight kitchen witch," of the latest "premium pattern;" and thus they start, father, mother, children, all on the high road — if persisted in — to a galloping consumption, which sooner or later conducts them to an air-tight dwelling, not soon to be changed. If such melancholy catastrophe be avoided, colds, catarrhs, headaches, and all sorts of bodily afflictions shortly make their appearance, and they wonder what is the matter! They live so snug! their house is so warm! they sleep so comfortable! how can it be? True, in the morning the air of their sleeping-rooms feels close, but then if a window is opened it will chill the rooms, and that will give them colds. What *can* be the matter? The poor creatures never dream that they have been breathing, for hour after hour, decomposed air, charged with poisonous gases, which cannot escape through the tight walls, or over the tight windows, or through the tight stoves; and thus they keep on in the sure course to infirmity, disease, and premature death — all for the want of a little ventilation! Better indeed, that instead of all this painstaking, a pane were knocked out of every window, or a panel out of every door in the house.

. We are not disposed to talk about cellar furnaces for heating a farmer's house. They have little to do in the farmer's inventory of goods at all, unless it be to give warmth to the hall — and even then a snug box stove, with its pipe passing into the nearest chimney is, in most cases, the better appendage. Fuel is usually abundant with the farmer; and where so, its benefits are much better dispensed in open stoves or fireplaces, than in heating furnaces or "air-tights."

We have slightly discussed this subject of firing in the farm house, in a previous page, but while in the vein, must crave another word. A farmer's house should *look* hospitable as well as *be* hospitable, both outside and in; and the broadest, most cheerful look of hospitality within doors, in cold weather, is an *open* fire in the chimney fireplace, with the blazing wood upon it. There is no *mistake* about it. It thaws you out, if cold; it stirs you up, if drooping; and is the welcome, winning introduction to the good cheer that is to follow

A short time ago we went to pay a former town friend a visit. He had removed out to a snug little farm, where he could indulge his agricultural and horticultural tastes, yet still attend to his town engagements, and enjoy the quietude of the country. We rang the door bell. A servant admitted us; and leaving overcoat and hat in the hall, we entered a lone room, with an "air-tight" stove, looking as black and solemn as a Turkish eunuch upon us, and giving out about the same degree of genial warmth as the said eunuch would have expressed had he been there — an emasculated warming machine truly! On the floor was a Wilton carpet, too fine to stand on; around the room were mahogany sofas and mahogany chairs, all too fine to sit on — at all events to *rest* one upon if he were fatigued. The blessed light of day was shut out by crimson and white curtains, held up by gilded arrows; and upon the mantle piece, and on the center and side tables were all sorts of gimcracks, costly and worthless. In short, there was no *comfort* about the whole concern. Hearing our friend coming up from his dining-room below, where too, was his *cellar kitchen*—that most abominable of all appendages to a farm house, or to any other country house, for that matter—we buttoned our coat up close and high, thrust our hands into our pockets, and walked the room, as he entered. "Glad to see you—glad to see you, my friend!" said he, in great joy; "but dear me, why so buttoned up, as if you were going? What's the matter?" "My good sir," we replied, "you asked us to come over and see you, 'a *plain farmer*,' and 'take a quiet family dinner with you.' We have done so; and here find you with all your town nonsense about you. No fire to warm by; no seat to rest in; no nothing like a farm or farmer about you; and it only needs your charming better half, whom we always admired, when she lived in town, to take down her enameled harp, and play

'In fairy bowers by moonlight hours,'

to convince one that instead of ruralizing in the country, you had gone a peg higher in town residence! No, no, we'll go down to farmer Jocelyn's, our old schoolfellow, and take a dinner of bacon and cabbage with him. If he does occupy a one-story house, he lives up in sunshine, has an open fireplace, with a blazing wood fire on a chilly day, and his 'latch string is always out.'"

Our friend was petrified—astonished! We meant

to go it rather strong upon him, but still kept a frank, good-humored face, that showed him no malice. He began to think he was not exactly in character, and essayed to explain. We listened to his story. His good wife came in, and all together, we had a long talk of their family and farming arrangements; how they had furnished their house; and how they proposed to live; but wound up with a sad story, that their good farming neighbors did'nt call on them the *second* time — kind, civil people they appeared, too — and while they were in, acted as though afraid to sit down, and afraid to stand up; — in short, they were dreadfully embarrassed; for why, our friends could n't tell, but now began to understand it. "Well, my good friends," said we, "you have altogether mistaken country life in the outset. To live on a farm, it is neither necessary to be vulgar, nor clownish, nor to affect ignorance. *Simplicity* is all you require, in manners, and equal simplicity in your furniture and appointments. Now just turn all this nonsense in furniture and room dressing out of doors, and let some of your town friends have it. Get some simple, comfortable, cottage furniture, much better for all purposes, than this, and you will settle down into quiet, natural country life before you are aware of it, and all will go 'merry as a marriage bell' with you, in a little time"— for they both loved the country, and were truly excellent people. We continued, "I came to spend the day and the night, and I will stay; and this evening we'll go down to your neighbor Jocelyn's; and you, Mrs. N——, shall go with us; and we will see how quietly and comfortably he and his family take the world in a farmer's way."

We did go; not in carriage and livery, but walked the pleasant half mile that lay between them; the exercise of which gave us all activity and good spirits. Jocelyn was right glad to see us, and Patty, his staid and sober wife, with whom we had romped many an innocent hour in our childhood days, was quite as glad as he. But they *looked* a little surprised that such "great folks" as their new neighbors, should drop in so unceremoniously, and into their common "keeping room," too, to chat away an evening. However, the embarrassment soon wore off. We talked of farming; we talked of the late elections; we talked of the fruit trees and the strawberry beds; and Mrs. Jocelyn, who was a pattern of good housekeeping, told Mrs. N——how *she* made her apple jellies, and her currant tarts, and cream cheeses; and before we left they had exchanged ever so many engagements,— Mrs. Patty to learn her new friend to do half a dozen nice little matters of household pickling and preserving; while she, in turn, was to teach Nancy and Fanny, Patty's two rosy-cheeked daughters, almost as pretty as their mother was at their own age, to knit a bead bag and work a fancy chair seat! And then we had apples and nuts, all of the very best — for Jocelyn was a rare hand at grafting and managing his fruit trees, and knew the best apples all over the country. We had, indeed, a capital time! To cut the story short, the next spring our friend sent his *fancy* furniture to auction, and provided his house with simple cottage furnishings, at less than half the cost of the other; which both he and his wife afterward declared was infinitely better, for all house-keeping purposes. He also threw a neat wing on to the cottage, for an upper kitchen and its offices, and they now live like sensible country folks; and with their healthy, frolicksome children, are worth the envy of all the dyspeptic, town-fed people in existence.

A long digression, truly; but so true a story, and one so apt to our subject can not well be omitted. But what has all this to do with ventilation? We'll tell you. Jocelyn's house was *ventilated* as it should be;—for he was a methodical, thoughtful man, who planned and built his house himself—not the mechanical work, but directed it throughout, and saw that it was faithfully done; and that put us in mind of the story.

To be perfect in its ventilation, every room in the house, even to the closets, should be so arranged that a current of air *may* pass through, to keep it pure and dry. In living rooms, fresh air in sufficient quantity may usually be admitted through the doors. In sleeping rooms and closets, when doors may not be left open, one or more of the lower panels of the door may be filled by a rolling blind, opening more or less, at pleasure; or a square or oblong opening for that purpose, may be left in the base board, at the floor, and covered by a wire netting. And in all rooms, living apartments, as well as these, an opening of at least sixty-four square inches should be made in the wall, near the ceiling, and leading into an air flue, to pass into the garret. Such opening may be filled by a rolling blind, or wire screen, as below, and closed or kept open, at pleasure. Some builders prefer an air register to be placed in the chimney, over the fireplace or stove, near the ceiling; but the liability to annoyance, by smoke escaping through it into the room, if not thoroughly done, is an objection to this latter method, and the other may be made, in its construction, rather ornamental than otherwise, in appearance. All such details as these should be planned when the building is commenced, so that the several flues may be provided as the building proceeds. In a stone or brick house, a small space may be left in the walls, against which these air registers may be required; and for inner rooms, or closets, they may pass off into the openings of the partitions, and so up into the garret; from which apertures of escape may be left, or made at the gables, under the roof, or by a blind in a window.

For the admission of air to the first floor of the house, a special opening through the walls, for that purpose, can hardly be necessary; as the doors leading outside are usually opened often enough for such object. One of the best ventilated houses we have ever seen, is that owned and occupied by Samuel Cloon, Esq., of Cincinnati. It is situated on his farm, three miles out of the city, and in its fine architectural appearance and finished appointments, as a rural residence and first-class farm house, is not often excelled. Every closet is ventilated through rolling blinds in the door panels; and foul air, either admitted or created within them, is passed off at once by flues near the ceiling overhead, passing into conductors leading off through the garret.

'Where chambers are carried into the roof of a house, to any extent, they are sometimes incommoded by the summer heat which penetrates them, conducted by the chamber ceiling overhead. This heat can best be obviated by inserting a small window at each opposite peak of the garret, by which the outside air can circulate through, above the chambers, and so pass off the heated air, which will continually ascend. All this is a simple matter, for which any builder can provide, without particular expense or trouble.

INTERIOR ACCOMMODATION OF HOUSES.

Ground, in the country, being the cheapest item which the farmer can devote to building purposes, his object should be to *spread over*, rather than to go deeply into it, or climb high in the air above it. We repudiate cellar kitchens, or under-ground rooms for house work, altogether, as being little better than a nuisance — dark, damp, unhealthy, inconvenient, and expensive. The several rooms of a farm dwelling house should be compact in arrangement, and contiguous as may be to the principally-occupied apartments. Such arrangement is cheaper, more convenient, and labor-saving; and in addition, more in accordance with a good and correct taste in the outward appearance of the house itself.

The general introduction of cooking stoves, and other stoves and apparatus for warming houses, within the last twenty years, which we acknowledge to be a great acquisition in comfort as well as in convenience and economy, has been carried to an extreme, not only in shutting up and shutting out the time-honored open fireplace and its broad hearthstone, with their hallowed associations, but also in prejudice to the health of those who so indiscriminately use them, regardless of other arrangements which ought to go with them. A farm house should never be built without an ample, open fireplace in its kitchen, and other *principally* occupied rooms; and in all rooms where stoves are placed, and fires are daily required, the *open* Franklin should take place of the close or air-tight stove, unless extraordinary ventilation to such rooms be adopted also. The great charm of the farmer's winter evening is the open fireside, with its cheerful blaze and glowing embers; not wastefully expended, but giving out that genial warmth and comfort which, to those who are accustomed to its enjoyment, is a pleasure not made up by any invention whatever; and although the cooking stove or range be required—which, in addition to the fireplace, we would always recommend, to lighten female labor—it can be so arranged as not to interfere with the enjoyment or convenience of the open fire.

In the construction of the chimneys which appear in the plans submitted, the great majority of them—particularly those for northern latitudes—are placed in the interior of the house. They are less liable to communicate fire to the building, and assist greatly in warming the rooms through which they pass. In southern houses they are not so necessary, fires being required for a much less period of the year. Yet even there they may be oftentimes properly so placed. Where holes, for the passage of stovepipes through floors, partitions, or into chimneys, are made, stone, earthen, or iron thimbles should be inserted; and, except in the chimneys, such holes should be at least one to two inches larger than the pipe itself. The main flues of the chimney conducting off the smoke of the different fires, should be built separate, and kept apart by a partition of one brick in thickness, and carried out independently, as in no other way will they rid the house of smoky rooms.

An illustration in point: Fifteen years ago we purchased and removed into a most substantial and well-built stone house, the chimneys of which were constructed with open fireplaces, and the flues carried up separately to the top, where they all met upon the same level surface, as chimneys in past times usually were built, thus. Every fireplace in the house (and some of them had stoves in,) smoked intolerably; so much so that when the wind was in some quarters the fires had to be put out in every room but the kitchen, which, as good luck would have it, smoked less — although it did smoke there — than the others. After balancing the matter in our own mind some time, whether we should pull down and rebuild the chimneys altogether, or attempt an alteration; as we had given but little thought to the subject of chimney draft, and to try an experiment was the cheapest, we set to work a bricklayer, who, under our direction, simply built over each discharge of the several flues a separate top of fifteen inches high, in this wise: The remedy was perfect. We have had no smoke in the house since, blow the wind as it may, on any and all occasions. The chimneys *can't* smoke; and the whole expense for four chimneys, with their twelve flues, was not twenty dollars! The remedy was in giving each outlet a *distinct* current of air all around, and on every side of it.

CHIMNEY TOPS.

Nothing adds more to the outward expression of a dwelling, than the style of its chimneys. We have just shown that independent chimney tops pass off their smoke more perfectly, than when only partitioned inside to the common point of outlet. Aside from the architectural beauty which a group of chimney flues adds to the building, we have seen that they are really useful, beyond the formal, square-sided piles so common throughout the country. They denote good cheer social firesides, and a generous hospitaity within — features which should always mark the country dwelling; and more particularly that of the farmer.

The style and arrangement of these chimney groups may be various, as comporting with the design of the house itself; and any good architect can arrange them as fitted to such design. Our illustrations will show them of different kinds, which are generally cheap in construction, and simple, yet expressive in their arrangement.

PRELIMINARY TO OUR DESIGNS.

We have discussed with tolerable fullness, the chief subjects connected with farm buildings — sufficiently so, we trust, to make ourselves understood as desiring to combine utility with commendable ornament in all that pertains to them. The object has been, thus far, to give hints, rather than models, in description. But as the point to which we have endeavored to arrive will be but imperfectly understood without illustration, we shall submit a few plans of houses and outbuildings, as carrying out more fully our ideas.

We are quite aware that different forms or fashions of detail and finish, to both outside and inside work, prevail among builders in different sections of the United States. Some of these fashions are the result of climate, some of conventional taste, and some of education. With them we are not disposed to quarrel. In many cases they are immaterial to the main objects of the work, and so long as they please the taste or partialities of those adopting them, are of little consequence. There are, however, certain matters of *principle*, both in general construction and in the detail of finish, which should not be disregarded; and these, in the designs submitted, and in the explanations which follow, will be fully discussed, each in its place. The particular form or style of work we have not directed, because, as before remarked, we are no professional builder, and of course free from the dogmas which are too apt to be inculcated in the professional schools and workshops. We give a wide berth, and a free toleration in all such matters, and are not disposed to raise a hornet's nest about our ears by interfering in matters where every tyro of the drafting board and work-bench assumes to be, and probably may be, our superior. All minor subjects we are free to leave to the skill and ingenuity of the builder — who, fortunately for the country, is found in almost every village and hamlet of the land.

Modes and styles of finish, both inside and outside of buildings, change; and that so frequently, that what is laid down as the reigning fashion to-day, may be superseded by another fashion of to-morrow — immaterial in themselves, only, and not affecting the shape, arrangement, and accommodation of the building itself, which in these, must ever maintain their relation with the use for which it is intended. The northern dwelling, with its dependencies and appointments, requires a more compact, snug, and connected arrangement than that of the south; while one in the middle states may assume a style of arrangement between them both, each fitted for their own climate and country, and in equally good taste. The designs we are about to submit are intended to be such as may be modified to any section of the country, although some of them are made for extremes of north and south, and are so distinguished. Another object we have had in view is, to give to every farmer and country dweller of moderate means the opportunity of possessing a cheap work which would guide him in the general objects which he wishes to accomplish in building, that he may *have his own notions* on the subject, and not be subject to the caprice and government of such as profess to exclusive knowledge in all that appertains to such subjects, and in which, it need not be offensive to say, that although clever in their way, they are sometimes apt to be mistaken.

Therefore, without assuming *to instruct* the professional builder, our plans will be submitted, not without the hope that he even, may find in them something worthy of consideration; and we offer them to the owner and future occupant of the buildings themselves, as models which he may adopt, with the confidence that they will answer all his reasonable purposes.

Design I.

We here present a farm house of the simplest and most unpretending kind, suitable for a farm of twenty, fifty, or an hundred acres. Buildings somewhat in this style are not unfrequently seen in the New England States, and in New York; and the plan is in fact suggested, although not copied, from some farm houses which we have known there, with improvements and additions of our own.

This house may be built either of stone, brick, or wood. The style is rather rustic than otherwise, and intended to be altogether plain, yet agreeable in outward appearance, and of quite convenient arrangement. The body of this house is 40×30 feet on the ground, and 12 feet high, to the plates for the roof; the lower rooms nine feet high; the roof intended for a pitch of 35°—but, by an error in the drawing, made less—thus affording very tolerable chamber room in the roof story. The L, or rear projection, containing the wash-room and wood-house, juts out two feet from the side of the house to which it is attached, with posts 7½ feet high above the floor of the main house; the pitch of the roof being the same. Beyond this is a building 32×24 feet, with 10 feet posts, partitioned off into a swill-room, piggery, workshop, and wagon-house, and a like roof with the others. A light, rustic porch,

FARM HOUSE. Pages 73-4.

12×8 feet, with lattice work, is placed on the front of the house, and another at the side door, over which vines, by way of drapery, may run; thus combining that sheltered, comfortable, and home-like expression so desirable in a rural dwelling. The chimney is carried out in three separate flues, sufficiently marked by the partitions above the roof. The windows are hooded, or sheltered, to protect them from the weather, and fitted with simple sliding sashes with 7×9 or 8×10 glass. Outer blinds may be added, if required; but it is usually better to have these *inside*, as they are no ornament to the outside of the building, are liable to be driven back and forth by the wind, even if fastenings are used, and in any event are little better than a continual annoyance.

INTERIOR ARRANGEMENT.

The front door, over which is a single sash-light across, opens into a hall or entry 9×7 feet, from which a door opens on either side into a sitting-room and parlor, each 16×15 feet, lighted by a double, plain window, at the ends, and a single two-sash window in front. Between the entrance door and stove, are in each room a small pantry or closet for dishes, or otherwise, as may be required. The chimney stands in the center of the house, with a separate flue for each front room, into which a thimble is inserted to receive the stovepipes by which they are warmed; and from the inner side of these rooms each has a door passing to the kitchen, or chief living room. This last apartment

W.H. 16x14	PIG 16x12
W.S. 16x10	SWILL 16x12

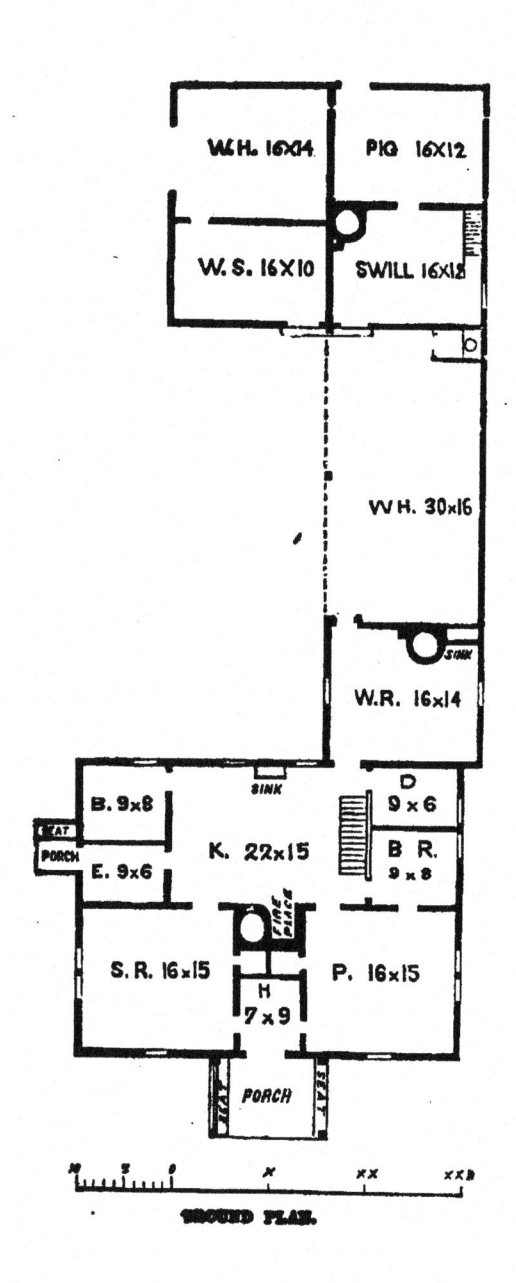

W.H. 30x16

W.R. 16x14

B. 9x8		SINK	D 9x6	
SEAT PORCH	E. 9x6	K. 22x15	B.R. 9x8	
	S.R. 16x15	FIRE PLACE	P. 16x15	
		H 7x9		

PORCH

GROUND PLAN.

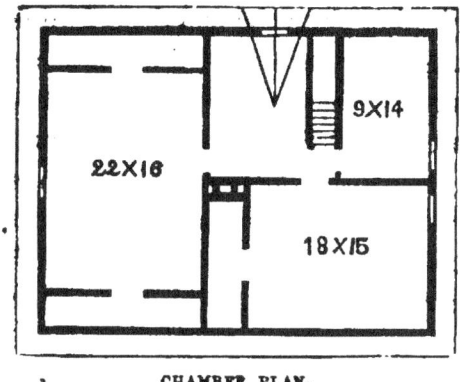

CHAMBER PLAN.

is 22×15 feet, with a broad fireplace containing a crane, hooks, and trammel, if required, and a spacious family oven—affording those homely and primitive comforts still so dear to many of us who are not ready to concede that all the virtues of the present day are combined in a "perfection" cooking stove, and a "patent" heater; although there is a chance for these last, if they should be adopted into the peaceful atmosphere of this kitchen.

On one side of the kitchen, in rear of the stairs, is a bedroom, 9×8 feet, with a window in one corner. Adjoining that, is a buttery, dairy-room, or closet, 9×6 feet, also having a window. At the inner end of the stairway is the cellar passage; at the outer end is the chamber passage, landing above, in the highest part of the roof story. Opposite the chamber stairs is a door leading to the wash-room. Between the two windows, on the rear side of the kitchen, is a sink, with a waste pipe passing out through the wall. At the further corner a door opens into a snug bedroom 9×8 feet, lighted by a window in rear; and adjoining this is a side entry leading from the end door, 9×6 feet in area; thus making every room in the house accessible at once from the kitchen, and giving the greatest possible convenience in both living and house-work.

The roof story is partitioned into convenient-sized bedrooms; the ceiling running down the pitch of the roof to within two feet of the floor, unless they are cut short by inner partitions, as they are in the largest chamber, to give closets. The open area in the center, at the head of the stairs, is lighted by a small gable window inserted in the roof, at the rear, and serves as a lumber room; or, if necessary, a bed may occupy a part of it.

In rear of the main dwelling is a building 44×16 feet, occupied as a wash-room and wood-house. The wash-room floor is let down eight inches below the kitchen, and is 16×14 feet, in area, lighted by a window on each side, with a chimney, in which is set a boiler, and fireplace, if desired, and a sink in the corner adjoining. This room is 7½ feet in height. A door passes from this wash-room into the wood-house, which is 30×16 feet, open in front, with a water-closet in the further corner.

The cellar is 7½ feet in height—and is the whole size of the house, laid with good stone wall, in lime mortar, with a flight of steps leading outside, in rear of the kitchen, and two or more sash-light windows at the ends. If not in a loose, gravelly, or sandy soil, the cellar should be kept dry by a drain leading out on to lower ground.

The building beyond, and adjoining the wood-house,

contains a swill-house 16×12 feet, with a window in one end; a chimney and boiler in one corner, with storage for swill barrels, grain, meal, potatoes, &c., for feeding the pigs, which are in the adjoining pen of same size, with feeding trough, place for sleeping, &c., and having a window in one end and a door in the rear, leading to a yard.

Adjoining these, in front, is a workshop and tool-house, 16×10 feet, with a window at the end, and an entrance door near the wood house. In this is a joiner's work-bench, a chest of working tools, such as saw, hammer, augers, &c., &c., necessary for repairing implements, doing little rough jobs, or other wood work, &c., which every farmer ought to do for himself; and also storing his hoes, axes, shovels, hammers, and other small farm implements. In this room he will find abundant rainy-day employment in repairing his utensils of various kinds, making his beehives, hencoops, &c., &c. Next to this is the wagon-house, 16×14 feet, with broad doors at the end, and harness pegs around the walls.

The posts of this building are 10 feet high; the rooms eight feet high, and a low chamber overhead for storing umber, grain, and other articles, as may be required. Altogether, these several apartments make a very complete and desirable accommodation to a man with the property and occupation for which it is intended.

On one side and adjoining the house, should be the garden, the clothes-yard, and the bee-house, which last should always stand in full sight, and facing the most frequented room — say the kitchen — that they can be seen daily during the swarming season, as those performing household duties may keep them in view.

MISCELLANEOUS.

In regard to the surroundings, and approach to this dwelling, they should be treated under the suggestions already given on these subjects. This is an exceedingly *snug* tenement, and everything around and about it should be of the same character. No pretension or frippery whatever. A neat garden, usefully, rather than ornamentally and profusely supplied; a moderate court-yard in front; free access to the end door, from the main every-day approach by vehicles — not on the highway, but on the farm road or lane — the business entrance, in fact; which should also lead to the barns and sheds beyond, not far distant. Every feature should wear a most domestic look, and breathe an air of repose and content. Trees should be near, but not so near as to cover the house. A few shrubs of simple kind — some standing roses — a few climbing ones; a syringa, a lilac, a snow ball, and a little patch or two of flowers near the front porch, and the whole expression is given; just as one would wish to look upon as a simple, unpretending habitation.

It is not here proposed to give working plans, or estimates, to a nicety; or particular directions for building any design even, that we present. The material for construction best suited to the circumstances and locality of the proprietor must govern all those matters; and as good builders are in most cases at hand, who are competent to give estimates for the cost of any given plan, when the material for construction is once settled, the question of expense is readily fixed. The same sized house, with the same accommodation, may be made to cost fifty to one hundred per cent. over an economical estimate, by the increased style, or manner of its finish; or it may be kept within bounds by a rigid adherence to the plan first adopted.

In western New York this house and attachments complete, the body of stone, the wood-house, wagon-house, &c., of wood, may be built and well finished in a plain way for $1,500. If built altogether of wood, with grooved and matched vertical boarding, and battens, the whole may be finished and painted for $800, to $1,200. For the lowest sum, the lumber and work would be of a rough kind, with a cheap wash to color it; but the latter amount would give good work, and a lasting coat of mineral paint both outside and within.

As a *tenant* house on a farm of three, four, or even five hundred acres, where all who live in it are laborers in the field or household, this design may be most conveniently adopted. The family inhabiting it in winter may be well accommodated for sleeping under the main roof, while they can at all seasons take their meals, and be made comfortable in the several rooms. In the summer season, when a larger number of laborers are employed, the lofts of the carriage or wagon-house and work-shop may be occupied with beds, and thus a large share of the expense of house building for a very considerable farm be saved. Luxury is a quality more or less consulted by every one who builds for his *own* occupation on a farm, or elsewhere; and the tendency in building is constantly to expand, to give a higher finish, and in fact, to over-build. Indeed, if we were to draw the balance, on our *old* farms, between scantily-accommodated houses, and houses with needless room in them, the latter would preponderate. Not that these latter houses either are too good, or too convenient for the purpose for which they were built, but they have *too much* room, and that room badly appropriated and arranged.

On a farm proper, the whole establishment is a *workshop*. The shop *out of doors*, we acknowledge, is not always *dry*, nor always warm; but it is exceedingly well aired and lighted, and a place where industrious people dearly love to labor. Within doors it is a work-shop too. There is always labor and occupation for the family, in the *general business* of the farm; therefore but little room is wanted for either luxury or leisure, and the farm house should be fully occupied, with the exception, perhaps, of a single room on the main floor, (and that not a large one,) for some regular business purpose. All these accommodated, and the requirements of the house are ended. Owners of *rented* farms should reflect, too, that expensive houses on their estates entail expensive repairs, and that continually. Many tenants are careless of highly-finished houses. Not early accustomed to them, they misappropriate, perhaps, the best rooms in the house, and pay little attention to the purposes for which the owner designed them, or to the *manner* of using them. It is therefore a total waste of money to build a house on a tenant estate anything beyond the mere comfortable wants of the family occupying it, and to furnish the room necessary for the accommodation of the crops, stock, and farm furniture, in the barns and other out-buildings — all in a cheap, tidy, yet substantial way.

So, too, with the grounds for domestic purposes around the house. A kitchen garden, sufficient to grow the family vegetables — a few plain fruits — a *posey* bed or two for the girls — and the story is told. Give a larger space for these things — anything indeed, for elegance — and ten to one, the plow is introduced, a corn or potato patch is *set out*, field culture is adopted, and your choice grounds are torn up, defaced, and sacrificed to the commonest uses.

Notwithstanding these drawbacks, a cheerful, home-expression may be given, and should be given to the homestead, in the character and construction of the buildings, be they ever so rough and homely. We can call to mind many instances of primitive houses — *log* cabins even — built when none better could be had, that presented a most comfortable and life-enjoying picture — residences once, indeed, of those who swayed "the applause of listening senates," but under the hands of taste, and a trifle of labor, made to look comfortable, happy, and sufficient. We confess, therefore, to a profound veneration, if not affection, for the humble farm house, as truly American in character, and which, with a moderate display of skill, may be made equal to the main purposes of life and enjoyment for all such as do not aspire to a high display, and who are content to make the most of moderate means

Design II.

This is the plan of a house and out-buildings based chiefly on one which we built of wood some years since on a farm of our own, and which, in its occupation, has proved to be one of exceeding convenience to the purposes intended. As a farm *business* house, we have not known it excelled; nor in the ease and facility of doing up the house-work within it, do we know a better. It has a subdued, quiet, unpretending look; yet will accommodate a family of a dozen workmen, besides the females engaged in the household work, with perfect convenience; or if occupied by a farmer with but his own family around him, ample room is afforded them for a most comfortable mode of life, and sufficient for the requirements of a farm of two, to three or four hundred acres.

This house is, in the main body, 36×22 feet, one and a half stories high, with a projection on the rear 34×16 feet, for the kitchen and its offices; and a still further addition to that, of 26×18 feet, for washroom. The main body of the house is 14 feet high to the plates; the lower rooms are 9 feet high; the roof has a pitch of 35° from a horizontal line, giving partially-upright chambers in the main building, and *roof* lodging rooms in the rear. The rear, or kitchen part,

FARM HOUSE.

See Page 84.

is one story high, with 10 feet posts, and such pitch of roof (which last runs at right angles to the main body, and laps on to the main roof,) as will carry the peak up to the same air line. This addition should retreat 6 inches from the line of the main building, on the side given in the design, and 18 inches on the rear. The rooms on this kitchen floor are 8 feet high, leaving one foot above the upper floor, under the roof, as a chamber garret, or lumber-room, as may be required. Beyond this, in the rear, is the other extension spoken of, with posts 9 feet high, for a buttery, closet, or dairy, or all three combined, and a wash-room; the floor of which is on a level with the last, and the roof running in the same direction, and of the same pitch. In front of this wash-room, where not covered by the woodhouse, is an open porch, 8 feet wide and 10 feet long, the roof of which runs out at a less angle than the others — say 30° from a horizontal line. Attached to this is the wood-house, running off by way of L, at right angles, 36×16 feet, of same height as the wash-room.

Adjoining the wood-house, on the same front line, is a building 50×20 feet, with 12 feet posts, occupied as a workshop, wagon-house, stable, and store-room, with a lean-to on the last of 15×10 feet, for a piggery. The several rooms in this building are 8 feet high, affording a good lumber room over the workshop, and hay storage over the wagon-house and stable. Over the wagon-house is a gable, with a blind window swinging on hinges, for receiving hay, thus relieving the long, uniform line of roof, and affording ample accommodation on each side to a pigeon-house or dovecote, if required.

The style of this establishment is of plain Italian, or bracketed, and may be equally applied to stone, brick, or wood. The roofs are broad, and protect the walls by their full projection over them, 2½ feet. The small gable in the front roof of the main dwelling relieves it of its otherwise straight uniformity, and affords a high door-window opening on to the deck of the veranda, which latter should be 8 or 10 feet in width. The shallow windows, also, over the wings of the veranda give it a more cheerful expression. The lower *end* windows of this part of the house are hooded, or sheltered by a cheap roof, which gives them a snug and most comfortable appearance. The veranda may appear more ornamental than the plain character of the house requires; but any superfluous work upon it may be omitted, and the style of finish conformed to the other. The veranda roof is flatter than that of the house, but it may be made perfectly tight by closer shingling, and paint; while the deck or platform in the centre may be roofed with zinc, or tin, and a coat of sanded paint laid upon it. The front chimney is plain, yet in keeping with the general style of the house, and may be made of ordinary bricks. The two parts of the chimney, as they appear in the front rooms, are drawn together as they pass through the chamber above, and become one at the roof. The kitchen chimneys pass up through the peaks of their respective roofs, and should be in like character with the other

CHAMBER PLAN.   GROUND PLAN.

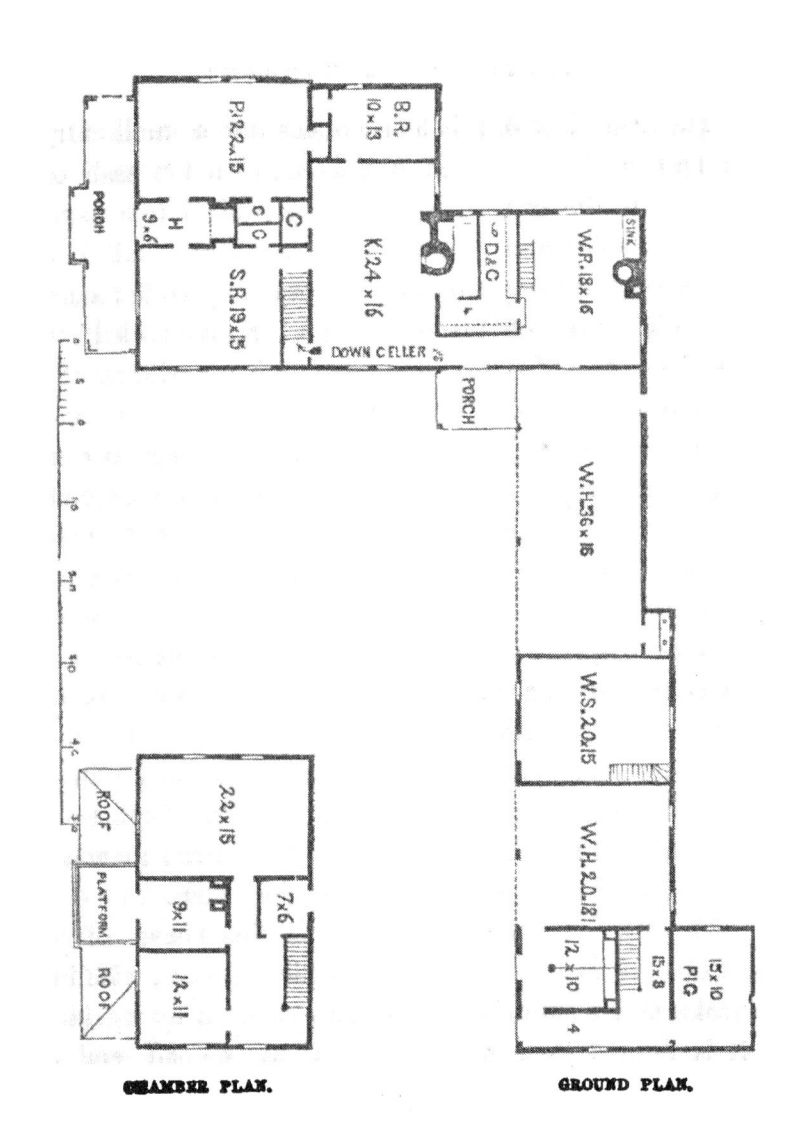

INTERIOR ARRANGEMENT.

The front door of this house opens into a small entry or hall, 9×6 feet, which is lighted by a low sash of glass over the front door. A door leads into a room on each side; and at the inner end of the hall is a recess between the two chimneys of the opposite rooms, in which may be placed a table or broad shelf to receive hats and coats. On the left is a parlor 22×15 feet, lighted on one side by a double window, and in front by a single plain one. The fireplace is centrally placed on one side of the room, in the middle of the house. On one side of the fireplace is a closet, three feet deep, with shelves, and another closet at the inner end of the room, near the kitchen door; or this closet may be dispensed with for the use of this parlor, and given up to enlarge the closet which is attached to the bedroom. Another door opens directly into the kitchen. This parlor is 9 feet high between joints. The sitting-room is opposite to the parlor, 19×15 feet, and lighted and closeted in nearly the same manner, as will be seen by referring to the floor plan.

The kitchen is the grand room of this house. It is 24×16 feet in area, having an ample fireplace, with its hooks and trammels, and a spacious oven by its side. It is lighted by a double window at one end, and a single window near the fireplace. At one end of this kitchen is a most comfortable and commodious family bedroom, 13×10 feet, with a large closet in one corner, and lighted by a window in the side. Two windows may be inserted if wanted. A passage leads by the side of the oven to a sink-room, or recess, behind the chimney, with shelves to dry dishes on, and lighted by the half of a double window, which accommodates with its other half the dairy, or closet adjoining. A door also opens from this recess into the closet and dairy, furnished with broad shelves, that part of which, next the kitchen, is used for dishes, cold meat and bread cupboards, &c.; while the part of it adjoining the window beyond, is used for milk. This room is 14×6 feet, besides the L running up next to the kitchen, of 6×4 feet. From the kitchen also opens a closet into the front part of the house for any purpose needed. This adjoins the parlor, and sitting-room, closets. In the passage to the sitting-room also opens the stairway leading to the chambers, and beneath, at the other end of it, next the outside wall, is a flight leading down cellar. The cellar is excavated under the whole house, being 36×22, and 34×16 feet, with glass windows, one light deep by four wide, of 8×10 glass; and an outer door, and flight of steps outside, under either the sitting-room or kitchen windows, as may be most convenient. A door opens, also, from the kitchen, into a passage 4 feet wide and 12 feet long leading to the wash-room, 18×16 feet, and by an outside door, through this passage to the porch. In this passage may be a small window to give it light.

In the wash-room are two windows. A chimney at the far end accommodates a boiler or two, and a fireplace, if required. A sink stands adjoining the chimney. A flight of stairs, leading to a garret over head on one side.

and to the kitchen chamber on the other, stands next the dairy, into which last a door also leads. In this wash-room may be located the cooking stove in warm weather, leaving the main kitchen for a family and eating room. A door also leads from the wash-room into the wood-house.

The wood-house stands lower than the floor of th wash-room, from which it falls, by steps. This is large, because a plentiful store of wood is needed for a dwelling of this character. If the room be not all wanted for such purpose, a part of it may devoted to other necessary uses, there seldom being too much shelter of this kind on a farm; through the rear wall of this woodhouse leads a door into the garden, or clothes-yard, as the case may be; and at its extreme angle is a water closet, 6×4 feet, by way of lean-to, with a hipped roof, 8 feet high, running off from both the wood-house and workshop. This water-closet is lighted by a sliding sash window.

On to the wood-house, in a continuous front line, joins the workshop, an indispensable appendage to farm convenience. This has a flight of stairs leading to the lumber-room above. For the furnishing of this apartment, see description of Design I. Next to the workhouse is the wagon and tool-house, above which is the hay loft, also spread over the stable adjoining; in which last are stalls for a pair of horses, which may be required for uses other than the main labors of the farm—to run to market, carry the family to church, or elsewhere. A pair of horses for such purposes should always be kept near the house. The horse-stalls occupy a space of 10×12 feet, with racks and feeding boxes. The plans of these will be described hereafter. The door leading out from these stalls is 5 feet wide, and faces the partition, so that each horse may be led out or in at an easy angle from them. Beyond the stalls is a passage 4 feet wide, leading to a store-room or area, from which a flight of rough stairs leads to the hay loft above. Beyond this room, in which is the oat bin for the horses, is a small piggery, for the convenience of a pig or two, which are always required to consume the daily wash and offal of the house; and not for the general *pork* stock of the farm;* which, on one of this size, may be expected to require more commodious quarters.

The chamber plan of this house is commodious, furnishing one large room and three smaller ones. The small chamber leading to the deck over the porch, may, or may not be occupied as a sleeping room. The small one near the stairs may contain a single bed, or be occupied as a large clothes-closet. Through this, a door leads into the kitchen chamber, which may serve as one, or more laborers' bed-chambers. They may be lighted by one or more windows in the rear gable.

If 'more convenient to the family, the parlor and sitting-room, already described, may change their occupation, and one substituted for the other.

The main business approach to this house should be by a lane, or farm road opening on the side next the stable and wagon-house. The yard, in front of these last named buildings, should be separated from the lawn, or front door-yard of the dwelling. The establishment should stand some distance back from the traveled highway, and be decorated with such trees, shrubbery and cultivation, as the taste of the owner may direct. No *general* rules or directions can be applicable to this design beyond what have already been given; and the subject must be treated as circumstances may suggest. The unfrequented side of the house should, however, be flanked with a garden, either ornamental, or fruit and vegetable; as buildings of this character ought to command a corresponding share of attention with the grounds by which they are surrounded.

This house will appear equally well built of wood, brick, or stone. Its cost, according to materials, or finish, may be $1,000 or $1,500. The out-buildings attached, will add $400 to $600, with the same conditions as to finish; but the whole may be substantially and well built of either stone, brick, or wood, where each may be had at equal convenience, for $2,000 in the interior of New York. Of course, it is intended to do all the work plain, and in character for the occupation to which it is intended.

MISCELLANEOUS DETAILS.

At this point of our remarks a word or two may be offered on the general subject of inside finish to farm houses, which may be applicable more or less to any one, or all of the designs that may come under our observation; therefore what is here said, may be applied at large. Different sections of the United States have their own several *local* notions, or preferences as to the mode of finish to their houses and out-buildings, according to climate, education, or other circumstances. In all these matters neither taste, fashion, nor climate should be arbitrary. The manner of finish may be various, without any departure from truth or propriety—always keeping in mind the object for which it is intended. The *material* for a country house should be *strong*, and *durable*, and the work simple in its details, beyond that for either town or suburban houses. It should be *strong*, for the reason that the interior of the farm house is used for purposes of industry, in finishing up and perfecting the labors of the farm; labors indispensable too, and in amount beyond the ordinary housekeeping requirements of a family who have little to do but merely to live, and make themselves comfortable. The material should be *durable*, because the distance at which the farm house is usually located from the residences of building mechanics, renders it particularly troublesome and expensive to make repairs, and alterations. The work should be *simple*, because cheaper in the first place, in construction, and finish; quite as appropriate and satisfactory in appearance; and demanding infinitely less labor and pains to care for, and protect it afterward. Therefore all mouldings, architraves, *chisel*-work, and gewgawgery in interior finish should be let alone in the living and daily occupied rooms of the house. If, to a single parlor, or *spare* bedchamber a little *ornamental* work be permitted, let even that be in moderation, and just enough to teach the active mistress and her daughters what a world of scrubbing and elbow work they have saved themselves in the enjoyment of a plainly-finished house, instead of one full of gingerbread work and finery. None but the initiated can tell the affliction that *chiseled* finishing entails on housekeepers in the spider, fly, and other insect lodgment which it invites — frequently the cause of more annoyance and *daily* disquietude in housekeeping, because unnecessary, than real griefs from which we may not expect to escape. Bases, casings, sashes, doors — all should be plain, and painted or stained a quiet *russet* color — a color natural to the woods used for the finish, if it can be, showing, in their wear, as little of dust, soiling, and fly dirt as possible. There is no poetry about common housekeeping. Cooking, house-cleaning, washing, scrubbing, sweeping, are altogether matter-of-fact duties, and usually considered *work*, not recreation; and these should all be made easy of performance, and as seldom to be done as possible; although the first item always was, and always *will* be, and the last item *should* be, an every-day vocation for *somebody;* and the manner of inside finish to a house has a great deal to do with all these labors.

In a stone, or brick house, the inside walls should be firred off for plastering. This may be done either by "plugging," that is, driving a plug of wood strongly into the mortar courses, into which the firring should be nailed, or by laying a strip of thin board in the mortar course, the entire length of each wall. This is better than *blocks* laid in for such purpose, because it is effectually *bound* by the stone, or brick work; whereas, a block may get loose by shrinking, but the nails which hold the firring to the plug, or to the thin strip of board will split and *wedge* it closer to the mason work of the outside wall. This is an important item. It makes close work too, and leaves no room for rats, mice, or other vermin; and as it admits a *space*—no matter how thin—so that no outside damp from the walls can communicate into, or through the inner plastering, it answers all purposes. The inside, and partition walls should be of coarse, strong mortar, *floated off* as smoothly as may be, not a *hard finish*, which is fine, and costly; and then papered throughout for the better rooms, and the commonly-used rooms whitewashed. Paper gives a most comfortable look to the rooms, more so than paint, and much less expensive, while nothing is so sweet, tidy, and cheerful to the *working* rooms of the house as a *lime* wash, either white, or softened down with some agreeable tint, such as *light* blue, green, drab, fawn, or russet, to give the shade desired, and for which every *professional* painter and whitewasher in the vicinity, can furnish a proper recipe applicable to the place and climate. On such subjects we choose to prescribe, rather than to play the apothecary by giving any of the thousand and one recipes extant, for the composition.

Our remarks upon the strength and durability of *material* in house-building do not apply exclusively to brick and stone. Wood is included also; and of this, there is much difference in the kind. Sound *white* oak, is, perhaps the best material for the heavy framework of any house or out-building, and when to be had at a moderate expense, we would recommend it in preference to any other. If *white* oak cannot be had, the other varieties of oak, or chesnut are the next best. In *light* frame-timbers, such as studs, girts, joists, or rafters, oak is inclined to spring and warp, and we would prefer hemlock, or chesnut, which holds a nail equally as well, or, in its absence, pine, (which holds a nail badly,) whitewood, or black walnut. The outside finish to a wooden house, may be *lighter* than in one of stone or brick. The wood work on the outside of the latter should always be heavy, and in character with the walls, giving an air of firmness and stability to the whole structure. No elaborate carving, or beadwork should be permitted on the outside work of a country house at all; and only a sufficient quantity of ornamental *tracery* of any kind, to break the monotony of a plainness that would otherwise give it a formal, or uncouth expression, and relieve it of what some would consider a pasteboard look. A farm house, in fact, of any degree, either cheap or expensive, should wear the same appearance as a well-dressed person of either sex; so that a stranger, not looking at them for the purpose of inspecting their garb, should, after an interview, be unable to tell what particular sort of dress they wore, so perfectly in keeping was it with propriety,

In the design now under discussion, a cellar is made under the whole body of the house; and this cellar is a *shallow* one, so far as being sunk into the ground is concerned, say 5½ feet, leaving 2½ feet of cellar wall above ground — 8 feet in all. A part of the wall above ground should be covered by the excavated earth, and sloped off to a level with the surrounding surface. A commodious, well-lighted, and well-ventilated cellar is one of the most important apartments of the farm house. It should, if the soil be compact, be well drained from some point or corner within the walls into a lower level outside, to which point within, the whole floor surface should incline, and the bottom be floored with water-lime cement. This will make it hard, durable, and dry. It may then be washed and scrubbed off as easily as an upper floor. If the building site be high, and in a gravelly, or sandy soil, neither drain nor flooring will be required. The cellar may be used for the storage of root crops, apples, meats, and household vegetables. A partitioned room will accommodate either a summer or a winter dairy, if not otherwise provided, and a multitude of conveniences may be made of it in all well arranged farmeries. But in all cases the cellar should be well lighted, ventilated, and dry. Even the ash-house and smoke-house may be made in it with perfect convenience, by brick or stone partitions, and the smoke-house flue be carried up into one of the chimney flues above, and thus make a more snug and compact arrangement than to have separate buildings for those objects. A wash-room, in which, also, the soap may be made, the tallow and lard tried up, and other extraordinary labor when fire heat is to be used, may properly be made in a cellar, particularly when on a sloping ground, and easy of access to the ground level on one side. But, as a general rule, such room is better on a level with the main floor of the dwelling, and there are usually sufficient occupations for the cellar without them.

All cellar walls should be at least 18 inches thick, for even a wooden house, and from that to 2 feet for a stone or brick one, and well laid in strong lime-mortar. Unmortared cellar walls are frequently laid under wooden buildings, and *pointed* with lime-mortar inside; but this is sometimes dug out by rats, and is apt to crumble and fall out otherwise. A *complete* cellar wall should be thoroughly laid in mortar.

FARM HOUSE.

Design III.

We here present the reader with a substantial, plain, yet highly-respectable stone or brick farm house, of the second class, suitable for an estate of three, to five hundred acres, and accommodation for a family of a dozen or more persons. The style is mixed rural Gothic, Italian, and bracketed; yet in keeping with the character of the farm, and the farmer's standing and occupation.

The main body of this house is 42×24 feet on the ground, and one and three quarter stories high — the chambers running two or three feet into the roof, as choice or convenience may direct. The roof has a pitch of 30 to 40° from a horizontal line, and broadly spread over the walls, say two and a half feet, showing the ends of the rafters, bracket fashion. The chimneys pass out through the peak of the roof, where the hips of what would otherwise be the gables, connect with the long sides of the roof covering the front and rear. On the long front is partly seen, in the perspective, a portico, 16×10 feet — not the *chief* entrance front, but rather a side front, practically, which leads into a lawn or garden, as may be most desirable, and from which the best view from the house is commanded. Over this porch is a small gable running into the roof, to break its monotony, in which is a door-window leading from the upper hall on to the deck of the porch. This gable has the same finish as the main roof, by brackets. The chamber windows are two-thirds or three-quarters the size of the lower ones; thus showing the upper story not full height below the plates, but running two to four feet into the garret. The rear wing, containing the entrance or business front, is 24×32 feet, one and a half stories high, with a pitch of roof not less than 35°, and spread over the walls both at the eaves and gable, in the same proportion as the roof to the main body. In front of this is a porch or veranda eight feet wide, with a low, hipped roof. In the front and rear roofs of this wing is a dormar window, to light the chambers. The gable to this wing is bold, and gives it character by the breadth of its roof over the walls, and the strong brackets by which it is supported. The chimney is thrown up strong and boldly at the point of the roof, indicating the every-day uses of the fire-places below, which, although distinct and wide apart in their location on the ground floors, are drawn together in the chambers, thus showing only one escape through the roof.

The wood-house in the rear of the wing has a roof of the same character, and connects with the long building in the rear, which has the same description of roof, but hipped at one end. That end over the workshop, and next the wood-house, shows a bold gable like the wing of the house, and affords room and light to the lumber room over the shop, and also gives variety and relief to the otherwise too great sameness of roof-appearance on the further side of the establishment.

GROUND PLAN.

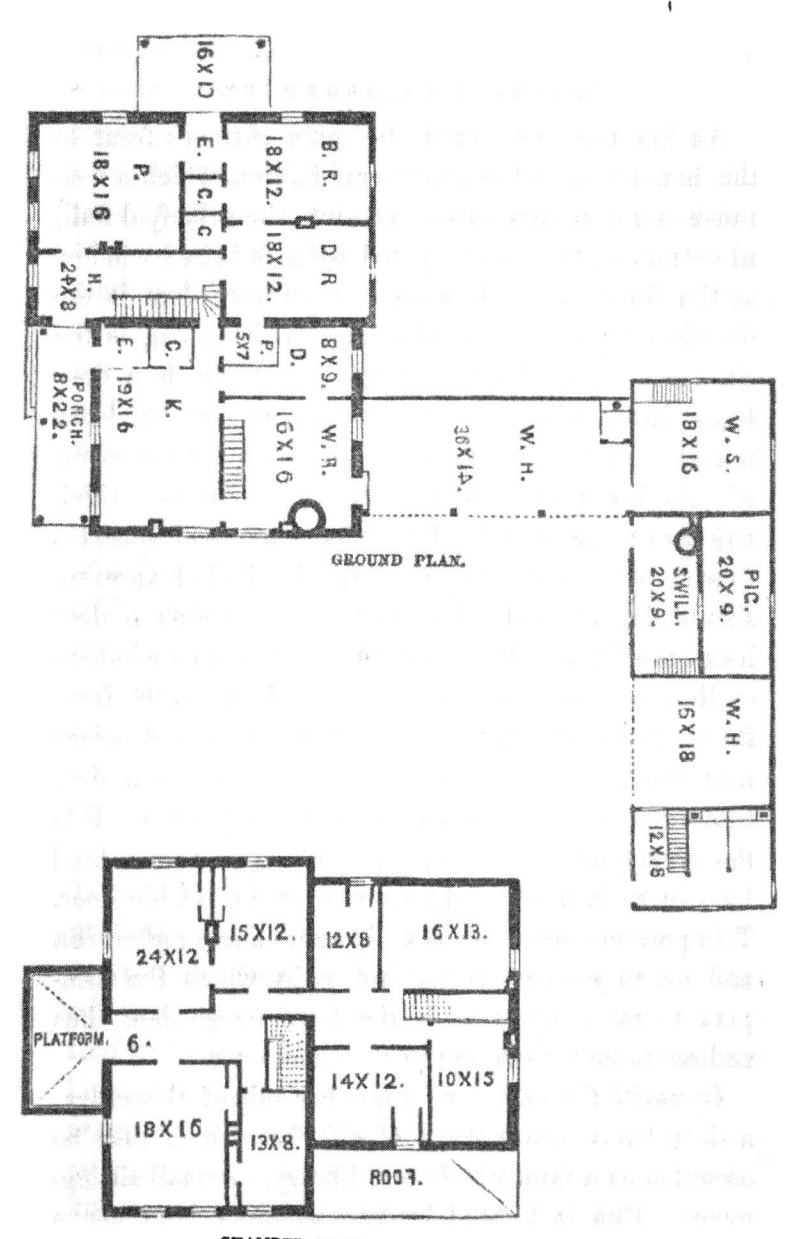

CHAMBER PLAN.

INTERIOR ARRANGEMENT.

As has been remarked, the main entrance front to this house is from the wing veranda, from which a well finished and sizeable door leads into the principal hall, 24×8 feet in area, and lighted by a full-sized window at the front end. Opposite the entrance door is the door leading into the parlor; and farther along is the staircase, under the upper landing of which a door leads into a dining or sitting-room, as may be determined. This hall is 10 feet high, as are all the rooms of this lower main story. In the chimney, which adjoins the parlor side of this hall, may be inserted a thimble for a hall stovepipe, if this method of warming should be adopted. The parlor, into which a door leads from the hall, is 18×16 feet, with two windows on the side, shown in perspective, and one on the front facing the lawn, or garden. It has also a fireplace near the hall door. At the further angle is a door leading to an entry or passage on to the portico. E is the entry just mentioned, six feet square, and lighted by a short sash, one light deep, over the outside door. This portico may be made a pleasant summer afternoon and evening resort for the family, by which the occupied rooms connect with the lawn or garden, thus adding to its retired and private character.

Opposite the parlor, on the other side of this entry, a door leads into a room 18×12 feet, which may be occupied as a family bedroom, library, or small sitting-room. This is lighted by two windows, and has a closet of 6×5 feet. A fireplace is on the inner side of this room; and near to that, a door connects with a dining-room of the same size, having a window in one end, and a fireplace, and closet of the same size as the last. Through the rear wall is a door leading into a pantry, which also communicates with the kitchen; and another door leads to the hall, and from the hall, under the staircases, (which, at that point, are sufficiently high for the purpose,) is a passage leading to the kitchen.

Under the wing veranda, near the point of intersection of the wing with the main body of the house, is an *every-day* outer door, leading into a small entry, 6×5 feet, and lighted by a low, one-sash window over the door. By another door, this leads to the kitchen, or family room, which is lighted by three windows. An ample fireplace, with oven, &c., accommodates this room at the end. A closet, 7×5 feet, also stands next to the entry; and beyond that, an open passage, to the left, leading out under the front hall stairs to the rooms of the main building. A door also leads from that passage into a *best* pantry, for choice crockery, sweetmeats, and tea-table comforts. Another door, near the last, leads into a dairy or milk-room, 9×8 feet, beyond the passage; in which last, also, may be placed a tier of narrow shelves. This milk, or dairy-room, is lighted by a window in the end, and connects also, by a door in the side, with the *outer* kitchen, or wash-room. Next to this milk-room door, in the front kitchen, is another door leading down cellar; and through this door, passing by the upper, broad stair of the flight of cellar steps, is another door into the wash-room. At

5*

the farther angle of the kitchen is still another door, opening into a passage four feet wide; and, in that passage, a door leading up a flight of stairs into the wing chambers. This passage opens into the back kitchen, or wash-room, 16×16 feet in area, and lighted by two windows, one of which looks into the wood-house. In this wash-room is a chimney with boilers and fireplace, as may be required. The cellar and chamber stairs, and the milk-room are also accessible direct, by doors leading from this wash-room.

The chamber plan will be readily understood, and requires no particular description. The space over the wing may be partitioned off according to the plan, or left more open for the accommodation of the "work folks," as occasion may demand. But, as this dwelling is intended for substantial people, "well to do in the world," and who extend a generous hospitality to their friends, a liberal provision of sleeping chambers is given to the main body of the house. The parlor chamber, which is the best, or *spare* one, is 18×16 feet, with roomy side-closets. Besides this, are other rooms for the daughters Sally, and Nancy, and Fanny, and possibly Mary and Elizabeth—who want their own chambers, which they keep so clean and tidy, with closets full of nice bedclothes, table linen, towels, &c., &c., for certain events not yet whispered of, but quite sure to come round. And then there are Frederick, and Robert, and George, fine stalwart boys coming into manhood, intending to be "somebody in the world," one day or another; they must have *their* rooms—and good ones too; for, if any people are to be well lodged, why not those who toil for it? All such accommodation every farm house of this character should afford. And we need not go far, or look sharp, to see the best men and the best women in our state and nation graduating from the wholesome farm house thus tidily and amply provided. How delightfully look the far-off mountains, or the nearer plains, or prairies, from the lawn porch of this snug farm house! The distant lake; the shining river, singing away through the valley; or the wimpling brook, stealing through the meadow! Aye, enjoy them all, for they are God's best, richest gifts, and we are made to love them.

The wood-house strikes off from the back kitchen, retreating two feet from its gable wall, and is 36×14 feet in size. A bathing room may be partitioned off 8×6 feet, on the rear corner next the wash-room, if required, although not laid down in the plan. At the further end is the water-closet, 6×4 feet. Or, if the size and convenience of the family require it, a part of the wood-house may be partitioned off for a wash-room, from which a chimney may pass up through the peak of the roof. If so, carry it up so high that it will be above the eddy that the wind may make in passing over the adjoining wing, not causing it to smoke from that cause.

At the far end of the wood-house is the workshop and tool-house, 18×16 feet, lighted by two windows, and a door to enter it from beneath the wood-house. Over this, is the lumber and store-room.

Next to this is the swill-room and pigsty for the

house pigs, as described in the last design; and over it a loft for farm seeds, small grains, and any other storage required.

Adjoining this is the wagon and carriage-house; and above, the hayloft, stretching, also, partly over the stable which stands next, with two stalls, 12×5 feet each, with a flight of stairs leading to the loft, in the passage next the door. In this loft are swinging windows, to let in hay for the horses.

This completes the household establishment, and we leave the surroundings to the correct judgment and good taste of the proprietor to complete, as its position, and the variety of objects with which it may be connected, requires.

Stone and brick we have mentioned as the proper materials for this house; but it may be also built of wood, if more within the means and limits of the builder. There should be no pinching in its proportions, but every part carried out in its full breadth and effect.

The cost of the whole establishment may be from $2,000, to $3,000; depending somewhat upon the material used, and the finish put upon it. The first-named sum would build the whole in an economical and plain manner, while the latter would complete it amply in its details.

MISCELLANEOUS.

It may be an objection in the minds of some persons to the various plans here submitted, that we have connected the out-buildings *immediately* with the offices of the dwelling itself. We are well aware that such is not always usual; but many years observation have convinced us, that in their use and occupation, such connection is altogether the most convenient and economical. The only drawback is in the case of fire; which, if it occur in any one building, the whole establishment is liable to be consumed. This objection is conceded; but we take it, that it is the business of every one not able to be his own insurer, to have his buildings insured by others; and the additional cost of this insurance is not a tithe of what the extra expense of time, labor, and exposure is caused to the family by having the out-buildings disconnected, and at a *fire-proof* distance from each other. There has, too, in the separation of these out-buildings, (we do not now speak of barns, and houses for the stock, and the farmwork proper,) from the main dwelling, crept into the construction of such dwellings, by modern builders, *some* things, which in a country establishment, particulariy, ought never to be there, such as privies, or *water-closets*, as they are more *genteelly* called. These last, in our estimation, have no business *in a farmer's* house. They are an *effeminacy*, only, and introduced by *city* life. An *appendage* they should be, but separated to some distance from the living rooms, and accessible by sheltered passages to them. The wood-house should adjoin the outer kitchen, because the fuel should always be handy, and the outer kitchen, or wash-room is a sort of *slop-room*, of necessity; and the night wood, and that for the morning fires may be deposited in it for immediate use. The workshop, and small tool-house naturally comes next to that, as being chiefly used in stormy weather. Next to this last, would, more conveniently, come the carriage or wagon-house, and of course a stable for a horse or two for family use, always accessible at night, and convenient at unseasonable hours for farm labor. In the same close neighborhood, also, should be a small pigsty, to accommodate a pig or two, to eat up the kitchen slops from the table, refuse vegetables, parings, dishwater, &c., &c., which could not well be carried to the main piggery of the farm, unless the old-fashioned filthy mode of letting the hogs run in the road, and a trough set outside the door-yard fence, as seen in some parts of the country, were adopted. A pig can always be kept, and fatted in three or four months, from the wash of the house, with a little grain, in any well-regulated farmer's family. A few fowls may also be kept in a convenient hen-house, if desired, without offence — all constituting a part of the *household* economy of the place.

These out-buildings too, give a comfortable, domestic look to the whole concern. Each one shelters and protects the other, and gives an air of comfort and repose to the whole — a family expression all round. What so naked and chilling to the feelings, as to see a country dwelling-house all perked up, by itself standing, literally, out of doors, without any dependencies about it? No, no. First should stand the house, the chief structure, in the foreground; appendant to that, the kitchen wing; next in grade, the wood-house; covering in, also, the minor offices of the house. Then by way of setting up, partially on their own account, should come the workshop, carriage-house, and stable, as practically having a separate character, but still subordinate to the house and its requirements; and these too, may have their piggery and hen-house, by way of tapering off to the adjoining fence, which encloses a kitchen garden, or family orchard. Thus, each structure is appropriate in its way — and together, they form a combination grateful to the sight, as a complete rural picture. All objections, on account of filth or vermin, to this connection, may be removed by a cleanly keeping of the premises — a removal of all offal immediately as it is made, and daily or weekly taking it on to the manure heaps of the barns, or depositing it at once on the grounds where it is required. In point of health, nothing is more congenial to sound physical condition than the occasional smell of a stable, or the breath of a cow, not within the immediate contiguity to the occupied rooms of the dwelling. On the score of neatness, therefore, as we have placed them, no bar can be raised to their adoption.

Design IV.

This is perhaps a more ambitious house than either of the preceding, although it may be adapted to a domain of the same extent and value. It is plain and unpretending in appearance; yet, in its ample finish, and deeply drawn, sheltering eaves, broad veranda, and spacious out-buildings, may give accommodation to a larger family indulging a more liberal style of living than the last.

By an error in the engraving, the main roof of the house is made to appear like a double, or gambrel-roof, breaking at the intersection of the gable, or hanging roof over the ends. This is not so intended. The roofs on each side are a straight line of rafters. The Swiss, or hanging style of gable-roof is designed to give a more sheltered effect to the elevation than to run the end walls to a peak in the point of the roof.

By a defect in the drawing, the roof of the veranda is not sufficiently thrown over the columns. This roof should project at least one foot beyond them, so as to perfectly shelter the mouldings beneath from the weather, and conform to the style of the main roof of the house.

The material of which it is built may be of either stone, brick, or wood, as the taste or convenience of the proprietor may suggest. The main building is 44×36 feet, on the ground. The cellar wall may show

FARM HOUSE.

18 to 24 inches above the ground, and be pierced by windows in each end, as shown in the plan. The height of the main walls may be two full stories below the roof plates, or the chambers may run a foot or two into the garret, at the choice of the builder, either of which arrangements may be permitted.

The front door opens from a veranda 28 feet long by 10 feet in depth, dropping eight inches from the door-sill. This veranda has a hipped roof, which juts over the columns in due proportion with the roof of the house over its walls. These columns are plain, with brackets, or braces from near their tops, sustaining the plate and finish of the roof above, which may be covered either with tin or zinc, painted, or closely shingled.

The walls of the house may be 18 to 20 feet high below the plates; the roof a pitch of 30 to 45°, which will afford an upper garret, or store, or small sleeping rooms, if required; and the eaves should project two to three feet, as climate may demand, over the walls. A plain finish—that is, ceiled underneath—is shown in the design, but brackets on the ends of the rafters, beaded and finished, may be shown, if preferred. The gables are *Swiss-roofed*, or *truncated*, thus giving them a most sheltered and comfortable appearance, particularly in a northerly climate. The small gable in front relieves the roof of its monotony, and affords light to the central garret. The chimneys are carried out with partition flues, and may be topped with square caps, as necessity or taste may demand.

Retreating three feet from the kitchen side of the

house runs, at right angles, a wing 30×18 feet, one and a half stories high, with a veranda eight feet wide in front. Next in rear of this, continues a wood-house, 30×18 feet, one story high, with ten feet posts, and open in front, the ground level of which is 18 inches below the floor of the wing to which it is attached. The roof of these two is of like character with that of the main building.

Adjoining this wood-house, and at right angles with it, is a building 68×18 feet, projecting two feet outside the line of wood-house and kitchen. This building is one and a half stories high, with 12 feet posts, and roof in the same style and of equal pitch as the others.

INTERIOR ARRANGEMENT.

The front door from the veranda of the house opens into a hall, 18×8 feet, and 11 feet high, amply lighted by sash windows on the sides, and over the door. From the rear of this hall runs a flight of easy stairs, into the upper or chamber hall. On one side of the lower hall, a door leads into a parlor, 18 feet square, and 11 feet high, lighted by three windows, and warmed by an open stove, or fireplace, the pipe passing into a chimney flue in the rear. A door passes from this parlor into a rear passage, or entry, thus giving it access to the kitchen and rear apartments. At the back end of the front hall, a door leads into the rear passage and kitchen; and on the side opposite the parlor, a door opens into the sitting or family room, 18×16 feet in

RURAL ARCHITECTURE. 119

area, having an open fireplace, and three windows. On the hall side of this room, a door passes into the kitchen, 22×16 feet, and which may, in case the requirements of the family demand it, be made the chief family or living room, and the last one described converted into a library. In this kitchen, which is

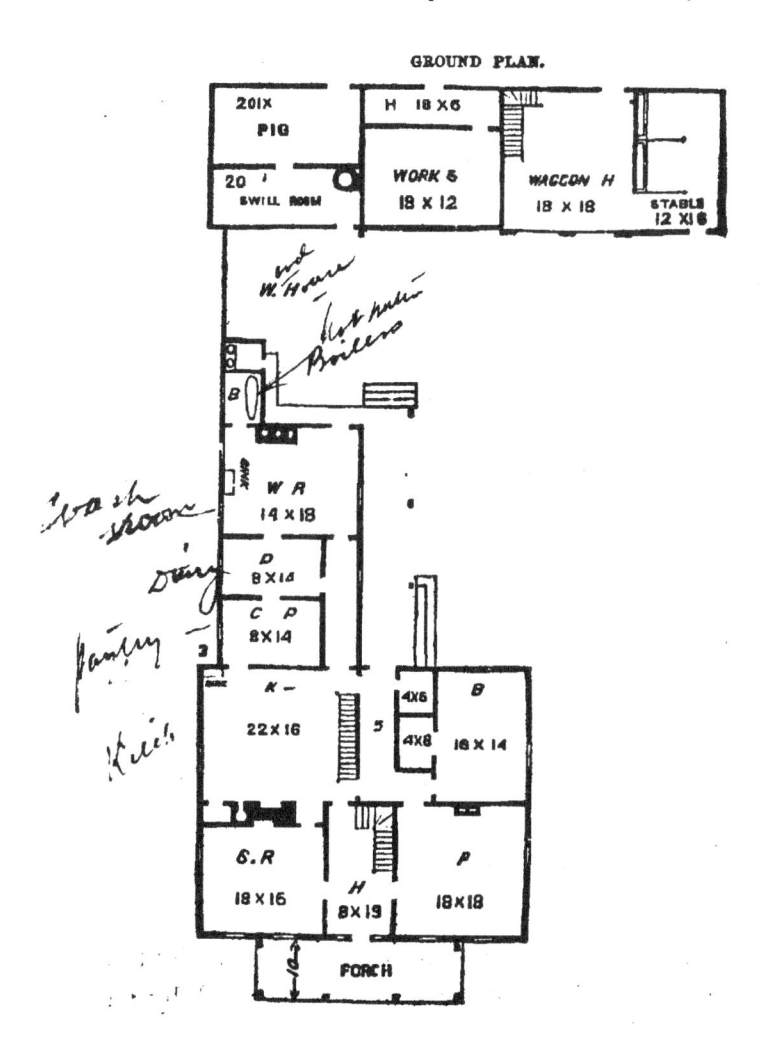

GROUND PLAN.

CHAMBER PLAN.

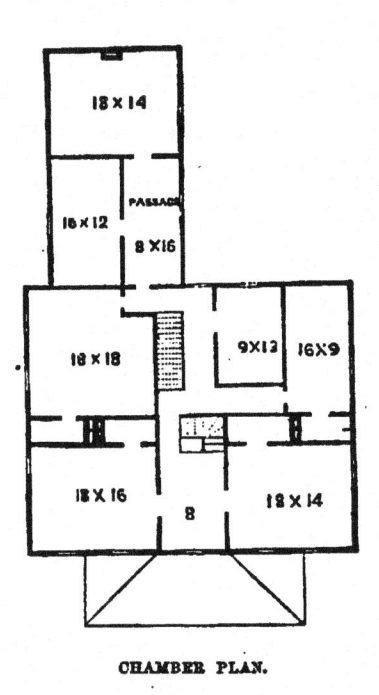

lighted by two windows, is a liberal open fireplace, with an ample oven by its side, and a sink in the outer corner. A flight of stairs, also, leads to the rear chambers above; and a corresponding flight, under them, to the cellar below. A door at each end of these stairs, leads into the back entry of the house, and thus to the other interior rooms, or through the rear outer door to the back porch. This back entry is lighted by a single sash window over the outside door leading to the porch. Another door, opposite that leading down cellar, opens into the passage through the wing. From the rear hall, which is 16×5 feet, the innermost passage leads into a family bedroom, or nursery, 16×14 feet, lighted by a window in each outside wall, and warmed by an open fireplace, or stove, at pleasure. Attached to this bedroom is a clothes-closet, 8×4 feet, with shelves, and drawers. Next the outer door, in rear end of the hall, is a small closet opening from it, 6×4 feet in dimensions, convertible to any use which the mistress of the house may direct.

Opening into the wing from the kitchen, first, is a large closet and pantry, supplied with a table, drawers, and shelves, in which are stored the dishes, table furniture, and edibles necessary to be kept at a moment's access. This room is 14×8 feet, and well lighted by a window of convenient size. If necessary, this room may have a partition, shutting off a part from the everyday uses which the family requires. In this room, so near to the kitchen, to the sink, to hot-water, and the other little domestic accessories which good housewives know so well how to arrange and appreciate, all the nice little table-comforts can be got up, and perfected, and stored away, under lock and key, in drawer, tub, or jar, at their discretion, and still their eyes not be away from their subordinates in the other departments. Next to this, and connected by a door, is the dairy, or milk-room, also 14×8 feet; which, if necessary, may be sunk three or four feet into the ground, for additional coolness in the summer season, and the floor reached by steps. In this are ample shelves for the milkpans, conveniences of churning, &c., &c. But, if the dairy be a prominent object of the farm, a separate establishment will be required, and the excavation may not be necessary for ordinary household uses. Out of this milk-room, a door leads into a wash-room, 18×14 feet. A passage from the kitchen also leads into this. The wash-room is lighted by two windows in rear, and one in front. A sink is between the two rear windows, with conductor leading outside, and a closet beneath it, for the iron ware. In the chimney, at the end, are boilers, and a fireplace, an oven, or anything else required, and a door leading to a platform in the wood-house, and so into the yard. On the other side of the chimney, a door leads into a bathing-room, 7×6 feet, into which hot water is drawn from one of the boilers adjoining, and cold water may be introduced, by a hand-pump, through a pipe leading into the well or cistern.

As no more convenient opportunity may present itself, a word or two will be suggested as to the location of the bath-room in a country house. In city houses, or country houses designed for the summer occupancy of city dwellers, the bathing-rooms are usually placed in the second or chamber story, and the water for their supply is drawn from cisterns still above *them*. This arrangement, in city houses, is made chiefly from the want of room on the ground floor; and, also, thus arranged in the city-country houses, *because* they are so constructed in the city. In the farm house, or in the country house proper, occupied by whom it may be, such arrangement is unnecessary, expensive, and inconvenient. Unnecessary, because there is no want of room on the ground; expensive, because an upper cistern is always liable to leakages, and a consequent wastage of water, wetting, and rotting out the floors, and all the slopping and dripping which such accidents occasion; and inconvenient, from the continual up-and-down-stair labor of those who occupy the bath, to say nothing of the piercing the walls of the house, for the admission of pipes to lead in and let out the water, and the thousand-and-one vexations, by way of plumbers' bills, and expense of getting to and from the house itself, always a distance of some miles from the mechanic.

The only defence for such location of the bath-room and cisterns is, the convenience and privacy of access to them, by the females of the family. This counts but little, if anything, over the place appropriated in this, and the succeeding designs of this work. The access is almost, if not quite as private as the other, and, in case of ill-health, as easily approachable to invalids. And on the score of economy in construction, repair, or accident, the plan here adopted is altogether preferable. In this plan, the water is drawn from the boiler by the turning of a cock; that from the cistern, by a minute's labor with the hand-pump. It is let off by the drawing of a plug, and discharges, by a short pipe, into the adjoining garden, or grassplat, to moisten and invigorate the trees and plants which require it, and the whole affair is clean and sweet again. A screen for the window gives all the privacy required, and the most fastidious, shrinking female is as retired as in the shadiest nook of her dressing-room.

So with water-closets. A fashion prevails of thrusting these noisome things into the midst of sleeping chambers and living rooms — pandering to effeminacy, and, at times, surcharging the house — for they cannot, at *all* times, and under *all* circumstances, be kept perfectly close — with their offensive odor. *Out* of the house they belong; and if they, by any means, find their way within its walls proper, the fault will not be laid at our door.

To get back to our description. This bathing-room occupies a corner of the wood-house.

A raised platform passes from the wash-room in, past the bath-room, to a water-closet, which may be divided into two apartments, if desirable. The vaults are accessible from the rear, for cleaning out, or introducing lime, gypsum, powdered charcoal, or other deodorizing material. At the extreme corner of the wood-house, a door opens into a feed and swill-room, 20×8 feet, which is reached by steps, and stands quite eighteen inches above the ground level, on a stone under-pinning, or with a stone cellar beneath, for the storage of roots in winter. In one corner of this is a boiler and chimney, for cooking food for the pigs and chickens. A door leads from this room into the piggery, 20×12 feet, where half-a-dozen swine may be kept. A door leads from this pen into a yard, in the rear, where they will be less offensive than if confined within. If necessary, a flight of steps, leading to the loft overhead, may be built, where corn can be stored for their feeding.

Next to this is the workshop and tool-house, 18×14 feet; and, in rear, a snug, warm house for the family chickens, 18×6 feet. These chickens may also have the run of the yard in rear, with the pigs, and apartments in the loft overhead for roosting.

Adjoining the workshop is the carriage-house, 18×18 feet, with a flight of stairs to the hayloft above, in which is, also, a dovecote; and, leading out of the carriage floor, is the stable, 18×12 feet, with stalls for two or four horses, and a passage of four feet wide, from the carriage-house into it; thus completing, and drawing under one continuous roof, and at less exposure than if separated, the chief every-day requirements of living, to a well-arranged and highly-respectable family.

The chamber plan of the dwelling will be readily understood by reference to its arrangement. There are a sufficiency of closets for all purposes, and the whole are accessible from either flight of stairs. The rooms over the wing, of course, should be devoted to the male domestics of the family, work-people, &c.

SURROUNDING PLANTATIONS, SHRUBBERY, WALKS, ETC.

After the general remarks made in the preceding pages, no *particular* instructions can be given for the manner in which this residence should be embellished in its trees and shrubbery. The large forest trees, always grand, graceful, and appropriate, would become such a house, throwing a protecting air around and over its quiet, unpretending roof. Vines, or climbing roses, might throw their delicate spray around the columns of the modest veranda, and a varied selection of familiar shrubbery and ornamental plants checker the immediate front and sides of the house looking out upon the lawn; through which a spacious walk, or carriage-way should wind, from the high road, or chief approach.

There are, however, so many objects to be consulted in the various sites of houses, that no one rule can be laid down for individual guidance. The surface of the ground immediately adjoining the house must be considered; the position of the house, as it is viewed from surrounding objects; its altitude, or depression, as affected by the adjacent lands; its command upon surrounding near, or distant objects, in the way of prospect; the presence of water, either in stream, pond, or lake, far or near, or the absence of water altogether— all these enter immediately into the manner in which the lawn of a house should be laid out, and worked and planted. But as a rule, all *filagree* work, such as serpentine paths, and tortuous, unmeaning circles, artificial piles of rock, and a multitude of small *ornaments*—so esteemed, by some—should never be introduced into the lawn of a *farm* house. It is unmeaning, in the first place; expensive in its care, in the second place; unsatisfactory and annoying altogether. Such things about a farm establishment are neither dignified nor useful, and should be left to town's-people, having but a stinted appreciation of what constitutes *natural* beauty, and wanting to make the most of the limited piece of ground of which they are possessed.

Nor would we shut out, by these remarks, the beauty and odor of the flower-borders, which are so appropriately the care of the good matron of the household and her comely daughters. To them may be devoted a **well-dug plat beneath the windows, or in the garden**

Enough, and to spare, they should always have, of such cheerful, life-giving pleasures. We only object to their being strewed all over the ground,—a tussoc of plant here, a patch of posey there, and a scattering of both everywhere, without either system or meaning. They lower the dignity and simplicity of the country dwelling altogether.

The business approach to this house is, of course, toward the stables and carriage-house, and from them should lead off the main farm-avenue.

The kitchen garden, if possible, should lie on the kitchen side of the house, where, also, should be placed the bee-house, in full sight from the windows, that their labors and swarming may be watched. In fact, the entire economy of the farm house, and its appendages, should be brought close under the eye of the household, to engage their care and watchfulness, and to interest them in all the little associations and endearments — and they are many, when properly studied out — which go to make agricultural life one of the most agreeable pursuits, if not altogether so, in which our lot in life may be cast.

A fruit-garden, too, should be a prominent object near this house. We are now advancing somewhat into the *elegances* of agricultural life; and although fruit trees, and *good* fruits too, should hold a strong place in the surroundings of even the humblest of all country places — sufficient, at least, for the ample use of the family — they have not yet been noticed, to any extent, in those already described. It may be remarked, that the fruit-*garden* — the *orchard*, for market purposes, is not here intended — should be placed in near proximity to the house. All the *small* fruits, for household use, such as strawberries, raspberries, currants, gooseberries, blackberries, grapes, as well as apricots, plums, nectarines, peaches, pears, apples, quinces, or whatever fruits may be cultivated, in different localities, should be close by, for the convenience of collecting them, and to protect them from destruction by vermin, birds, or the depredations of creatures *called* human.

A decided plan of arrangement for all the plantations and grounds, should enter into the composition of the site for the dwelling, out-houses, gardens, &c., as they are to appear when the whole establishment is completed; and nothing left to accident, chance, or after-thought, which can be disposed of at the commencement. By the adoption of such a course, the entire composition is more easily perfected, and with infinitely greater expression of character, than if left to the chance designs, or accidental demands of the future.

Another feature should be strictly enforced, in the outward appointments of the farm house,— and that is, the entire withdrawal of any use of the highway in its occupation by the stock of the farm, except in leading them to and from its enclosures. Nothing looks more slovenly, and nothing can be more unthrifty, in an *enclosed* country, than the running of farm stock in the highway. What so untidy as the approach to a house, with a herd of filthy hogs rooting about the fences, basking along the sidewalk, or feeding at a huge, uncouth, hollowed log, in the road near the dwelling It may be out of place here to speak of it, but this disgusting spectacle has so often offended our sight, at the approach of an otherwise pleasant farm establishment, that we cannot forego the opportunity to speak of it. The road lying in front, or between the different sections of the farm, should be as well, and as cleanly kept as any portion of the enclosures, and it is equally a sin against good taste and neighborhood-morality, to have it otherwise.

TREE-PLANTING IN THE HIGHWAY.

This is frequently recommended by writers on country embellishment, as indispensable to a finished decoration of the farm. Such may, or may not be the fact. Trees shade the roads, when planted on their sides, and so they partially do the fields adjoining, making the first muddy, in bad weather, by preventing the sun drying them, and shading the crops of the last by their overhanging foliage, in the season of their growth. Thus they are an evil, in moist and heavy soils. Yet, in light soils, their shade is grateful to the highway traveler, and not, perhaps, injurious to the crops of the adjoining field; and when of proper kinds, they add grace and beauty to the domain in which they stand.

We do not, therefore, indiscriminately recommend them, but leave it to the discretion of the farmer, to decide for himself, having seen estates equally pleasant with, and without trees on the roadside. Nothing, however, can be more beautiful than a clump of trees in a pasture-ground, with a herd, or a flock beneath them, near the road; or the grand and overshadowing branches of stately tree, in a rich meadow, leaning, perhaps, over the highway fence, or flourishing in its solitary grandeur, in the distance—each, and all, imposing features in the rural landscape. All such should be preserved, with the greatest care and solicitude, as among the highest and most attractive ornaments which the farm can boast.

Design V.

We here present a dwelling of a more ambitious and pretending character than any one which we have, as yet, described, and calculated for a large and wealthy farmer, who indulges in the elegances of country life, dispenses a liberal hospitality, and is every way a country gentleman, such as all our farmers of ample means should be. It will answer the demands of the retired man of business as well; and is, perhaps, as full in its various accommodation as an American farm or country house may require. It claims no distinct style of architecture, but is a composition agreeable in effect, and appropriate to almost any part of the country, and its climate. Its site may be on either hill or plain—with a view extensive, or restricted. It may look out over broad savannas, cultivated fields, and shining waters; it may nestle amid its own quiet woods and lawn in its own selected shade and retirement, or lord it over an extensive park, ranged by herds and flocks, meandered by its own stream, spreading anon into the placid lake, or rushing swiftly over its own narrow bed—an independent, substantial, convenient, and well-conditioned home, standing upon its own broad acres, and comporting with the character and standing of its occupant, among his friends and neighbors.

The main building is 50×40 feet in area upon the ground, two stories high; the ground story 11 feet high, its floor elevated 2½ or 3 feet above the level of the surrounding surface, as its position may demand; the chambers 9 feet high, and running 2 feet into the roof. The rear wing is one and a half stories high, 36×16 feet; the lower rooms 11 feet high, with a one story lean-to range of closets, and small rooms on the weather side, 8 feet in width and 9 feet high. In the rear of these is a wood-house, 30×20 feet, with 10 feet posts, dropped to a level with the ground. At the extremity of this is a building, by way of an L, 60×20 feet, one and a half stories high, with a lean-to, 12×30 feet, in the rear. The ground rooms of this are elevated 1½ feet above the ground, and 9 feet high. A broad roof covers the whole, standing at an angle of 40 or 45° above a horizontal line, and projecting widely over the walls, 2½ to 3 feet on the main building, and 2 feet on the others, to shelter them perfectly from the storms and damps of the weather. A small cupola stands out of the ridge of the rear building, which may serve as a ventilator to the apartments and lofts below, and in it may be hung a bell, to summon the household, or the field laborers, as the case may be, to their duties or their meals.

The design, as here shown, is rather florid, and perhaps profusely ornamental in its finish, as comporting with the taste of the day; but the cut and moulded trimmings may be left off by those who prefer a plain finish, and be no detriment to the general effect which the deep friezes of the roofs, properly cased beneath, may give to it. Such, indeed, is our own taste; but this full finish has been added, to gratify such as wish the full ornament which this style of building may admit.

INTERIOR ARRANGEMENT.

The front of this house is accommodated by a porch, or veranda, 40 feet long, and 10 feet wide, with a central, or entrance projection of 18 feet in length, and 12 feet in width, the floor of which is eight inches below the main floor of the house. The wings, or sides of this veranda may be so fitted up as to allow a pleasant conservatory on each side of the entrance area in winter, by enclosing them with glass windows, and the introduction of heat from a furnace under the main hall, in the cellar of the house. This would add to its general effect in winter, and, if continued through the summer, would not detract from its expression of dignity and refinement. From the veranda, a door in the center of the front, with two side windows, leads into the main hall, which is 26×12 feet in area, two feet in the width of which is taken from the rooms on the right of the main entrance. On the left of the hall a door opens into a parlor or drawing-room, marked P, 20 feet square, with a bay window on one side, containing three sashes, and seats beneath. A single window lights the front opening on to the veranda. On the opposite side to this is the fireplace, with blank walls on each side. On the opposite side of the hall is a library, 18×16 feet, with an end window, and a

GROUND PLAN.

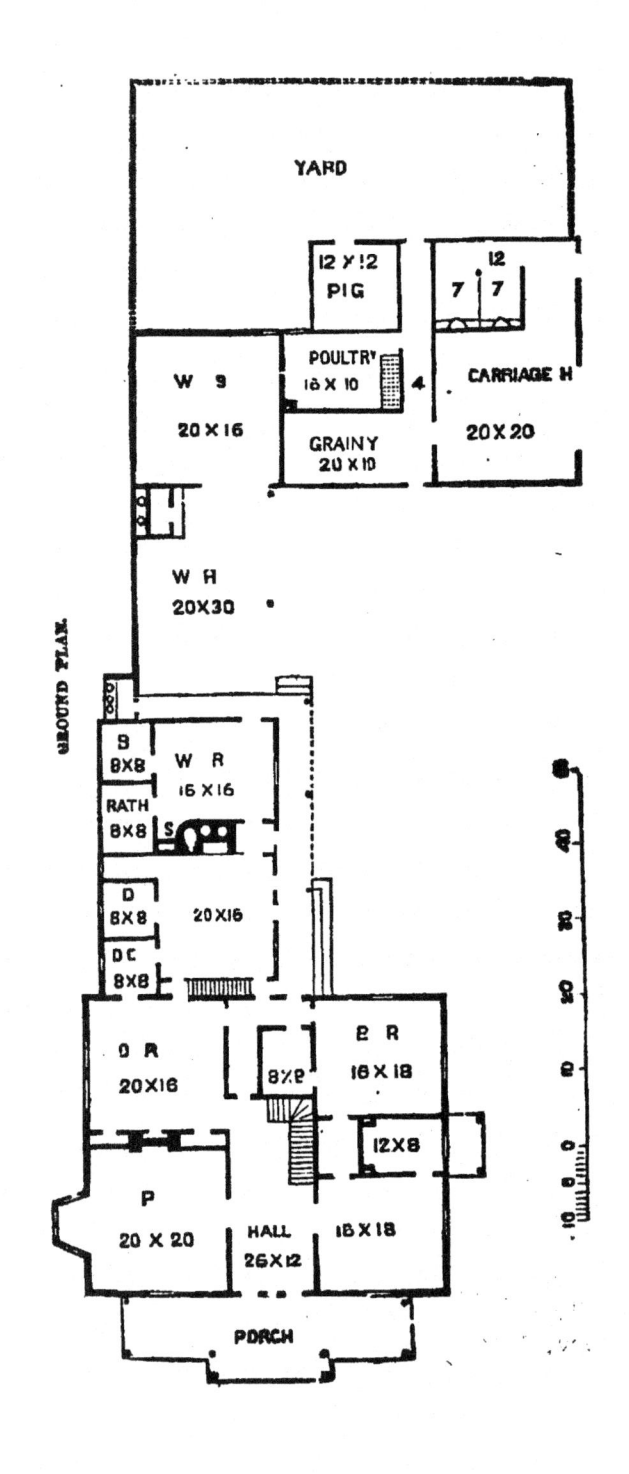

YARD

12 × 12 PIG		12 7 7
W 9 20×16	POULTRY 18×10	CARRIAGE H 20×20
	GRAINY 20×10	

W R 20×30

B 8×8	W R 16×16
BATH 8×8	S
D 8×8	20×16
DC 8×8	

D R 20×16		P R 16×18
	8×8	
		12×8
P 20×20	HALL 26×12	18×18

PORCH

corresponding one to the parlor, in front, looking out on the veranda. In case these portions of the veranda, opposite the two front windows are occupied as conservatories, these windows should open to the floor, to admit a walk immediately into them. At the farther corner of the library a narrow door leads into an office, or business apartment, 12×8 feet, and opening by a broad door, the upper half of which is a lighted sash. This door leads from the office out on a small porch, with a floor and two columns, 8×5 feet, and nine feet high, with a gable and double roof of the same pitch as the house. Between the chimney flues, in the rear of this room may be placed an iron safe, or chest for the deposit of valuable papers; and, although small, a table and chairs sufficient to accommodate the business requirements of the occupant, may be kept in it. A chimney stands in the center of the inner wall of the library, in which may be a fireplace, or a flue to receive a stovepipe, whichever may be preferred for warming the room.

Near the hall side of the library a door opens into a passage leading into the family bedroom, or nursery. A portion of this passage may be shelved and fitted up as a closet for any convenient purpose. The nursery is 18×16 feet in size, lighted by two windows. It may have an open fireplace, or a stove, as preferred, let into the chimney, corresponding to that in the library. These two chimneys may either be drawn together in the chambers immediately above, or carried up separately into the garret, and pass out of the roof in one stack, or they may be built in one solid mass from the cellar bottom; but they are so placed here, as saving room on the floors, and equally accommodating, in their separate divisions, the stovepipes that may lead into them. On the inner side of the nursery, a door leads into a large closet, or child's sleeping-room, 9×8 feet; or it may be used as a dressing-room, with a sash inserted in the door to light it. A door may also lead from it into the small rear entry of the house, and thus pass directly out, without communicating with the nursery. On the extreme left corner of the nursery is a door leading into the back entry, by which it communicates either with the rear porch, the dining-room, or the kitchen. Such a room we consider indispensable to the proper accommodation of a house in the country, as saving a world of up-and-down-stairs' labor to her who is usually charged with the domestic cares and supervision of the family.

On the right of the main hall an ample staircase leads into the upper hall by a landing and broad stair at eight feet above the floor, and a right-angled flight from that to the main floor above. Under this main hall staircase, a door and stairs may lead into the cellar. Beyond the turning flight below, a door leads into the back hall, or entry, already mentioned, which is 13×4 feet in area, which also has a side passage of 8×4 feet, and a door leading to the rear porch, and another into the kitchen at its farther side, near the outer one. Opposite the turning flight of stairs, in the main hall, is also a door leading to the dining-room, 20×16 feet. This is lighted by a large double window at the end. A fireplace, or stove flue is in the center wall, and on each side a closet for plate, or table furniture. These closets come out flush with the chimney. At the extreme right corner a door leads into the rear entry — or this may be omitted, at pleasure. Another door in the rear wall leads into the kitchen, past the passage down into the cellar — or this may be omitted, if thought best. Still another door to the left, opens into a large dining closet of the back lean-to apartments, 8×8 feet. This closet is lighted by a window of proper architectural size, and fitted up with a suite of drawers, shelves, table, and cupboards, required for the preparation and deposit of the lighter family stores and edibles. From this closet is also a door leading into the kitchen, through which may be passed all the meats and cookery for the table, either for safe-keeping, or immediate service. Here the thrifty and careful housekeeper and her assistants may, shut apart, and by themselves, get up, fabricate, and arrange all their table delicacies with the greatest convenience and privacy, together with ease of access either to the dining-room or kitchen — an apartment most necessary in a liberally-arranged establishment.

From the rear entry opens a door to the kitchen, passing by the *rear* chamber stairs. This flight of stairs may be entered directly from the kitchen, leading either to the chamber, or under them, into the cellar, without coming into the passage connecting with the entry or dining-room, if preferred. In such case, a broad stair of thirty inches in width should be next the door, on which to turn, as the door would be at right angles with the stairs, either up or down.

The kitchen is 20×16 feet, and 11 feet high. It has an outer door leading on the rear porch, and a window on each side of that door; also a window, under which is a sink, on the opposite side, at the end of a passage four feet wide, leading through the lean-to. It has also an open fireplace, and an oven by the side of it—old fashion. It may be also furnished with a cooking range, or stove—the smoke and fumes leading by a pipe into a flue into the chimney. On the lean-to side is a milk or dairy-room, 8×8 feet, lighted by a window. Here also the kitchen furniture and meats may be stored in cupboards made for the purpose. In rear of the kitchen, and leading from it by a door through a lighted passage next the rear porch, is the wash-room, 16×16 feet, lighted by a large window from the porch side. A door also leads out of the rear on to a platform into the wood-house. Another door leads from the wash-room into a bath-room in the lean-to 8×8 feet, into which warm water is drawn by a pipe and pump from the boiler in the wash-room; or, if preferred, the bath-room may be entered from the main kitchen, by the passage next the sink. This bath-room is lighted by a window. Next to the bath-room is a bedroom for a man servant who has charge of the fires, and heavy house-work, wood, &c., &c. This bedroom is also 8×8 feet, and lighted by a window in the lean-to. In front of this wash-room and kitchen is a porch, eight inches below the floor, six feet wide, with a railing, or not, as may be preferred. (The railing is made in the cut.) A platform, three feet wide, leads from the back door of the wash-room to a water-closet for the family *proper*. The wood-house is open in front, with a single post supporting the center of the roof. At the extreme outer angle is a water-closet for the domestics of the establishment.

Adjoining the wood-house, and opening from it into the L before mentioned, is a workshop, and small-tool-house, 20×16 feet, lighted by a large double window at one end. In this should be a carpenter's work-bench and tool-chest, for the repairs of the farming utensils and vehicles. Overhead is a store-room for lumber, or whatever else may be necessary for use in that capacity. Next to this is a granary or feed-room, 20×10 feet, with a small chimney in one corner, where may be placed a boiler to cook food for pigs, poultry, &c., as the case may be. Here may also be bins for storage of grain and meal. Leading out of this is a flight of stairs passing to the chamber above, and a passage four feet wide, through the rear, into a yard adjoining. At the further end of the stairs a door opens into a poultry house, 16×10 feet, including the stairs. The poultry room is lighted at the extreme left corner, by a broad window. In this may be made roosts, and nesting places, and feeding troughs. A low door under the window may be also made for the fowls in passing to the rear yard. Adjoining the granary, and leading to it by a door, is the carriage-house, 20×20 feet, at the gable end of which are large doors for entrance. From the carriage-house is a broad passage of six feet, into the stables, which are 12 feet wide, and occupy the lean-to. This lean-to is eight feet high below the eaves, with two double stalls for horses, and a door leading into the *side* yard, with the doors of the carriage-house. A window also lights the rear of the stables. A piggery 12 feet square occupies the remainder of the lean-to in rear of the poultry-house, in which two or three pigs can always be kept, and fatted on the offal of the house, for *small* pork, at any season, apart from the swine stock of the farm. A door leads out of the piggery into the rear yard, where range also the poultry. As the *shed* roof shuts down on to the pigsty and stables, no loft above them is necessary. In the loft over the granary, poultry, and carriage-house is deposited the hay, put in there through the doors which appear in the design.

CHAMBER PLAN.—This is easily understood. At the head of the stairs, over the main hall, is a large passage leading to the porch, and opening by a door-window on the middle deck of the veranda, which is nearly level, and tinned, or coppered, water-tight, as are also the two sides. On either side of this upper hall is a door leading to the front sleeping chambers, which are well closeted, and spacious. If it be desirable to construct more sleeping-rooms, they can be partitioned laterally from the hall, and doors made to enter them. A rear hall is cut off from the front, lighted by a window over the lower rear porch, and a door leads into a further passage in the wing, four feet wide, which leads down a flight of stairs into the kitchen below. At the head of this flight is a chamber 20×12 feet, for the female domestic's sleeping-room, in which may be placed a stove, if necessary, passing its pipe into the kitchen chimney which passes through it.

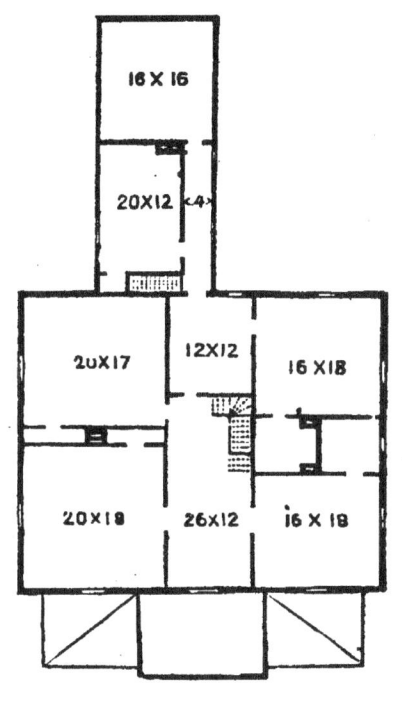

CHAMBER PLAN.

It is also lighted by a window over the lean-to, on the side. Back of this, at the end of the passage, is the sleeping-room, 16 feet square, for the "men-folks," lighted on both sides by a window. This may also be warmed, if desired, by a stove, the pipe passing into the kitchen chimney.

The cellar may extend under the entire house and wing, as convenience or necessity may require. If it be constructed under the main body only, an offset should be excavated to accommodate the cellar stairs, three feet in width, and walled in with the rest. A wide, *outer* passage, with a flight of steps should also be made under the rear nursery window, for taking in and passing out bulky articles, with double doors to shut down upon it; and partition walls should be built to support the partitions of the large rooms above. Many minor items of detail might be mentioned, all of which are already treated in the general remarks, under their proper heads, in the body of the work, and which cannot here be noticed — such as the mode of warming it, the construction of furnaces, &c.

It may, by some builders, be considered a striking defect in the interior accommodation of a house of this character, that the chief entrance hall should not be extended through, from its front to the rear, as is common in many of the large mansions of our country. We object to the large, open hall for more than one reason, except, possibly, in a house for *summer* occupation only. In the first place it is uncomfortable, in subjecting the house to an unnecessary draught of air when it is not needed, in cold weather. Secondly, it cuts the house into two distinct parts, making them inconvenient of access in crossing its wide surface. Thirdly, it is uneconomical, in taking up valuable room that can be better appropriated. For summer ventilation it is unnecessary; that may be given by simply opening the front door and a chamber window connected with the hall above, through which a current of fresh air will always pass. Another thing, the hall belongs to the front, or *dress* part of the house, and should be *cut off* from the more domestic and common apartments by a partition, although accessible to them, and not directly communicating with such apartments, which cannot of necessity, be in keeping with its showy and pretending character. It should contain only the *front* flight of stairs, as a part of its appointments, besides the doors leading to its best apartments on the ground floor, which should be centrally placed — its rear door being of a less pretending and subordinate character. Thus, the hall, with its open doors, connecting the best rooms of the house on each side, with its ample flight of stairs in the background, gives a distinct expression of superiority in occupation to the other and humbler portions of the dwelling.

In winter, too, how much more snug and comfortable is the house, shut in from the prying winds and shivering cold of the outside air, which the opposite outer doors of an open hall cannot, in their continual opening and shutting, altogether exclude! Our own experience, and, we believe, the experience of most housekeepers will readily concede its defects; and after full reflection we have excluded it as both unnecessary and inconvenient.

Another objection has been avoided in the better class of houses here presented, which has crept into very many of the designs of modern builders; which is, that of using the living rooms of the family, more or less, as passages from the kitchen apartments in passing to and from the front hall, or chief entrance. Such we consider a decided objection, and hence arose, probably, the older plans of by-gone years, of making the main hall reach back to the kitchen itself. This is here obviated by a cutting up of the rear section of the hall, by which a passage, in all cases of the better kind of dwelling, is preserved, without encroaching upon the occupied rooms in passing out and in. To be sure, the front door is not the usual passage for the laborers or servants of the house, but they are subject, any hour of the day, to be called there to admit those who may come, and the continual opening of a private room for such purposes is most annoying. Therefore, as matter of convenience, and as a decided improvement on the designs above noticed, we have adhered strictly to the separate rear passage.

The *garret*, also, as we have arranged our designs, is either altogether left out, or made a quite unimportant part of the dwelling. It is but a *lumber* room, at best; and should be approached only by a flight of steps from a rear chamber or passage, and used as a receptacle for useless traps, or cast-off furniture, seldom wanted. It is hot in summer, and cold in winter, unfit for decent lodging to any human being in the house, and of little account any way. We much prefer running the chambers partially into the roof, which we think gives them a more comfortable expression, and admits of a better ventilation, by carrying their ceilings higher without the expense of high *body* walls to the house, which would give them an otherwise naked look. If it be objected that thus running the chambers above the plates of the roof prevents the insertion of proper ties or beams to hold the roof plates together to prevent their spreading, we answer, that he must be a poor mechanic who cannot, in framing the chamber partitions so connect the opposite plates as to insure them against all such difficulty. A *sheltered, comfortable* aspect is that which should distinguish every farm house, and the *cottage* chamber is one of its chiefest characteristics; and this can only be had by running such apartments into the roof, as in our design.

CONSTRUCTION.

A house of this kind must, according to its locality, and the material of which it is built, be liable to wide differences of estimate in its cost; and from our own experience in such matters, any estimate here made we know cannot be reliable as a rule for other localities, where the prices of material and labor are different from our own. Where lumber, stone, and brick abound, and each are to be had at reasonable prices, the cost of an establishment of this kind would not vary much in the application of either one of these materials for the walls, if well and substantially constructed. There should be no *sham*, nor slight, in any part of the building. As already observed, the design shows a high degree of finish, which, if building for ourself, we should not indulge in. A plain style of cornice, and veranda finish, we should certainly adopt. But the roof should not be contracted in its projecting breadth over the walls, in any part of the structure — if anything, it should be more extended. The bay-window is an appendage of luxury, only. Great care should be had, in attaching its roof to the adjoining outer wall, to prevent leakage of any kind. If the walls be of brick, or stone, a beam or lintel of wood should be inserted in the wall over the window-opening, quite two inches — three would be better — back from its outer surface, to receive the casing of the window, that the drip of the wall, and the driving of the storms may fall *over* the connecting joints of the window roof, beyond its point of junction with it. Such, also, should be the case with the intersection of the veranda or porch roof with the wall of the house, wherever a veranda, or porch is adopted; as, simply joined on to a *flush* surface, as such appendages usually are — even if ever so well done — leakage and premature decay is inevitable.

The style of finish must, of course, influence, in a considerable degree, its cost. It may, with the plainest finish, be done for $4,000, and from that, up to $6,000. Every one desirous to build, should apply to the best mechanics of his neighborhood for information on that point, as, in such matters, they are the best judges, and from experience in their own particular profession, of what the cost of building must be.

The rules and customs of housekeeping vary, in different sections of the United States, and the Canadas. These, also, enter into the estimates for certain departments of building, and must be considered in the items of expenditure.

The manner in which houses should be warmed, the ventilation, accommodation for servants and laborers, the appropriations to hospitality — all, will have a bearing on the expense, of which we cannot be the proper judge.

A sufficient time should be given, to build a house of this character. A house designed and built in a hurry, is never a satisfactory house in its occupation. A year is little enough, and if two years be occupied in its design and construction, the more acceptable will probably be its finish, and the more comfort will be added in its enjoyment.

GROUNDS, PLANTATIONS, AND SURROUNDINGS.

A house of this kind should never stand in vulgar and familiar contact with the highway, but at a distance from it of one hundred to a thousand yards; or even, if the estate on which it is built be extensive, a much greater distance. Breadth of ground between the highway and the dwelling adds dignity and character to its appearance. An ample lawn, or a spreading park, well shaded with trees, should lay before it, through which a well-kept avenue leads to its front, and most frequented side. The various offices and buildings of the farm itself, should be at a respectable distance from it, so as not to interfere with its proper keeping as a genteel country residence. Its occupant is not to be supposed as under the necessity of toiling with his daily laborers in the fields, and therefore, although he may be strictly a man of business, he has sufficient employment in planning his work, and managing his estate through a foreman, in the various labor-occupations of the estate. His horse may be at his door in the earliest morning hours, that he may inspect his fields, and give timely directions to his laborers, or view his herds, or his flocks, before his breakfast hour; or an early walk may take him to his stables, his barns, or to see that his previous directions are executed.

The various accommodation appurtenant to the dwelling, makes ample provision for the household convenience of the family, and the main business of the farm may be at some distance, without inconvenience to the owner's every-day affairs. Consequently, the indulgence of a considerable degree of ornament may be given, in the surroundings of his dwelling, which the occupant of a less extensive estate would neither require, nor his circumstances warrant. A natural forest of stately trees, properly thinned out, is the most appropriate spot on which to build a house of this character. But that not at hand, it should be set off with plantations of forest trees, of the largest growth, as in keeping with its own liberal dimensions. A capacious kitchen garden should lead off from the rear apartments, well stocked with all the family vegetables, and culinary fruits, in their proper seasons. A luxuriant fruit-garden may flank the least frequented side of the house. Neat and tasteful flower beds may lie beneath the windows of the rooms appropriated to the leisure hours of the family, to which the smaller varieties of shrubbery may be added, separated from the chief lawn, or park, only by a wire fence, or a simple railing, such as not to cut up and *checker* its simple and dignified surface; and all these shut in on the rear from the adjoining fields of the farm by belts of large shrubbery.

closely planted, or the larger orchards, thus giving it a style of its own, yet showing its connection with the pursuits of the farm and its dependence upon it.

These various appointments, however, may be either carried out or restricted, according to the requirements of the family occupying the estate, and the prevailing local taste of the vicinity in which it is situated; but no narrow or stingy spirit should be indicated in the general plan or in its execution. Every appointment connected with it should indicate a liberality of purpose in the founder, without which its effect is painfully marred to the eye of the man of true taste and judgment. Small yards, picketed in for small uses, have no business in sight of the grounds in front, and all minor concerns should be thrown into the rear, beyond observation from the main approach to the dwelling. The trees that shade the entrance park, or lawn, should be chiefly forest trees, as the oak, in its varieties, the elm, the maple, the chestnut, walnut, butternut, hickory, or beech. If the soil be favorable, a few weeping willows may throw their drooping spray around the house; and if exotic, or foreign trees be permitted, they should take their position in closer proximity to it than the natural forest trees, as indicating the higher care and cultivation which attaches to its presence. The Lombardy poplar, albeit a tree of disputed taste with modern planters, we would now and then throw in, not in stiff and formal rows, as guarding an avenue, but occasionally in the midst of a group of others, above which it should rise like a church spire from amidst a block of contiguous houses—

a cheerful relief to the monotony of the rounder-headed branches of the more spreading varieties. If a stream of water meander the park, or spread into a little pond, trees which are partial to moisture should shadow it at different points, and low, water shrubs should hang over its border, or even run into its margin. Aquatic herbs, too, may form a part of its ornaments, and a boat-house, if such a thing be necessary, should, under the shade of a hanging tree of some kind, be a conspicuous object in the picture. An overhanging rock, if such a thing be native there, may be an object of great attraction to its features, and its outlet may steal away and be hid in a dense mass of tangled vines and brushwood. The predominating, *natural* features of the place should be *cultivated*, not rooted out, and metamorphosed into something foreign and unfamiliar. It should, in short, be *nature* with her *hair combed* out straight, flowing, and graceful, instead of pinched, puffed, and curling—a thing of luxuriance and beauty under the hand of a master.

The great difficulty with many Americans in getting up a new place of any considerable extent is, that they seem to think whatever is common, or natural in the features of the spot must be so changed as to show, above all others, their own ingenuity and love of expense in fashioning it to their peculiar tastes. Rocks must be sunk, or blasted, trees felled, and bushes grubbed, crooked water-courses straightened — the place gibbeted and put into stocks; in fact, that their own boasted handiwork may rise superior to the wisdom of Him who fashioned it in his own good pleasure; forgetting that a thousand points of natural beauty upon the earth on which they breathe are

"When unadorned, adorned the most;"

and our eye has been frequently shocked at finding the choicest gems of nature sacrificed to a wanton display of expense in perverting, to the indulgence of a mistaken fancy, that, which, with an eye to truth and propriety, and at a trifling expense, might have become a spot of abiding interest and contentment.

Design VI.

A Southern or Plantation House.—The proprietor of a plantation in the South, or South-west, requires altogether a different kind of residence from the farmer of the Northern, or Middle States. He resides in the midst of his own principality, surrounded by a retinue of dependents and laborers, who dwell distant and apart from his own immediate family, although composing a community requiring his daily care and superintendence for a great share of his time. A portion of them are the attachés of his household, yet so disconnected in their domestic relations, as to require a separate accommodation, and yet be in immediate contiguity with it, and of course, an arrangement of living widely different from those who mingle in the same circle, and partake at the same board.

The usual plan of house-building at the South, we are aware, is to have *detached* servants' rooms, and offices, and a space of some yards of uncovered way intervene between the family rooms of the chief dwelling and its immediate dependents. Such arrangement, however, we consider both unnecessary and inconvenient; and we have devised a plan of household accommodation which will bring the family of the planter himself, and their servants, although under

FARM HOUSE.

Pages 155-156.

different roofs, into convenient proximity with each other. A design of this kind is here given.

The style is mainly Italian, plain, substantial, yet, we think, becoming. The broad veranda, stretching around three sides, including the front, gives an air of sheltered repose to what might otherwise appear an ambitious structure; and the connected apartments beyond, show a quiet utility which divests it of an over attempt at display. Nothing has been attempted for appearance, solely, beyond what is necessary and proper in the dwelling of a planter of good estate, who wants his domestic affairs well regulated, and his family, and servants duly provided with convenient accommodation. The form of the main dwelling is nearly square, upright, with two full stories, giving ample area of room and ventilation, together with that appropriate indulgence to ease which the enervating warmth of a southern climate renders necessary. The servants' apartments, and kitchen offices are so disposed, that while connected, to render them easy of access, they are sufficiently remote to shut off the familiarity of association which would render them obnoxious to the most fastidious — all, in fact, under one shelter, and within the readiest call. Such should be the construction of a planter's house in the United States, and such this design is intended to give.

A stable and carriage-house, in the same style, is near by, not connected to any part of the dwelling, as in the previous designs — with sufficient accommodation for coachman and grooms, and the number of saddle and carriage horses that may be reqrired for either business or pleasure; and to it may be connected, in the rear, in the same style of building, or plainer, and less expensive, further conveniences for such domestic animals as may be required for family use.

The whole stands in open grounds, and may be separated from each other by enclosures, as convenience or fancy may direct.

The roofs of all the buildings are broad and sweeping, well protecting the walls from storm and frosts, as well as the glaring influences of the sun, and combining that comfortable idea of shelter and repose so grateful in a well-conditioned country house. It is true, that the dwelling might be more extensive in room, and the purposes of luxury enlarged; but the planter on five hundred, or five thousand acres of land can here be sufficiently accommodated in all the reasonable indulgences of family enjoyment, and a liberal, even an elegant and prolonged hospitality, to which he is so generally inclined.

The chimneys of this house, different from those in the previous designs, are placed next the outer walls, thus giving more space to the interior, and not being required, as in the others, to promote additional warmth than their fireplaces will give, to the rooms. A deck on the roof affords a pleasant look-out for the family from its top, guarded by a parapet, and giving a finish to its architectural appearance, and yet making no ambitious attempt at expensive ornament. It is, in fact, a plain, substantial, respectable mansion for a gentleman of good estate, and nothing beyond it.

INTERIOR ARRANGEMENT.

This house stands 50 × 40 feet on the ground. The front door opens from the veranda into a hall, 24 × 14 feet, in which is a flight of stairs leading to the chambers above. On the left a door leads into a library, or

GROUND PLAN.

business room, 17×17 feet, lighted by three windows. A fireplace is inserted in the outer wall. Another door leads into a side hall, six feet wide, which separates the library from the dining-room, which is also 17×17 feet in area, lighted and accommodated with a fireplace like the other, with a door leading into it from the side hall, and another door at the further right hand corner leading into the rear hall, or entry.

On the right of the chief entrance hall, opposite the library, a door opens into the parlor or drawing-room, 23×19 feet in area, lighted by three windows, and having a fireplace in the side wall. A door leads from the rear side of the parlor into a commodious nursery, or family bedroom, 19×16 feet in size, lighted by a window in each outer wall. A fireplace is also inserted on the same line as in the parlor. From the nursery a door leads into and through a large closet, 9×7 feet, into the rear hall. This closet may also be used as a sleeping-room for the children, or a confidential servant-maid, or nurse, or devoted to the storage of bed-linen for family use. Further on, adjoining, is another closet, 7×6 feet, opening from the rear hall, and lighted by a window.

Leading from the outer door of the rear hall is a covered passage six feet wide, 16 feet long, and one and a half stories high, leading to the kitchen offices, and lighted by a window on the left, with a door opening in the same side beyond, on to the side front of the establishment. On the right, opposite, a door leads on to the kitchen porch, which is six feet wide, passing on to the bath-room and water-closet, in the far rear. At the end of the connecting passage from the main dwelling, a door opens into the kitchen, which is 24×18 feet in size, accommodated with two windows looking on to the porch just described. At one end is an open fireplace with a cooking range on one side, and an oven on the other. At the left of the entrance door is a large, commodious store-room and pantry, 12×9 feet, lighted by a window; and adjoining it, (and may be connected with it by a door, if necessary,) a kitchen closet of the same size, also connected by a corresponding door from the opposite corner of the kitchen. Between these doors is a flight of stairs leading to the sleeping-rooms above, and a cellar passage beneath them. In the farther right corner of the kitchen a door leads into a smaller closet, 8×6 feet, lighted by a small window looking on to the rear porch at the end. A door at the rear of the kitchen leads out into the porch of the wash-room beyond, which is six feet wide, and another door into the wash-room itself, which is 20×16 feet, and furnished with a chimney and boilers. A window looks out on the extreme right hand, and two windows on to the porch in front. A door opens from its rear wall into the wood-house, 32×12 feet, which stands open on two sides, supported by posts, and under the extended roof of the wash-room and its porch just mentioned. A servants' water-closet is attached to the extreme right corner of the wood-house, by way of lean-to.

The bath-room is 10×6 feet in area, and supplied with water from the kitchen boilers adjoining. The water-closet beyond is 6 feet square, and architecturally in its roof, may be made a fitting termination to that of the porch leading to it.

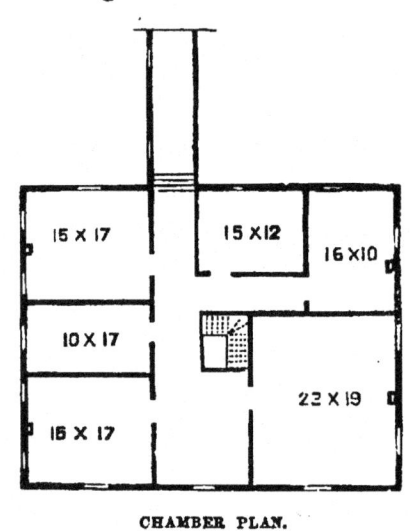

CHAMBER PLAN.

The main flight of stairs in the entrance hall leads on to a broad landing in the spacious upper hall, from which doors pass into the several chambers, which may be duly accommodated with closets. The passage connecting with the upper story of the servants' offices, opens from the rear section of this upper hall, and by the flight of rear stairs communicates with the kitchen and out-buildings. A garret flight of steps may be made in the rear section of the main upper hall, by which that apartment may be reached, and the upper deck of the roof ascended.

The sleeping-rooms of the kitchen may be divided off as convenience may dictate, and the entire structure thus appropriated to every accommodation which a well-regulated family need require.

CARRIAGE HOUSE.

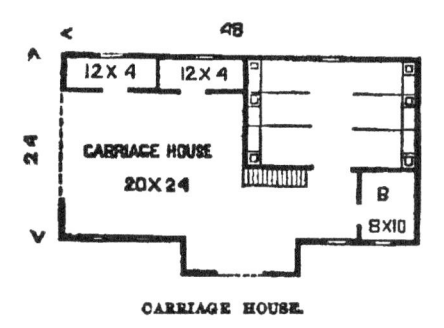

The carriage-house is 48×24 feet in size, with a projection of five feet on the entrance front, the door of which leads both into the carriage-room and stables. On the right is a bedroom, 10×8 feet, for the grooms, lighted by a window; and beyond are six stalls for horses, with a window in the rear wall beyond them. A flight of stairs leads to the hayloft above. In the rear of the carriage-room is a harness-room, 12×4 feet, and a granary of the same size, each lighted by a window. If farther attachments be required for the accommodation of out-building conveniences, they may be continued indefinitely in the rear.

MISCELLANEOUS.

It may strike the reader that the house just described has a lavish appropriation of veranda, and a needless side-front, which latter may detract from the *precise* architectural keeping that a dwelling of this pretension should maintain. In regard to the first, it may be remarked, that no feature of the house in a southern climate can be more expressive of easy, comfortable enjoyment, than a spacious veranda. The habits of southern life demand it as a place of exercise in wet weather, and the cooler seasons of the year, as well as a place of recreation and social intercourse during the fervid heats of the summer. Indeed, many southern people almost live under the shade of their verandas. It is a delightful place to take their meals, to receive their visitors and friends; and the veranda gives to a dwelling the very expression of hospitality, so far as any one feature of a dwelling can do it. No equal amount of accommodation can be provided for the same cost. It adds infinitely to the *room* of the house itself, and is, in fact, indispensable to the full enjoyment of a southern house.

The side front in this design is simply a matter of convenience to the owner and occupant of the estate, who has usually much office business in its management; and in the almost daily use of his library, where such business may be done, a side door and front is both appropriate and convenient. The *chief* front entrance belongs to his family and guests, and should be devoted to their exclusive use; and as a light fence may be thrown off from the extreme end of the side porch, separating the front lawn from the rear approach to the house, the veranda on that side may be reached from its rear end, for business purposes, without intruding upon the lawn at all. So we would arrange it.

Objections may be made to the *sameness* of plan, in the arrangement of the lower rooms of the several designs which we have submitted, such as having the nursery, or family sleeping-room, on the main floor of the house, and the uniformity, in location, of the others; and that there are no *new* and *striking* features in them. The answer to these may be, that the room appropriated for the nursery, or bedroom, may be used for other purposes, equally as well; that when a mode of accommodation is already as convenient as may be, it is poorly worth while to make it less convenient, merely for the sake of variety; and, that utility and convenience are the main objects to be attained in any well-ordered dwelling. These two requisites, utility and convenience, attained, the third and principal one — comfort — is secured. Cellar kitchens — the most abominable nuisances that ever crept into a country dwelling — might have been adopted, no doubt, to the especial delight of some who know nothing of the experimental duties of housekeeping; but the recommendation of these is an offence which we have no stomach to answer for hereafter. Steep, winding, and complicated staircases might have given a new feature to one or another of the designs; dark closets, intricate passages, unique cubby-holes, and all sorts of inside gimcrackery might have amused our pencil; but we have avoided them, as well as everything which would stand in the way of the simplest, cheapest, and most direct mode of reaching the object in view: a convenient, comfortably-arranged dwelling within, having a respectable, dignified appearance without — and such, we trust, have been thus far presented in our designs.

LAWN, AND PARK SURROUNDINGS.

The trees and shrubbery which ornament the approach to this house, should be rather of the graceful varieties, than otherwise. The weeping-willow, the horse-chesnut, the mountain-ash, if suitable to the climate; or the china-tree of the south, or the linden, the weeping-elm, and the silver-maple, with its long slender branches and hanging leaves, would add most to the beauty, and comport more closely with the character of this establishment, than the more upright, stiff, and unbending trees of our American forests. The Lombardy-poplar — albeit, an object of fashionable derision with many tree-fanciers in these more *tasty* days, as it was equally the admiration of our fathers, of forty years ago — would set off and give effect to a mansion of this character, either in a clump at the back-ground, as shown in the design, or occasionally shooting up its spire-like top through a group of the other trees. Yet, if built in a fine natural park or lawn of oaks, with a few other trees, such as we have named, planted immediately around it, this house would still show with fine effect.

The style of finish given to this dwelling may appear too ornate and expensive for the position it is supposed to occupy. If so, a plainer mode of finish may be adopted, to the cheapest degree consistent with the manner of its construction. Still, on examination, there will be found little intricate or really expensive work upon it. Strength, substance, durability, should all enter into its composition; and without these elements, a house of this appearance is a mere bauble, not fit to stand upon the premises of any man of substantial estate.

If a more extensive accommodation be necessary, than the size of this house can afford, its style will admit of a wing, of any desirable length, on each side, in place of the rear part of the side verandas, without prejudice to its character or effect. Indeed, such wings may add to its dignity, and consequence, as comporting with the standing and influence which its occupant may hold in the community wherein he resides. A man of mark, indeed, should, if he live in the country, occupy a dwelling somewhat indicating the position which he holds, both in society and in public affairs. By this remark, we may be treading on questionable ground, in our democratic country; but, practically, there is a fitness in it which no one can dispute. Not that extravagance, pretension, or any other *assumption* of superiority should mark the dwelling of the distinguished man, but that his dwelling be of like character with himself: plain, dignified, solid, and, as a matter of course, altogether respectable.

It is a happy feature in the composition of our republican institutions, both social and political, that we can afford to let the flashy men of the *day* — not of *time* — flaunter in all their purchased fancy in house-building, without prejudice to the prevailing sober sentiment of their neighbors, in such particulars. The man of money, simply, may build his "villa," and squander his tens of thousands upon it. He may riot within it, and fidget about it for a few brief years; he may even hang his coat of arms upon it, if he can fortunately do so without stumbling over a lapstone, or greasing his coat against the pans of a cook-shop; but it is equally sure that no child of his will occupy it after him, even if his own changeable fancy or circumstances permi him to retain it for his natural life. Such are th episodes of country house-building, and of frequen attempts at agricultural life, by those who affect it as a matter of ostentation or display. For the subjects of these, we do not write. But there is something exceedingly grateful to the feelings of one of stable views in life, to look upon an estate which has been long in an individual family, still maintaining its primitive character and respectability. Some five-and-twenty years ago, when too young to have any established opinions in matters of this sort, as we were driving through one of the old farming towns in Massachusetts, about twenty miles west of Boston, we approached a comfortable, well-conditioned farm, with a tavern-house upon the high road, and several great elms standing about it. The road passed between two of the trees, and from a cross-beam, lodged across their branches, swung a large square sign, with names and dates painted upon it — name and date we have forgotten; it was a good old Puritan name, however — in this wise:

"John Endicott, 1652."
"John Endicott, 1696."
"John Endicott, 1749."
"John Endicott, 1784."
"John Endicott, 1817."

As our eyes read over this list, we were struck with the stability of a family who for many consecutive generations had occupied, by the same name, that venerable spot, and ministered to the comfort of as many generations of travelers, and incontinently took off our hat in respect to the record of so much worth, drove our horse under the shed, had him fed, went in, and took a quiet family dinner with the civil, good-tempered host, and the equally kind-mannered hostess, then in the prime of life, surrounded with a fine family of children, and heard from his own lips the history of his ancestors, from their first emigration from England — not in the Mayflower, to whose immeasurable accommodations our good New England ancestors are so prone to refer — but in one of her early successors.

All over the old thirteen states, from Maine to Georgia, can be found agricultural estates now containing families, the descendants of those who founded them — exceptions to the general rule, we admit, of American stability of residence, but none the less gratifying to the contemplation of those who respect a deep love of home, wherever it may be found. For the moral of our episode on this subject, we cannot refrain from a description of a fine old estate which we have frequently seen, minus now the buildings which then existed, and long since supplanted by others equally respectable and commodious, and erected by the successor of the original occupant, the late Dr. Boylston, of Roxbury, who long made the farm his summer residence. The description is from an old work, "The History of the County of Worcester, in the

State of Massachusetts, by the Rev. Peter Whitney, 1793:"

"Many of the houses (in Princeton,) are large and elegant. This leads to a particular mention, that in this town is the country seat of the Hon. Moses Gill, Esq., ('Honorable' meant something in those days,) who has been from the year 1775 one of the Judges of the Court of Common Pleas for the county of Worcester, and for several years a counsellor of this commonwealth. His noble and elegant seat is about one mile and a quarter from the meeting-house, to the south. The farm contains upwards of three thousand acres. The county road from Princeton to Worcester passes through it, in front of the house, which faces to the west. The buildings stand upon the highest land of the whole farm; but it is level round about them for many rods, and then there is a very gradual descent. The land on which these buildings stand is elevated between twelve hundred and thirteen hundred feet above the level of the sea, as the Hon. James Winthrop, Esq. informs me. The mansion house is large, being 50×50 feet, with four stacks of chimnies. The farm house is 40 feet by 36: In a line with this stand the coach and chaise-house, 50 feet by 36. This is joined to the barn by a shed 70 feet in length—the barn is 200 feet by 32. Very elegant fences are erected around the mansion house, the out-houses, and the garden.

"The prospect from this seat is extensive and grand, taking in a horizon to the east, of seventy miles, at least. The blue hills in Milton are discernible with the naked eye, from the windows of this superb edifice, distant not less than sixty miles; as also the waters in the harbor of Boston, at certain seasons of the year. When we view this seat, these buildings, and this farm of so many hundred acres, now under a high degree of profitable cultivation, and are told that in the year 1766 it was a perfect wilderness, we are struck with wonder, admiration, and astonishment. The honorable proprietor thereof must have great satisfaction in contemplating these improvements, so extensive, made under his direction, and, I may add, by his own active industry. Judge Gill is a gentleman of singular vivacity and activity, and indefatigable in his endeavors to bring forward the cultivation of his lands; of great and essential service, by his example, in the employment he finds for so many persons, and in all his attempts to serve the interests of the place where he dwells, and in his acts of private munificence, and public generosity, and deserves great respect and esteem, not only from individuals, but from the town and country he has so greatly benefited, and especially by the ways in which he makes use of that vast estate wherewith a kind Providence has blessed him."

Such was the estate, and such the man who founded and enjoyed it sixty years ago; and many an equal estate, founded and occupied by equally valuable men, then existed, and still exist in all our older states; and if our private and public virtues are preserved, will ever exist in every state of our union. Such pictures, too, are forcible illustrations of the *morals* of correct building on the ample estates of many of our American planters and farmers. The mansion house, which is so graphically described, we saw but a short time before it was pulled down — then old, and hardly worth repairing, being built of wood, and of style something like this design of our own, bating the extent of veranda.

The cost of this house may be from $5000 to $8000, depending upon the material of which it is constructed, the degree of finish given to it, and the locality where it is built. All these circumstances are to be considered, and the estimates should be made by practical and experienced builders, who are competent judges in whatever appertains to it.

FARM HOUSE.

Pages 173-174.

Design VII.

A Plantation House.— Another southern house is here presented, quite different in architectural design from the last, plain, unpretending, less ornate in its finish, as well as less expensive in construction. It may occupy a different site, in a hilly, wooded country of rougher surface, but equally becoming it, as the other would more fitly grace the level prairie, or spreading plain in the more showy luxury of its character.

This house stands 46×44 feet on the ground, two stories high, with a full length veranda, 10 feet wide in front, and a half length one above it, connecting with the main roof by an open gable, under which is a railed gallery for summer repose or recreation, or to enjoy the scenery upon which it may open. The roof is broad and overhanging, thoroughly sheltering the walls, and giving it a most protected, comfortable look. Covering half the rear is a lean-to, with shed roof, 16 feet wide, communicating with the servants' offices in the wing, the hall of which opens upon a low veranda on its front, and leading to the minor conveniences of the establishment. The main servants' building is 30×20 feet, one and a half stories high, with a roof in keeping with the main dwelling, and a chimney in the center. In rear of this is attached a wood-house, with a shed roof, thus sloping off, and giving it a reposed, quiet air from that point of view. A narrow porch, 23 feet long and 8 feet wide, also shades the remaining rear part of the main dwelling, opening on to the approach in rear.

INTERIOR ARRANGEMENT.

The front door opens into a hall 34 feet long and 10 feet wide, with a flight of stairs. On the left of this opens a parlor or dining-room, 22×18 feet, lighted by two windows in front and one on the side, and connecting with the dining-room beyond, which is 18×16 feet, with two small dining closets between. The dining-room has two windows opening on to the rear veranda. Under the cross flight of stairs in the hall, a partition separates it from the rear hall, into which is a door. On the right of the entrance hall is a library, 18×18 feet, lighted by three windows. At the farther end is a closet, and by the side of it a small entry leading into the nursery or family bedroom, 18×15 feet in size, which also has a corresponding closet with the library. On the rear of the nursery is a flight of back stairs opening from it. Under these stairs, at the other end, a door opens to another flight leading into the cellar below. A door also leads out from the nursery into the rear passage, to the offices; another door on the further side of the room opens into the rear hall of the house. The nursery should have two windows, but

GROUND PLAN.

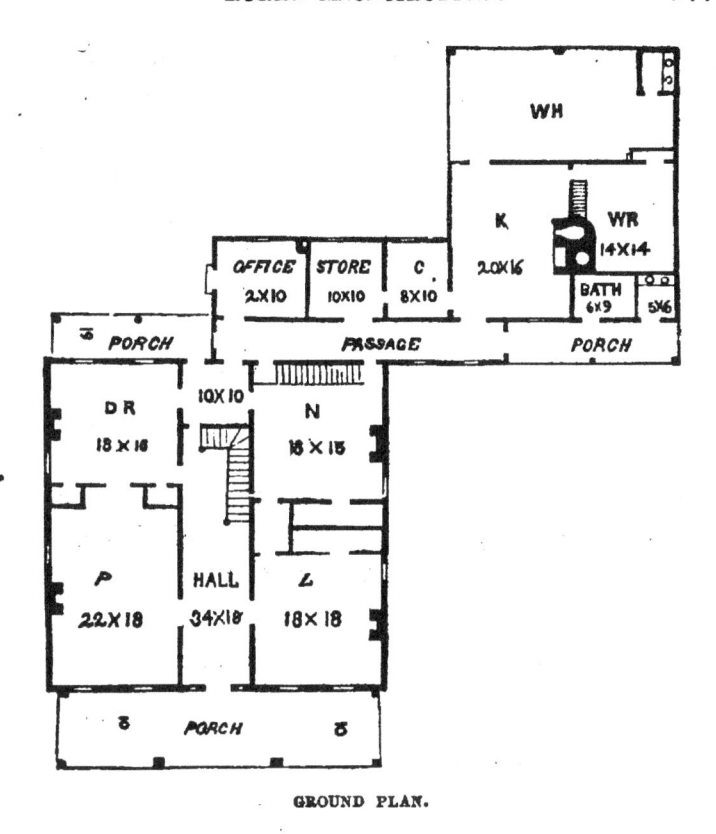

the drawing, by an error, gives only one. From this rear hall a door opens on the rear veranda, and another into the passage to the rear offices. This passage is six feet wide and 34 feet long, opening at its left end on to the veranda, and on the right, to the servants' porch, and from its rear side into three small rooms, 10 feet square each, the outer one of which may be a business room for the proprietor of the estate; the next, a store-room for family supplies; and the other a kitchen closet. Each of these is lighted by a window on the rear. A door also leads from the rear passage into the kitchen, 20×16 feet in area, with a window looking out in front and two others on the side and rear, and a door into the wood-house. In this is placed a large chimney for the cooking establishment, oven, &c., &c. A flight of stairs and partition divides this from the wash-room, which is 14×14 feet, with two windows in the side, and a door into the wood-house. This wood-house is open on two sides, and a water-closet is in the far corner. The small veranda, which is six feet wide, fronting the kitchen apartments, opens into the bath-room, 9×6 feet, into which the water is drawn from the kitchen boilers in the adjoining chimney. Still beyond this is the entrance to the water-closets, 6×5 feet.

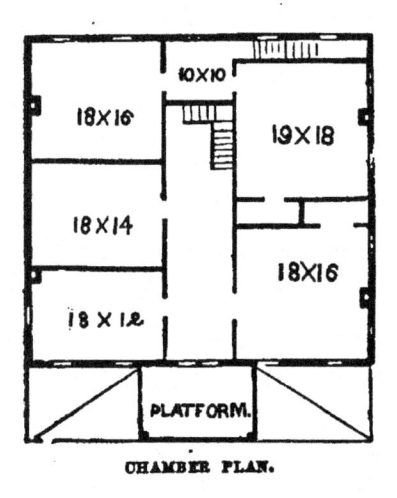

CHAMBER PLAN.

The chamber plan is simple, and will be readily comprehended. If more rooms are desirable, they can be cut off from the larger ones. A flight of garret stairs may also be put in the rear chamber hall. The main hall of the chambers, in connection with the upper veranda, may be made a delightful resort for the summer, where the leisure hours of the family may be passed in view of the scenery which the house may command, and thus made one of its most attractive features.

MISCELLANEOUS.

We have given less veranda to this house than to the last, because its style does not require it, and it is a cheaper and less pains-taking establishment throughout, although, perhaps, quite as convenient in its arrangement as the other. The veranda may, however, be continued round the two ends of the house, if required. A screen, or belt of privet, or low evergreens may be planted in a circular form from the front right-hand corner of the dwelling, to the corresponding corner of the rear offices, enclosing a clothes drying yard, and cutting them off from too sightly an exposure from the lawn in front. The opposite end of the house, which may be termed its *business* front, may open to the every-day approach to the house, and be treated as convenience may determine.

For the *tree* decoration of this establishment, evergreens may come in for a share of attraction. Their conical, tapering points will correspond well with its general architecture, and add strikingly to its effect; otherwise the remarks already given on the subject of park and lawn plantation will suffice. As, however, in the position where this establishment is supposed to be erected, land is plenty, ample area should be appropriated to its convenience, and no pinched or parsimonious spirit should detract from giving it the fullest effect in an allowance of ground. Nor need the ground devoted to such purposes be at all lost, or unappropriated; various uses can be made of it, yielding both pleasure and profit, to which a future chapter will refer; and it is one of the chief pleasures of retired residence to cultivate, in the right place, such incidental objects of interest as tend to gratify, as well as to instruct, in whatever appertains to the elevation of our thoughts, and the improvement of our condition. All these, in their place, should be drawn about our dwellings, to render them as agreeable and attractive as our ingenuity and labor may command.

LAWNS, GROUNDS, PARKS, AND WOODS.

Having essayed to instruct our agricultural friends in the proper modes of erecting their houses, and providing for their convenient accommodation within them, a few remarks may be pardoned touching such collateral subjects of embellishment as may be connected with the farm residence in the way of plantations and grounds in their immediate vicinity.

We are well aware that small farms do not permit any considerable appropriation of ground to *waste* purposes, as such spots are usually called which are occupied with wood, or the shade of open trees, near the dwelling. But no dwelling can be complete in all its appointments without trees in its immediate vicinity. This subject has perhaps been sufficiently discussed in preceding chapters; yet, as a closing course of remark upon what a farm house, greater or less in extent, should be in the amount of shade given to it, a further suggestion or two may be permitted. There are, in almost all places, in the vicinity of the dwelling, portions of ground which can be appropriated to forest trees without detriment to other economical uses, if applied in the proper way. Any one who passes along a high road and discovers the farm house, seated on the margin or in the immediate vicinity of a pleasant grove, is immediately struck with the peculiarly rural and picturesque air which it presents, and thinks to himself that he should love such a spot for his own home, without reflecting that he might equally as well create one of the same character. Sites already occupied, where different dispositions are made of contiguous ground, may not admit of like advantages; and such are to be continued in their present arrangement, with such course of improvement as their circumstances will admit. But to such as are about to *select* the sites of their future homes, it is important to study what can best embellish them in the most effective shade and ornament.

In the immediate vicinity of our large towns and cities it is seldom possible to appropriate any considerable breadth of land to ornamental purposes, excepting rough and unsightly waste ground, more or less occupied with rock or swamp; or plainer tracts, so sterile as to be comparatively worthless for cultivation. Such grounds, too, often lie bare of wood, and require planting, and a course of years to cover them with trees, even if the proprietor is willing, or desirous to devote them to such purpose. Still, there are vast sections of our country where to economize land is not important, and a mixed occupation of it to both ornament and profit may be indulged to the extent of the owner's disposition. All over the United States there are grand and beautiful sweeps and belts of cultivated country, interspersed with finely-wooded tracts, which offer the most attractive sites for the erection of dwellings on the farms which embrace them, and that require only the eye and hand of taste to convert them, with slight labor, into the finest-wooded lawns and forested parks imaginable. No country whatever produces finer trees than North America. The evergreens of the north luxuriate in a grandeur scarcely known elsewhere, and shoot their cones into the sky to an extent that the stripling pines and firs, and larches of England in vain may strive to imitate. The elm of New England towers up, and spreads out its sweeping arms with a majesty unwonted in the ancient parks or forests of Europe; while its maples, and birches, and beeches, and ashes, and oaks, and the great white-armed buttonwood, make up a variety of intervening growth, luxuriant in the extreme. Pass on through the Middle States, and into the far west, and there they still flourish with additional kinds—the tulip and poplar—the nut-trees, in all their wide variety, with a host of others equally grand and imposing, interspersed; and shrub-trees innumerable, are seen every where as they sweep along your path. Beyond the Alleghanies, and south of the great lakes, are vast natural parks, many of them enclosed, and dotted with herds of cattle ranging over them, which will show single trees, and clumps of forest that William the Conqueror would have given a whole fiefdom in his Hampshire spoliations to possess; while, stretching away toward the Gulf of Mexico, new varieties of tree are found, equally imposing, grand, and beautiful. throughout the whole vast range, and in almost every locality, susceptible of the finest possible appropriation to ornament and use. Many a one of these noble forests, and open, natural parks have been appropriated already to embellish the comfortable family establishment which has been built either on its margin, or within it; and thousands more are standing, as yet unimproved, but equally inviting the future occupant to their ample protection.

The moral influences, too, of lawns and parks around or in the vicinity of our dwellings, are worthy of consideration. Secluded as many a country dweller may be, away from the throng of society, there is a sympathy in trees which invites our thoughts, and draws our presence among them with unwonted interest, and in frequent cases, assist materially in stamping the feelings and courses of our future lives — always with pure and ennobling sentiments —

"The groves were God's first temples."

The thoughtful man, as he passes under their sheltering boughs, in the heat of summer, with uncovered brow, silently worships the Hand that formed them there, scarcely conscious that their presence thus elevates his mind to holy aspirations. Among them, the speculative man

"Finds tongues in trees, books in the running brooks,
Sermons in stones."

Even children, born and educated among groves of trees, drink in early impressions, which follow them for good all their days; and, when the toils of their after life are passed, they love to return to these grateful coverts, and spend their remaining days amid the tranquillity of their presence. Men habituated to the wildest life, too, enjoy the woods, the hills, and the mountains, beyond all the captivation and excitement of society, and are nowhere at rest, but when in their communion.

The love of forest scenery is a thing to be cultivated as a high accomplishment, in those whose early associations have not been among them. Indeed, country life is tame, and intolerable, without a taste, either natural or acquired, for fine landscape scenery; and in a land like this, where the country gives occupation to so great a proportion of its people, and a large share of those engaged in the active and exciting pursuits of populous towns, sigh and look forward to its enjoyment, every inducement should be offered to cultivate a taste for those things which make one of its chief attractions. Nor should seclusion from general society, and a residence apart from the bustling activity of the world, present a bar to the due cultivation of the taste in many subjects supposed to belong only to the throng of association. It is one of the advantages of rural life, that it gives us time to think; and the greatest minds of whose labors in the old world we have had the benefit, and of later times, in our own land, have been reared chiefly in the solitude of the country. Patrick Henry loved to range among the woods, admiring the leafy magnificence of nature, and to follow the meandering courses of the brooks, with his hook and line. Washington, when treading the vast solitudes of central Virginia, with his surveyor's instruments on his back, conceived the wonderful resources of the great empire of which he will ever be styled the "father." The dwelling of the late John C. Calhoun, sheltered by noble trees, stands on an elevated swell of a grand range of mountain land, and it was there that his prolific genius ripened for those burning displays of thought which drew to him the affections of admiring thousands. Henry Clay undoubtedly felt the germ of his future greatness while sauntering, in his boyhood days, through the wild and picturesque slashes of Hanover. Webster, born amid the rugged hills of New Hampshire; drew the delightful relish of rural life, for which he is so celebrated, from the landscapes which surrounded his early home, and laid the foundation of his mighty intellect in the midst of lone and striking scenery. Bryant could never have written his "Thanatopsis," his "Rivulet," and his "Green River," but from the inspiration drawn from his secluded youthful home in the mountains of Massachusetts. Nor, to touch a more sacred subject, could Jonathan Edwards ever have composed his masterly "Treatise on the Will," in a pent-up city; but owes his enduring fame to the thought and leisure which he found, while ministering, among the sublime mountains of the Housatonic, to a feeble tribe of Stockbridge Indians.

And these random names are but a few of those whose love of nature early imbibed, and in later life enjoyed in their own calm and retired homes, amid the serene beauty of woods and waters, which might be named, as illustrations of the influence which fine scenery may exercise upon the mind, to assist in moulding it to greatness. The following anecdote was told us many years ago, by a venerable man in Connecticut, a friend of the elder Hillhouse, of New Haven, to whom that city is much indebted for the magnificent trees by which it has become renowned as "the City of the Elms:" While a member of the General Assembly of that state, when Hillhouse was in Congress, learning that he had just returned home from the annual session, our informant, with a friend, went to the residence of the statesman, to pay him a visit. He had returned only that morning, and on their way there, they met him near his house, with a stout young tree on his shoulder, just taken from a neighboring piece of forest, which he was about to transplant in the place of one which had died during his absence. After the usual salutations, our friend expressed his surprise that he was so soon engaged in tree-planting, before he had even had time to look to his private and more pressing affairs. "Another day may be too late," replied the senator; "my tree well planted, it will grow at its leisure, and I can then look to my own concerns at my ease. So, gentlemen, if you will just wait till the tree is set, we'll walk into the house, and settle the affairs of state in our own way."

Walter Scott, whose deep love of park and forest scenery has stamped with his masterly descriptions, his native land as the home of all things beautiful and useful in trees and plantations, spent a great share of his leisure time in planting, and has written a most instructive essay on its practice and benefits. He puts into the mouth of "the Laird of Dumbiedikes," the advice, "Be aye sticking in a tree, Jock; it will be growing while you are sleeping." But Walter Scott had no American soil to plant his trees upon; nor do the grandest forest parks of Scotland show a tithe of the luxuriance and majesty of our American forests. Could he but have seen the variety, the symmetry, and the vast size of our oaks, and elms, and evergreens, a new element of descriptive power would have grown out of the admiration they had created within him; and he would have envied a people the possession of such exhaustless resources as we enjoy, to embellish their homes in the best imaginable manner, with such enduring monuments of grace and beauty.

To the miscellaneous, or casual reader, such course of remark may appear merely sublimated nonsense. No matter; we are not upon stilts, talking *down* to a class of inferior men, in a condescending tone, on a subject above their comprehension; but we are addressing men, and the sons of men, who are our equals — although, like ourself, upon their farms, taking their share in its daily toils, as well as pleasures — and can perfectly well understand our language, and sympathize with our thoughts. They are the thoughts of rural life everywhere. It was old Sam Johnson, the great lexicographer, who lumbered his unwieldy gait through the streets of cities for a whole life, and with all his vast learning and wisdom, had no appreciation of the charms of the country, that said, "Who feeds fat cattle should himself be fat;" as if the dweller on the farm should not possess an idea above the brutes around him. We wonder if he ever supposed a merchant should have any more brain than the parcel that he handled, or the bale which he rolled, or directed others to roll for him! But, loving the solitude of the farm, and finding a thousand objects of interest and beauty scattered in profusion, where those educated among artificial objects would see nothing beyond things, to them, vulgar and common-place, in conversing with our rural friends upon what concerns their daily comfort, and is to constitute the nursery of those who succeed them, and on the influences which may, in a degree, stamp their future character, we cannot forbear such suggestions, connected with the family Home, as may induce them to cultivate all those accessories around it, which may add to their pleasure and contentment. We believe it was Keats, who said,

"A thing of Beauty is a joy for ever."

And the thought that such "beauty" has been of our own creation, or that our own hands have assisted in its perpetuation, should certainly be a deep "joy" of our life.

We have remarked, that the farm house is the chief nursery on which our broad country must rely for that healthy infusion of stamina and spirit into those men who, under our institutions, guide its destiny and direct its councils. They, in the great majority of their numbers, are natives of the retired homestead. It is, therefore, of high consequence, that good taste, intelligence, and correct judgment, should enter into all that surrounds the birth-place, and early scenes of those who are to be the future actors in the prominent walks of life, either in public or private capacity; and as the love of trees is one of the leading elements of enjoyment amid the outward scenes of country-life, we commend most heartily all who dwell in the pure air and bright sunshine of the open land to their study and cultivation.

Every man who lives in the country, be he a practical farmer or not, should *plant* trees, more or less. The father of a family should plant, for the benefit of his children, as well as for his own. The bachelor and the childless man should plant, if for nothing more than to show that he has left *some* living thing to perpetuate his memory. Boys should early be made planters. None but those who love trees, and plant them, know the serene pleasure of watching their growth, and anticipating their future beauty and grandeur; and no one can so exquisitely enjoy their grateful shade, as he whose hand has planted and cared for them. Planting, too, is a most agreeable pastime to a reflecting mind. It may be ranked among the pleasures, instead of the toils of life. We have always so found it. There is no pleasanter sight of labor than to see a father, with his young lads about him, planting a tree. It becomes a landmark of their industry and good taste; and no thinking man passes a plantation of fine trees but inwardly blesses the man, or the memory of the man who placed them there.

Aside from all this, trees properly distributed, give a value to an estate far beyond the cost of planting and tending their growth, and which no other equal amount of labor and expense upon it can confer. Innumerable farms and places have been sold at high prices, over those of perhaps greater producing value, merely for the trees which embellished them. Thus, in a pecuniary light, to say nothing of the pleasure and luxury they confer, trees are a source of profitable investment.

It is a happy feature in the improving rural character of our country, that tree-planting and tree preservation for some years past have attracted much more attention than formerly; and with this attention a better taste is prevailing in their selection. We have gained but little in the introduction of many of the foreign trees among us, for ornament. Some of them are absolutely barbarous in comparison with our American forest trees, and their cultivation is only a demonstration of the utter want of good taste in those who apply them.

For ordinary purposes, but few exotics should be tolerated; and those chiefly in collections, as curiosities, or for arboretums — in which latter the farmer cannot often indulge; and for all the main purposes of shade, and use, and ornament, the trees of no country can equal our own.

Varied as our country is, in soils and climates, no particular directions can be given as to the individual varieties of tree which are to be preferred for planting. Each locality has its own most appropriate kinds, and he who is to plant, can best make the selections most fitted to his use. Rapid-growing trees, when of fine symmetry, and free from bad habits in throwing up suckers; not liable to the attacks of insects; of early, dense, and long-continued foliage, are most to be commended; while their opposites in character should be avoided in all well-kept grounds. It requires, indeed, but a little thought and observation to guide every one in the selection which he should make, to produce the best effect of which the tree itself is capable.

Giving the importance we have, to trees, and their planting, it may be supposed that we should discuss their position in the grounds to which they should be appropriated. But no specific directions can be given at large. All this branch of the subject must be left to the locality, position, and surface of the ground sought to be improved. A good tree can scarcely stand in a wrong place, when not injurious to a building by its too dense shade, or shutting out its light, or prospect. Still, the proper disposition of trees is a *study*, and should be well considered before they be planted. Bald, unsightly spots should be covered by them, when not devoted to more useful objects of the farm, either in pasturage or cultivation. A partial shading of the soil by trees may add to its value for grazing purposes, like the woodland pastures of Kentucky, where subject to extreme droughts, or a scorching sun.

If the planter feels disposed to consult authorities, as to the best disposition of his trees, works on Landscape Gardening may be studied; but these can give only general hints, and the only true course is to strive to make his grounds look as much like nature herself as possible—for nature seldom makes mistakes in her designs. To conclude a course of remark, which the plain farmer, cultivating his land for its yearly profit alone, may consider as foreign to the subject of our work, we would not recommend any one to plant trees who is not willing to spend the necessary time to nurse and tend them afterward, till they are out of harm's way, and well established in a vigorous growth. All this must be taken into the account, for it is better to have even but a few trees, and those what trees should be, than a whole forest of stinted things, writhing and pining through a course of sickly existence.

A chapter might also be written upon the proper mode of taking up and planting trees, but as this would lead us to a subject more directly belonging to another department, the proper authorities on that head must be consulted.

FRUIT GARDEN.--ORCHARDS.

As the fruit garden and orchards are usually near appendages to the dwelling and out-buildings, a few remarks as to their locality and distribution may be appropriate. The first should *always* be near the house, both for convenience in gathering its fruits, and for its due protection from the encroachments of those not entitled to its treasures. It should, if possible, adjoin the kitchen garden, for convenience of access; as fruit is, or should be, an important item in the daily consumption of every family where it can be grown and afforded. A sheltered spot, if to be had, should be devoted to this object; or if not, its margin, on the exposed side, should be set with the hardiest trees to which it is appropriated—as the apple. The fruit garden, proper, may also contain the smaller fruits, as they are termed, as the currant, gooseberry, raspberry, and whatever other shrub-fruits are grown; while the quince, the peach, the apricot, nectarine, plum, cherry, pear, and apple may, in the order they are named, stand in succession behind them, the taller and more hardy growth of each successive variety rising higher, and protecting its less hardy and aspiring neighbor. The soil for all these varieties of tree is supposed to be congenial, and our remarks will only be directed to their proper distribution.

The aspect for the fruit garden should, if possible, front the south, south-east, or south-west, in a northerly climate. In the Middle and Southern States the exposure is of less consequence. Currants, gooseberries raspberries, &c., should, for their most productive bearing, and the highest quality of their fruits, be set at least four feet apart, in the rows, and the rows six feet distant from each other, that there may be abundant room to cultivate them with the plow, and kept clean of weeds and grass. The quince, peach, apricot, nectarine, and plum should be 16 feet apart each way. The pear, if on quince stock, may be 12 feet apart, and if on its own stock, 20 to 24 feet; while the apple should always be 30 to 36 feet apart, to let in the requisite degree of sun and air to ripen as well as give growth, color, and flavor to its fruit. The tendency of almost all planters of fruit trees is to set them too close, and many otherwise fine fruit gardens are utterly ruined by the compact manner in which they are planted. Trees are great consumers of the atmosphere; every leaf is a lung, inhaling and respiring the gases, and if sufficient breathing room be not allowed them, the tree sickens, and pines for the want of it; therefore, every fruit tree, and fruit-bearing shrub should be so placed that the summer sun can shine on every part of its surface at some hour of the day. In such position, the fruit will reach its maximum of flavor, size, and perfection.

The ground, too, should be rich; and, to have the

greatest benefit of the soil, no crops should be grown among the trees, after they have arrived at their full maturity of bearing. Thus planted, and nursed, with good selections of varieties, both the fruit garden and the orchard become one of the most ornamental, as well as most profitable portions of the farm.

In point of position, as affecting the appearance of the homestead, the fruit garden should stand on the *weather-side* of the dwelling, so as, although protected, in its several varieties, by itself, when not altogether sheltered by some superior natural barrier, it should appear to shelter both the dwelling and kitchen gardens, which adjoin them.

As this is a subject intended to be but incidentally touched in these pages, and only then as immediately connected in its general character with the dwelling house and its attachments, we refrain from going into any particulars of detail concerning it. It is also a subject to which we are strongly attached, and gladly would we have a set chat with our readers upon it; but as the discussion for so broad a field as we should have to survey, would be in many points arbitrary, and unfitting to local information as to varieties, and particular cultivation, we refer the reader, with great pleasure, to the several treatises of Downing, and Thomas, and Barry, on this interesting topic, with which the public are fortunately in possession; observing, only, that there is no one item of rural economy to which our attention can be given, which yields more of luxury, health, and true enjoyment, both to the body and the mind, than the cultivation of good fruits.

HOW TO LAY OUT A KITCHEN GARDEN.

The kitchen garden yields more necessaries and comforts to the family, than any other piece of ground on the premises. It is, of consequence, necessary that it be so located and planned as to be ready of access, and yield the greatest possible quantity of products for the labor bestowed upon it; and as locality and plan have much to do with the labor bestowed upon it and the productions it may yield, both these subjects should be considered.

As to locality, the kitchen garden should lie in the *warmest* and *most sheltered* spot which may be convenient to the *kitchen* of the house. It should, in connection with that, be convenient of access to the dung-yards of the stables. The size may be such as your necessities or your convenience may demand. The shape, either a parallelogram or a square; for it will be recollected, that this is a place allotted, not for a *show* or *pleasure* ground, but for *profit*. If the garden be large, this shape will better allow the use of the plow to turn up the soil, which, in a large garden, is a much cheaper, and, when properly done, a better mode than to spade it; and if small, and it be worked with the spade, *right* lines are easier made with the spade than curved ones. One or more walks, at least eight feet wide, should be made, leading from a broad gate, or bars, through which a cart and horse, or oxen, may enter, to draw in manure, or carry out the vegetables; and if such walk, or walks, do not extend around the garden, which, if in a large one, they should do, a sufficient area should be thrown out at the farther extremity, to turn the cart upon. If the soil be free, and stony, the stones should be taken out *clean*, when large — and if small, down to the size of a hen's egg — and the surface made as level as possible, for a loose soil will need no draining. If the soil be a clay, or clayey loam, it should be underdrained two and a half feet, *to be perfect*, and the draining so planned as to lead off to a lower spot outside. This draining *warms* the soil, opens it for filtration, and makes it friable. Then, properly fenced, thoroughly manured, and plowed deep, and left rough — no matter how rough — in the fall of the year, and as late before the setting in of winter as you dare risk it, that part of the preparation is accomplished.

The *permanent* or wide walks of the garden, after being laid out and graded, should never be plowed nor disturbed, except by the hoe and rake, to keep down the weeds and grass; yet, if a close, and well-shorn grass turf be kept upon them, it is perhaps the cheapest and most cleanly way of keeping the walks. They need only cutting off close with the hand-hook, in summer.

We have known a great many people, after laying out a kitchen garden, and preparing it for use, fill it up with fruit trees, supposing that vegetables will grow quite as well with them as without. This is a wide mistake. *No tree larger than a currant or gooseberry bush should ever stand in a vegetable garden.* These fruits being partially used in the cooking department, as much in the way of vegetables, as of fruits, and small in size, may be permitted; and they, contrary to the usual practice, should always stand in *open* ground, where they can have all the benefits of the sun and rain to ripen the fruit to perfection, as well as to receive the cultivation they need, instead of being placed under fences around the sides of the garden, where they are too frequently neglected, and become the resort of vermin, or make prolific harbors for weeds.

Along the main walks, or alleys, the borders for perennial plants, as well as the currant and gooseberry bushes, should be made — for the plow should run parallel to, and not at right angles with them. Here may stand the rhubarbs, the sea kales, the various herbs, or even the asparagus beds, if a particular quarter be not set apart for them; and, if it be important, a portion of these main borders may be appropriated to the more common flowers and small shrubbery, if desired to cultivate them in a plain way; but not a peach, apricot, or any other larger tree than a currant or raspberry, should come within it. They not only shade the small plants, but suck up and rob them of their food and moisture, and keep off the sun, and prevent the circulation of air — than which nothing needs all these more than garden vegetables, to have them in high perfection. If it be necessary, by means of a cold exposure on the one side, to have a close plantation of shrubbery to screen the garden, let it be *outside* the fence, rather than within it; but if within, let there be a *broad* walk between such shrubbery and the garden beds, as their roots will extend under the vegetables, and rob them of their food.

A walk, alley, or cartway, on the sides of the garden, is always better *next to the fence*, than to fill that space with anything else, as it is usually shaded for a portion of the day, and may be better afforded for such *waste* purposes than the open, sunny ground within.

It will be observed that *market gardeners*, men who always strive to make the most profit from their land and labor, and obtain the *best* vegetables, cultivate them in open fields. Not a tree, nor even a bush is permitted to stand near the growing crop, if they can prevent it; and where one is not stinted in the area of his domain, their example should be followed.

A word upon *plowing* gardens. Clays, or clayey loams, should always be manured and plowed in the fall, just before the setting in of the winter frosts. A world of pounding and hammering of lumps, to make them fine, in spring, is saved by fall plowing, besides incorporating the manure more thoroughly with the soil, as well as freezing out and destroying the eggs of worms and insects which infest it. Thrown up deeply and roughly with the plow or spade, the frosts act mechanically upon the soil, and slack and pulverise it so thoroughly that a heavy raking in early spring, is all that becomes necessary to put it in the finest condition for seeds, and make it perhaps the very best and most productive of all garden soils whatever. A light sandy loam is better to lie compact in winter, and manured and turned up in early spring. Its friable nature leaves it always open and light, and at all times in the absence of frost, accessible to the spade or the hoe. On these accounts, it is usually the most desirable and convenient soil for the kitchen garden, and on the whole, generally preferred where either **kind may** be a matter simply of choice.

FLOWERS.

Start not, gentle reader! We are not about to inflict upon you a dissertation on Pelargoniums, Calla-Ethiopias, Japonicas, and such like unmentionable terms, that bring to your mind the green-house, and forcing-house, and all the train of expense and vexation attending them; but we desire to have a short familiar conversation about what is all around you, or if not around you, should be, and kept there, with very little pains or labor on your part. Still, if you dislike the subject, just hand this part of our book over to your excellent wife, or daughters, or sisters, as the case may be, and we will talk to them about this matter.

Flowers have their objects, and were made for our use and pleasure; otherwise, God would never have strewed them, as he has, so bountifully along our paths, and filled the world with their fragrance and beauty. Like all else beautiful, which He made, and pronounced "good," flowers have been objects of admiration and love since man's creation; and their cultivation has ever been a type of civilization and refinement among all people who have left written records behind them. Flowers equally become the cottage and the palace, in their decoration. The humblest cottager, and the mightiest monarch, have equally admired their beauty and their odor; and the whole train of mortals between, have devoted a portion of their time and thoughts to the development of their peculiar properties.

But let that pass. Plain country people as we are, there are enough of sufficient variety all around us, to engage our attention, and give us all that we desire to embellish our homes, and engage the time which we have to devote to them. Among the wild flowers, in the mountains and hills of the farthest North, on the margin of their hidden brooks, where

"Floats the scarce-rooted watercress;"

and on their barren sides, the tiny violet and the laurel bloom, each in their season, with unwonted beauty; and, sloping down on to the plains beneath, blush out in all their summer garniture, the wild rose and the honeysuckle. On, through the Middle States, the lesser flowers of early spring throw out a thousand brilliant dyes, and are surrounded by a host of summer plants, vieing with each other in the exuberance of their tints. On the Alleghanies, through all their vast range, grow up the magnificent dogwood, kalmia, and rhodendendron, spangling mile upon mile of their huge sides and tops with white, and covering crags and precipices of untold space with their blushing splendor. Further west, on the prairies, and oak openings, and in the deep woods, too, of the great lakes, and of the Mississippi valley, with the earliest grass, shoot up, all over the land, a succession of flowers, which in variety and profusion of shape, and color, and odor, outvie all the lilies of the gardens of Solomon; and so they continue till the autumnal frosts cut down both grass and flower alike. Further south, along the piney coast, back through the hills and over the vast reach of cotton and sugar lands, another class of flowers burst out from their natural coverts in equal glory; and the magnolia, and the tulip-tree, and the wild orange throw a perfume along the air, like the odors of Palestine. In the deep lagoons of the southern rivers, too, float immense water-lilies, laying their great broad leaves, and expanded white and yellow flowers, upon the surface, which the waters of the Nile in the days of Cleopatra never equaled. And these are nature's wild productions only.

Flowers being cultivated, not for profit, but for show and amusement, need not intrude upon the time which is required to the more important labors of the farm. A little time, given at such hours when it can be best spared, will set all the little flower-beds in order, and keep the required shrubbery of the place in trim — and should not be denied in any family who enjoy a taste for them. Even the simplest of their kind, when carefully disposed, produce a fine effect; and the hardy bulbous, and tuberous-rooted plants require but slight aid in producing the highest perfection of their bloom; while the fibrous-rooted perenials, and the flowering shrubs, bloom on from year to year, almost uncared for and untouched.

The annuals require the most attention. Their seeds must be planted and gathered every year; they must be weeded and nursed with more care than the others; yet they richly repay all this trouble in their fresh bloom when the others are gone, and will carry their rich flowers far into the frosts of autumn, when their hardier companions have composed themselves for a winter's rest.

The position of the flower-bed, or borders, may be various. As a matter of taste, however, they should be near the house, and in view of the windows of the most frequented rooms. They thus give more enjoyment in their sight, than when but occasionally seen in special visits; and such spots can usually be set apart for them. If not in the way of more important things, they should always be thus placed, where they are ever objects of interest and attraction.

The ground which flowering plants occupy should be devoted to them alone, and the soil be made deep and rich. They should not be huddled up, nor crowded, but stand well apart, and have plenty of breathing-room for their branches and leaves, and space for the spread of their roots. They are consumers of the fertilizing gases, and require, equally with other plants, their due supply of manures — which also adds to the brilliance and size of their bloom, as well as to the growth of their stems. Their roots should be protected in winter by coarse litter thrown over them, particularly the earlier flowering plants, as it gives them an early and rapid start in the spring.

In variety, we need scarcely recommend what may

be most desirable. The crocus, and snowdrop are among (if not quite) the earliest in bloom; and to these follow the hyacinth, and daffodil, the jonquil, and many-varied family of Narcissus, the low-headed hearts-ease, or pansy; with them, too, comes the flowering-almond, the lilac, and another or two flowering shrubs. Then follow the tulips, in all their gorgeous and splendid variety of single, double, and fringed. To these follow the great peonies, in their full, dashing colors of crimson, white and pink, and the tree-like snow-ball, or guelder-rose. By the side of these hangs out the monthly-trumpet-honeysuckle, gracing the columns of your veranda, porch, or window, and the large Siberian honeysuckle, with its white and pink flowers; and along with them, the various Iris family, or fleur-de-lis, reminding one of France and the Bourbons, the Prussian lilac, and the early phloxes. Then blush out, in all their endless variety of shade and tint, from the purest white to the deepest purple, the whole vast family of roses; and in stature, from the humblest twig that leans its frail stem upon the ground, up to the hardy climber, whose delicious clusters hang over your chamber window; and a month of fragrance and beauty of these completes the succession of bulbs, and tubers, and perennial plants and shrubs — scores of which have not been noticed.

Now commence the annuals, which may carry you a month further into the season, when the flaunting dahlia of every hue, and budding from its plant of every size, from the height of little Tommy, who is just toddling out with his mother to watch the first opening flower, up to the top of his father's hat, as he stands quite six feet, to hold the little fellow up to try to smell of another, which, like all the rest, has no sign of odor. Then come, after a long retinue of different things — among which we always count the morning-glory, or convolvulus, running up the kitchen windows,— the great sun-flower, which throws his broad disk high over the garden fence, always cheerful, and always glowing — the brilliant tribe of asters, rich, varied, and beautiful, running far into the autumnal frosts; and, to close our floral season, the chrysanthemum, which, well cared-for, blooms out in the open air, and, carefully taken up and boxed, will stay with us, in the house, till Christmas. Thus ends the blooming year. Now, if you would enjoy a pleasure perfectly pure, which has no alloy, save an occasional disappointment by casualty, and make home interesting beyond all other places, learn first to love, **then to get**, and next to cultivate **flowers**.

FARM COTTAGES.

Altogether too little attention has been paid in our country to these most useful appendages to the farm, both in their construction and appearance. Nothing adds more to the feeling of comfort, convenience, and *home* expression in the farm, than the snug-built laborers' cottage upon it. The cottage also gives the farm an air of respectability and dignity. The laborer should, if not so sumptuously, be as comfortably housed and sheltered as his employer. This is quite as much to the interest of such employer as it is beneficial to the health and happiness of the laborer. Building is so cheap in America, that the difference in cost between a snugly-finished cottage, and a rickety, open tenement, is hardly to be taken into consideration, as compared with the higher health, and increased enjoyment of the laborer and his family; while every considerate employer knows that cheerfulness and contentment of disposition, which are perhaps more promoted by good home accommodations for the workingman than by any other influence, are strong incentives to increased labor on his part, and more fidelity in its application.

A landed estate, of whatever extent, with its respectable farm house, in its own expressive style of construction, relieved and set off by its attendant cottages, either contiguous, or remote, and built in their proper character, leaves nothing wanting to fill the picture upon which one loves to gaze in the contemplation of country life; and without these last in due keeping with the chief structures of the estate, a blank is left in its completeness and finish. The little embellishments which may be given, by way of architectural arrangement, or the conveniences in accommodation, are, in almost all cases, appreciated by those who occupy them, and have an influence upon their character and conduct; while the trifling decorations which may be added in the way of shrubbery, trees, and flowering plants, costing little or nothing in their planting and keeping, give a charm to the humblest abode.

The position of cottages on a farm should be controlled by considerations of convenience to the place of labor, and a proper economy in their construction; and hardly a site can be inappropriate which ensures these requirements. In the plans which are submitted, due attention has been paid to the comfort of those who inhabit them, as well as to picturesque effect in the cottage itself. Decency, order, and respectability are thus given to the estate, and to those who inhabit the cottages upon it, as well as to those whose more fortunate position in life has given the enjoyment of a higher luxury in the occupancy of its chief mansion.

On all estates where the principal dwelling is located at any considerable distance from the public road, or where approached by a side road shut off from the highway by a gate, a small cottage, by way of lodge, or laborer's tenement, should be located at or near the entrance. Such appendage is not only ornamental in itself, but gives character to the place, and security to the enclosure; in guarding it from improper intrusion, as well as to receive and conduct into the premises those who either reside upon, or have business within it. It is thus a sort of sentry-box, as well as a laborer's residence.

COTTAGE.   Page 211.

Design I.

This cottage is 10 feet high, from the sill to the plates, and may be built of wood, with a slight frame composed of sills and plates only, and planked up and down (vertically) and battened; or grooved and tongued, and matched close together; or it may be framed throughout with posts and studs, and covered with rough boards, and over these clapboards, and lathed and plastered inside. The first mode would be the cheapest, although not so warm and durable as the other, yet quite comfortable when warmed by a stove. On the second plan of building, it will cost near or quite double the amount of the first, if neatly painted. A small brick chimney should rest upon the floor overhead, in the side of which, at least a foot above the chamber floor, should be inserted an earthen or iron thimble, to receive the stovepipe and guard against fire; unless a flat stone, 14 to 16 inches square, and 2 to 4 inches thick, with a pipe-hole — which is the better plan — should rest on the floor immediately over the pipe. This stone should be, also, the foundation of the chimney, which should pass immediately up through the ridge of the roof, and, for effect, in the center, longitudinally, of the house. Such position will not interfere with the location of the stove, which may be placed in any part of the room, the pipe reaching the chimney by one or more elbows.

INTERIOR ARRANGEMENT.

The main body of this cottage is 18×12 feet, with a lean-to, 8 feet wide, running its whole length in rear. This lean-to may be 8 or 9 inches lower, on the floor, than the main room, and divided into a passage, (leading to an open wood-house in rear, 10×12 feet, with a shed roof,) a large closet, and a bedroom, as may be required; or, the passage end may be left open at the side, for a wood shelter, or other useful purpose. The roof, which is raftered, boarded, and shingled in the usual mode, is well spread over the gables, as well as over the front and rear — say 18 inches. The porch in front will give additional convenience in summer, as a place to sit, or eat under, and its posts so fitted with grooves as to let in rough planks for winter enclosure in front and at one end, leaving the entrance only, at the least windy, or stormy side. The extra cost of such preparation, with the planks, which should be 1¼ or 1½ inches thick, and jointed, would not exceed ten or fifteen dollars. This would make an admirable wood-house for the winter, and a perfect snuggery for a small family. While in its summer dress, with the porch opened — the planks taken out and laid overhead, across the beams connecting the porch with the house — it would present an object of quiet comfort and beauty. A hop vine or honeysuckle might be trained outside the posts, and give it all the shade required.

In a stony country, where the adjoining enclosures are of stone, this cottage may be built of stone, also, at about double the cost of wood. This would save the expense of paint, or wash of any kind, besides the greater character of durability and substance it would add to the establishment. Trees, of course, should shelter it; and any little out-buildings that may be required should be nestled under a screen of vines and shrubbery near by.

This being designed as the humblest and cheapest kind of cottage, where the family occupy only a single room, the cost would be small. On the plan first named, stained with a coarse wash, it could be built for $100. On the second plan, well-framed of sills, plates, posts, studs, &c. &c., covered with vertical boarding and battens, or clapboarded, and well painted in oil, it might cost $150 to $200. Stone, or brick, without paint, would add but little, if anything in cost over the last sum. The ceiling of the main floor is 8 feet high, and a low chamber or garret is afforded above it, into which a swing-step ladder ascends; and when not in use, it may be hung to the ceiling overhead by a common hook and staples.

Design II.

This cottage is a grade beyond the one just described, both in appearance and accommodation. It is 20×16 feet on the ground, with a rear wing 26×8 feet in area. The main body is 10 feet high, to the roof, vertically boarded and battened. A snug, half-open (or it may be closed, as convenience may require,) porch shelters the front door, 5×4 feet in area. The cottage has a square or hipped roof, of a 30° pitch from a horizontal line, which spreads full two feet over the walls and bracketed beneath. The rear wing retreats two feet from the wall line of the main building, and has also a hipped roof of the same pitch as the main one, with eight-feet posts. The open end of the wing advances 6 feet toward the front of the main part for wood-house and storage. The construction of this is in the same style as Design I. The windows are plain, two-sashed, of six lights each, 8×12 glass in front, and 8×10 in the rear.

INTERIOR ARRANGEMENT.

The front door opens into a common living room, 16×12 feet, with two windows, in which is a stove-chimney running up from the main floor next the partition, or placed over it in the chamber, and running

Elevation.

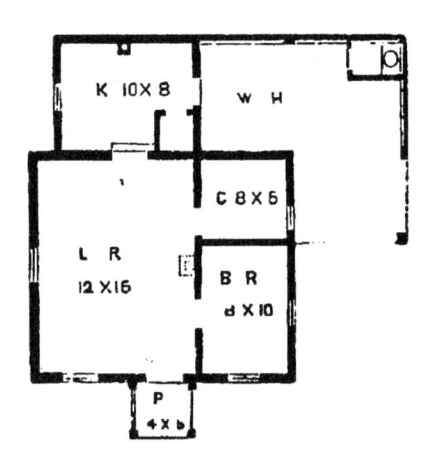

Plan.

COTTAGE.   Pages 217-218.

up through the center of the roof. On one side of the living room is a bedroom, 10×8 feet, with two windows. Next to this bedroom is a large closet, 8×6 feet, with one window, and shelves, and tight cupboard within. These rooms are 9 feet high, and over them is a chamber, or garret, 20×16 feet, entered by a swing step ladder, as in Design No. I. This garret is lighted by a small dormer window in the rear roof, over the shed or lean-to. A bed may be located in this chamber, or it may serve as a storage and lumber-room.

The wing contains a small kitchen, in case the living room be not occupied for that purpose, 10×8 feet, lighted by a side-window, and having a small chimney in the rear wall. It may contain, also, a small closet, 3 feet square. A door passes from this small kitchen into the wood-house, which is 16×8 feet, or with its advance L, 14 feet, in the extreme outer corner of which is a water-closet, 5×3 feet; thus, altogether, giving accommodation to a family of five or six persons.

The construction of this cottage is shown as of wood. Other material, either brick or stone, may be used, as most convenient, at a not much increased cost. The expense of this building may be, say fifty per cent. higher than that of No. I, according to the finish, and may be sufficiently well done and painted complete for $300; which may be reduced or increased, according to the style of finish and the taste of the builder.

A cellar may be made under this cottage, which can be reached by a trap-door from the living room, opening to a flight of steps below.

Design III.

This cottage is still in advance of No. II, in style and arrangement, and may accommodate not only the farm laborer or gardener, but will serve for a small farmer himself, or a village mechanic. It is in the French style of roof, and allied to the Italian in its brackets, and gables, and half-terraced front. The body of the cottage is 22×20 feet, with twelve-feet posts; the roof has a pitch of 50° from a horizontal line, in its straight dimensions, curving horizontally toward the eaves, which, together with the gables, project 3 feet over the walls. The terrace in front is 5 feet wide. On the rear is a wood-house, 18×16 feet in area, open at the house end, and in front, with a roof in same style as the main house, and posts, 8 feet high, standing on the ground, 2 feet below the surface of the cellar wall, which supports the main building.

INTERIOR ARRANGEMENT.

The front door opens, in the center of the front wall, into a hall, 12×8 feet, with a flight of stairs on one side, leading to the chamber above; under the stairs, at the upper end, is a passage leading beneath them into the cellar. On one side of this hall is a bedroom

Elevation.

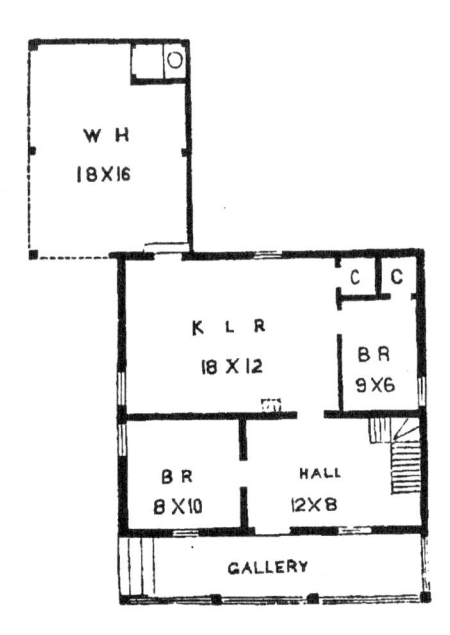

Plan.

8×10 feet, lighted by a window in front, and part of the hooded double window on the side. On the inner side, a door leads from the hall into the living room or kitchen, 18×12 feet. On one side of this is a bedroom, or pantry, as may be most desirable, 9×6 feet, from which leads a close closet, 3 feet square. This bedroom has a window on one side, next the hall. A door from the kitchen leads into a closet, 3 feet wide, which may contain a sink, and cupboard for kitchen wares. The living room is lighted by a part of the double hooded window on one side, and another on the rear. A door leads into the wood-house, which is 12×16 feet, in the extreme corner of which is the water-closet, 5×3 feet. The rooms in this cottage are 9 feet high. A chimney leads up from the floor of the living room, which may receive, in addition to its own fireplace, or stove, a pipe from the stove in the hall, if one is placed there.

The chamber has two feet of perpendicular wall, and the sharp roof gives opportunity for two good lodging rooms, which may be partitioned off as convenience may require, each lighted by a window in the gables, and a dormer one in the roof, for the passage leading into them.

The hall may serve as a pleasant sitting or dining-room, in pleasant weather, opening, as it does, on to the terrace, which is mostly sheltered by the overhanging roof.

The construction of this cottage may be of either stone, brick, or wood, and produce a fine effect. Although it has neither porch, nor veranda, the broad eaves and gables give it a well-sheltered appearance, and the hooded windows on the sides throw an air of protection over them, quite agreeable to the eye. The framing of this roof is no way different, in the rafters, from those made on straight lines, but the curve and projection is given by planks cut into proper shape, and spiked into the rafters, and apparently supported by the brackets below, which should be cut from two to three-inch plank, to give them a heavy and substantial appearance. The windows are in casement form, as shown in the design, but may be changed into the ordinary sash form, if preferred, which is, in this country, usually the better way. It will be observed, that we have in all cases adopted the usual square-sided form of glass for windows, as altogether more convenient and economical in building, simple in repairing, and, we think, quite as agreeable in appearance, as those out-of-the-way shapes frequently adopted to give a more picturesque effect.

In a hilly, mountainous, and evergreen country, this style of cottage is peculiarly appropriate. It takes additional character from bold and picturesque scenery, with which it is in harmony. The pine, spruce, cedar, or hemlock, or the evergreen laurel, planted around or near it, will give it increased effect, while among deciduous trees and shrubs, an occasional Lombardy poplar, and larch, will harmonize with the boldness of its outline. Even where hill or mountain scenery is wanting, plantations such as have been named, would render it a pleasing style of cottage, and give agreeable effect to its bold, sharp roof and projecting eaves

In a snowy country, the plan of roof here presented is well adapted to the shedding of heavy snows, on which it can find no protracted lodgment. Where massive stone walls enclose the estate, this style of cottage will be in character, as comporting with that strong and solid air which the rustic appearance of stone alone can give. It may, too, receive the same amount of outer decoration, in its shrubbery and plantations, given to any other style of building of like accommodation, and with an equally agreeable effect.

Design IV.

This cottage is still in advance of the last, in its accommodation, and is suitable for the small farmer, or the more liberal cottager, who requires wider room, and ampler conveniences than are allowed by the hitherto described structures. It is a first class dwelling, of its kind, and, in its details and finish, may be adapted to a variety of occupation, while it will afford a sufficient amount of expenditure to gratify a liberal outlay, to him who chooses to indulge his taste in a moderate extent of decoration and embellishment.

The ground plan of this cottage is 30×22 feet, in light rural-Gothic style, one and a half stories high, the posts 14 feet in elevation. It has two chimneys, passing out through the roof on each side of the ridge, uniformly, each with the other. The roof has a pitch of 45° from a horizontal line, giving it a bold and rather dashing appearance, and deeply sheltering the walls. The side gables give variety to the roof, and light to the chambers, and add to the finish of its appearance; while the sharp arched double window in the front gable adds character to the design.

The deep veranda in front covers three-quarters of its surface in length, and in the symmetry of its roof, and airiness of its columns, with their light braces,

Elevation.

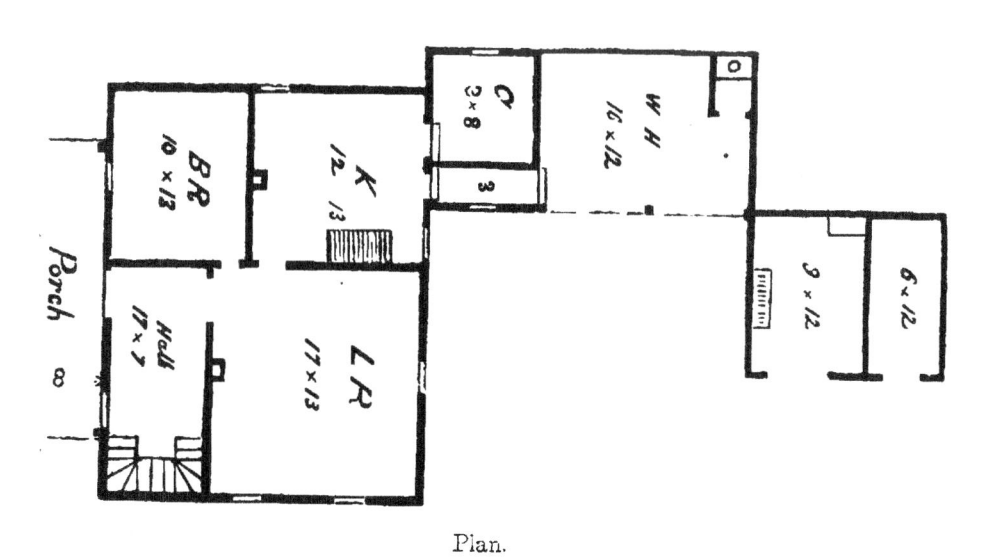

Plan.

COTTAGE.

Pages 227-228.

give it a style of completeness; and if creeping vines or climbing shrubs be trained upon them, will produce an effect altogether rural and beautiful.

Or, if a rustic style of finish be adopted, to render it cheaper in construction, the effect may still be imposing, and in harmony with the purposes to which it is designed. In fact, this model will admit of a variety of choice in finish, from the plainest to a high degree of embellishment, as the ability or fancy of the builder may suggest.

INTERIOR ARRANGEMENT.

From the veranda in the center of the front, a door opens into a hall, 17×7 feet, with a flight of stairs leading, in three different angles, to the chambers above. Opposite the front door is the passage into the living room, or parlor, 17×15 feet, lighted by three windows, two of which present an agreeable view of an adjacent stream and its opposite shores. At the line of partition from the hall, stands a chimney, with a fireplace, if desirable, or for a stove, to accommodate both this room and the hall with a like convenience; and under the flight of stairs adjoining opens a china closet, with spacious shelves, for the safe-keeping of household comforts. From this room, a door leads into a bedroom, 10×13 feet, lighted by a window opening into the veranda, also accommodated by a stove, which leads into a chimney at its inner partition. Next to this bedroom is the kitchen, 12×13 feet, accommodated with a chimney, where may be inserted an open fireplace, or a stove, as required. In this is a flight of back chamber and cellar stairs. This room is lighted by two windows—one in the side, another in the rear. A door leads from its rear into a large, roomy pantry, 8 feet square, situated in the wing, and lighted by a window. Next to this is a passage, 3 feet in width, leading to the wood-house, (in which the pantry just named is included,) 16×12 feet, with nine-feet posts, and roof pitched like the house, in the extreme corner of which is a water-closet, 5×3 feet. Cornering upon the wood-house beyond, is a small building, 15×12 feet, with ten-feet posts, and a roof in same style as the others—with convenience for a cow and a pig, with each a separate entrance. A flight of stairs leads to the hay-loft above the stables, in the gable of which is the hay-door; and under the stairs is the granary; and to these may be added, inside, a small accommodation for a choice stock of poultry.

The chamber plan is the same as the lower floor, mainly, giving three good sleeping-rooms; that over the kitchen, being a *back* chamber, need not have a separate passage into the upper hall, but may have a door passage into the principal chamber. The door to the front bedroom leads direct from the upper hall. Thus, accommodation is given to quite a numerous family. Closets may be placed in each of these chambers, if wanted; and the entire establishment made a most snug and compact, as well as commodious arrangement.

COTTAGE OUTSIDE DECORATION.

Nothing so perfectly sets off a cottage, in external appearance, as the presence of plants and shrubbery around it. A large tree or two, by giving an air of protection, is always in place; and creeping vines, and climbing shrubs about the windows and porch, are in true character; while a few low-headed trees, of various kinds, together with some simple and hardy annual and other flowers — to which should always be added, near by, a small, well-tended kitchen garden — fill up the picture.

In the choice of what varieties should compose these ornaments, one can hardly be at a loss. Flanking the cottage, and near the kitchen garden, should be the fruit trees. The elm, maples, oak, and hickory, in all their varieties, black-walnut, butternut — the last all the better for its rich kernel — are every one appropriate for shade, as *large* trees. The hop, morning-glory, running beans — all useful and ornamental as summer climbers; the clematis, bitter-sweet, ivy, any of the *climbing* roses; the lilac, syringa, snow-ball, and the *standard* roses; while marigolds, asters, pinks, the phloxes, peonies, and a few other of the thousand-and-one simple and charming annuals, biennials, and perennials, with now and then a gorgeous sunflower, flaunting in its broad glory, will fill up the catalogue. Rare and costly plants are not required, and indeed, are hardly in place in the grounds of an ordinary cottage, unless occupied by the professional gardener. They denote expense, which the laboring cottager cannot afford; and besides that, they detract from the simplicity of the life and purpose which not only the cottage itself, but everything around it, should express.

There is an affectation of *cottage* building, with some people who, with a seeming humilty, really aim at higher flights of style in living within them, than truth of either design or purpose will admit. But as such cases are more among villagers, and those temporarily retiring from the city for summer residence, the farm cottage has little to do with it. Still, such fancies are contagious, and we have occasionally seen the ambitious cottage, with its covert expression of humility, insinuating itself on to the farm, and for the farmer's own family occupation, too, which at once spoiled, to the eye, the *substantial reality* of the whole establishment. A farmer should discard all such things as *ornamental* cottages. They do not belong to the farm. If he live in a cottage himself, it should be a *plain* one; yet it may be very substantial and well finished—something showing that he means either to be content in it, in its character of plainness, or that he intends, at a future day, to build something better—when this may serve for the habitation of one of his laborers.

The cottage should never occupy a principal, or prominent site on the farm It should take a subordinate position of ground. This adds to its expression as subordinate in rank, among the lesser farm buildings. A cottage cannot, and should not aspire to be *chief* in either position or character. Such should be the farm house proper; although unpretending, still, in style, above the cottage; and if the latter, in addition, be required on the farm, it should so appear, both in construction and finish; just what it is intended for — a tenement for economical purposes.

There is another kind of cottage, the dwellers in which, these pages will probably never reach, that expresses, in its wild structure, and rude locality, the idea of Moore's pretty song —

"I knew by the smoke that so gracefully curled
Above the green elms, that a cottage was near."

Yet, in some parts of our country, landlords may build such, for the accommodation of tenants, which they may make useful on the outskirts of their estates, and add indirectly to their own convenience and interest in so doing. This may be indulged in, *poetically* too — for almost any thinking man has a spice of poetry in his composition — vagabondism, a strict, economizing utilitarian would call it. The name matters not. One may as well indulge his taste in this cheap sort of charitable expenditure, as another may indulge, in his dogs, and guns, his horses and equipages — and the first is far the cheapest. They, at the west and south, understand this, whose recreations are occasionally with their hounds, in chase of the deer, and the fox, and in their pursuit spend weeks of the fall and winter months, in which they are accompanied, and assisted, as boon companions for the time, by the rude tenants of the cottages we have described:

"A cheerful, simple, honest people."

Another class of cottage may come within the farm enclosures, half poetical, and half economical, such as Milton describes:

"Hard by a cottage chimney smokes,
From betwixt two aged oaks;"

and occupied by a family pensioner and his infirm old wife — we don't think *all* " poor old folks " ought to go to the alms-house, because they cannot work *every* day of the year — of which all long-settled families of good estate have, now and then, one near to, or upon their premises. Thousands of kind and liberal hearts among our farming and planting brethren, whose impulses are —

"Open as the day to melting charity,"

are familiar with the wants of those who are thus made their dependents; and in their accommodation, an eye may be kept to the producing of an agreeable effect in locating their habitations, and to rudely embellish, rather than to mar the domain on which they may be lodged.

In short, cottage architecture, in its proper character, may be made as effective, in all the ornament which it should give to the farm, as that of any other structure;

and if those who have occasion for the cottage will only be content to build and maintain it as it should be, and leave off that perpetual aspiration after something unnatural, and foreign to its purpose, which so many cottage builders of the day attempt, and let it stand in its own humble, secluded character, they will save themselves a world of trouble, and pass for—what they now do not—men possessing a taste for truth and propriety in their endeavors.

HOUSE AND COTTAGE FURNITURE.

This is a subject so thoroughly discussed in the books, of late, that anything which may here be said, would avail but little, inasmuch as our opinions might be looked upon as "old-fashioned," "out of date," and "of no account whatever,"—for wonderfully modern notions in room-furnishing have crept into the farm house, as well as into town houses. Indeed, we confess to altogether ancient opinions in regard to household furniture, and contend, that, with a few exceptions, "modern degeneracy" has reached the utmost stretch of absurdity, in house-furnishing, to which the ingenuity of man can arrive. Fashions in furniture change about as often as the cut of a lady's dress, or the shape of her bonnet, and pretty much from the same source, too — the fancy shops of Paré, once, in good old English, Paris, the capital city of France. A farmer, rich or poor, may spend half his annual income, every year of his life, in taking down old, and putting up new furniture, and be kept uncomfortable all the time; when, if he will, after a quiet, good-tempered talk with his better-half, agree with her upon the list of *necessary* articles to make them *really comfortable;* and then a catalogue of what shall comprise the *luxurious* part of their furnishings, which, when provided, they will fixedly make up their mind to keep, and be content with, they will remain entirely free from one great source of "the ills which flesh is heir to."

It is pleasant to see a young couple setting out in their housekeeping life, well provided with convenient and properly-selected furniture, appropriate to all the uses of the family; and then to keep, and use it, and enjoy it, like contented, sensible people; adding to it, now and then, as its wear, or the increasing wants of their family may require. Old, familiar things, to which we have long been accustomed, and habituated, make up a round share of our actual enjoyment. A family addicted to constant change in their household furniture, attached to nothing, content with nothing, and looking with anxiety to the next change of fashion which shall introduce something *new* into the house, can take no sort of comfort, let their circumstances be ever so affluent. It is a kind of dissipation in which some otherwise worthy people are prone to indulge, but altogether pernicious in the indulgence. It detracts, also, from the apparent respectability of a family to find nothing *old* about them — as if they themselves were of yesterday, and newly dusted out of a modern shop-keeper's stock in trade. The furniture of a house ought to look as though the family within it once had a grandfather — and as if old things had some veneration from those who had long enjoyed their service.

We are not about to dictate, of what fashion household furniture should be, when selected, any further than that of a plain, substantial, and commodious fashion, and that it should comport, so far as those requirements in it will admit, with the approved modes of the day. But we are free to say, that in these times the extreme of absurdity, and unfitness for *use*, is more the fashion than anything else. What so useless as the modern French chairs, standing on legs like pipe-stems, *garote*-ing your back like a rheumatism, and frail as the legs of a spider beneath you, as you sit in it; and a tribe of equally worthless incumbrances, which absorb your money in their cost, and detract from your comfort, instead of adding to it, when you have got them; or a bedstead so high that you must have a ladder to climb into it, or so low as to scarcely keep you above the level of the floor, when lying on it. No; give us the substantial, the easy, the free, and enjoyable articles, and the rest may go to tickle the fancy of those who have a taste for them. Nor do these flashy furnishings add to one's rank in society, or to the good opinion of those whose consideration is most valuable. Look into the houses of those people who are the *really* substantial, and worthy of the land. There will be found little of such frippery with them.

Old furniture, well-preserved, useful in everything, mark the well-ordered arrangement of their rooms, and give an air of quietude, of comfort, and of hospitality to their apartments. Children cling to such objects in after life, as heir-looms of affection and parental regard.

Although we decline to give specific directions about what varieties of furniture should constitute the furnishings of a house, or to illustrate its style or fashion by drawings, and content ourself with the single remark, that it should, in all cases, be strong, plain, and durable — no sham, nor ostentation about it — and such as is *made for use:* mere trinkets stuck about the room, on center tables, in corners, or on the mantel-piece, are the foolishest things imaginable. They are costly; they require a world of care, to keep them in condition; and then, with all this care, they are good for nothing, in any sensible use. We have frequently been into a country house, where we anticipated better things, and, on being introduced into the 'parlor," actually found everything in the furniture line so dainty and "prinked up," that we were afraid to sit down on the frail things stuck around by way of seats, for fear of breaking them; and everything about it looked so gingerly and inhospitable, that we felt an absolute relief when we could fairly get out of it, and take a place by the wide old fireplace, in the common living room, comfortably ensconced in a good old easy, high-backed, split-bottomed chair — there was positive comfort in that, when in the "parlor" there was nothing but restraint and *dis*comfort. No; leave all this vanity to town-folk, who have nothing better — or who, at least, think they have — to amuse themselves with; it has no fitness for a country dwelling, whatever. All this kind of frippery smacks of the boarding school, the pirouette, and the dancing master, and is out of character for the farm, or the sensible retirement of the country.

In connection with the subject of furniture, a remark may be made on the *room* arrangement of the house, which might, perhaps, have been more fittingly made when discussing that subject, in the designs of our houses. Some people have a marvellous propensity for introducing into their houses a *suite* of rooms, connected by wide folding-doors, which must always be opened into each other, furnished just alike, and devoted to extraordinary occasions; thus absolutely sinking the best rooms in the house, for display half a dozen times in the year, and at the sacrifice of the every-day comfort of the family. This is nothing but a bastard taste, of the most worthless kind, introduced from the city — the propriety of which, for city life, need not here be discussed. The presence of such arrangement, in a country house, is fatal to everything like domestic enjoyment, and always followed by great expense and inconvenience. No room, in any house, should be too good for occupation by the family themselves — not every-day, and common-place — but occupation at any and all times, when convenience or pleasure demand it. If a large room be required, let the single room itself be large; not sacrifice an extra room to the occasional extension of the choicer one, as in the use of folding-doors must be done. This "parlor" may be better furnished — and so it should be — than any other room in the house. Its carpet should be not too good to tread, or stand upon, or for the children to roll and tumble upon, provided their shoes and clothes be clean. Let the happy little fellows roll and tumble on it, to their heart's content, when their mother or elder sisters are with them — for it may be, perhaps, the most joyous, and most innocent pleasure of their lives, poor things! The hearth-rug should be in keeping with the carpet, also, and no floor-cloth should be necessary to cover it, for fear of soiling; but everything free and easy, with a comfortable, inviting, hospitable look about it.

Go into the houses of our great men — such as live in the country — whom God made great, not money — and see how *they* live. We speak not of statesmen and politicians alone, but great merchants, great scholars, great divines, great mechanics, and all men who, in mind and attainments, are head and shoulder above their class in any of the walks of life, and you find no starch, or flummery about them. We once went out to the country house — he lived there all the time, for that matter — of a distinguished banker of one of our great cities, to dine, and spend the day with him. He had a small farm attached to his dwelling, where he kept his horses and cows, his pigs, and his poultry. He had a large, plain two-story cottage house, with a piazza running on three sides of it, from which a beautiful view of the neighboring city, and water, and land, was seen in nearly all directions. He was an educated man. His father had been a statesman of distinguished ability and station at home, and a diplomatist abroad, and himself educated in the highest circles of business, and of society. His wife, too, was the daughter of a distinguished city merchant, quite his equal in all the accomplishments of life. His own wealth was competent; he was the manager of millions of the wealth of others; and his station in society was of the highest. Yet, with all this claim to pretension, his house did not cost him eight thousand dollars — and he built it by "days-work," too, so as to have it faithfully done; and the furniture in it, aside from library, paintings, and statuary, never cost him three thousand. Every room in it was a plain one, not more highly finished than many a farmer's house can afford. The furniture of every kind was plain, saving, perhaps, the old family plate, and such as he had added to it, which was all substantial, and made for use. The younger children — and of these, younger and older, he had several — we found happy, healthy, cheerful, and frolicking on the carpets; and their worthy mother, in the plainest, yet altogether appropriate garb, was sitting among them, at her family sewing, and kindly welcomed us as we took our seats in front of the open, glowing fireplace. "Why, sir," we exclaimed, rubbing our hands in the comfortable glow of warmth which the fire had given — for it was a cold December day — "you are quite plain, as well as wonderfully comfortable, in your country house — quite different from your former city residence!" "To be sure we are," was the reply; "we stood it as long as we could, amid the starch and the gimcracks of ——

street, where we rarely had a day to ourselves, and the children could never go into the streets but they must be tagged and tasselled, in their dress, into all sorts of discomfort, merely for the sake of appearance. So, after standing it as long as we could, my wife and I determined we would try the country, for a while, and see what we could make of it. We kept our townhouse, into which we returned for a winter or two; but gave it up for a permanent residence here, with which we are perfectly content. We see here all the friends we want to see; we all enjoy ourselves, and the children are healthy and happy." And this is but a specimen of thousands of families in the enjoyment of country life, including the families of men in the highest station, and possessed of sufficient wealth.

Why, then, should the farmer ape the fashion, and the frivolity of the butterflies of town life, or permit his family to do it? It is the sheerest possible folly in him to do so. Yet, it is a folly into which many are imperceptibly gliding, and which, if not reformed, will ultimately lead to great discomfort to themselves, and ruin to their families. Let thoughtless people do as they choose. Pay no attention to their extravagance; but watch them for a dozen years, and see how they come out in their fashionable career; and observe the fate of their families, as they get "established" in the like kind of life. He who keeps aloof from such temptation, will then have no cause to regret that he has maintained his own steady course of living, and taught his sons and daughters that a due attention to their own comfort, with economical habits in everything relating to housekeeping, will be to their lasting benefit in future.

But, we have said enough to convey the ideas in house-furnishing we would wish to impart; and the reader will do as he, or she, no doubt, would have done, had we not written a word about it—go and select such as may strike their own fancy.

We received, a day or two since, a letter from a person at the west, entirely unknown to us, whose ideas so entirely correspond with our own, that we give it a place, as showing that a proper taste *does* prevail among many people in this country, in regard to buildings, and house-furnishings; and which we trust he will pardon us for publishing, as according entirely with our own views, in conclusion:

———, ———, ILL., Dec. 18, 1851.

DEAR SIR,—I received, a few days since, a copy of the first number of a periodical called the "Plough," into which is copied the elevation of a design for a farm house, purporting to be from a forthcoming work of yours, entitled "Rural Architecture." Although a perfect stranger to you, you will perhaps allow me to make one or two suggestions.

I have seen no work yet, which seems fully to meet the wants of our country people in the matter of furniture. After having built their houses, they need showing how to furnish them in the cheapest, most neat, comfortable, convenient, and substantial manner. The furniture should be designed for use, not merely for show. I would have it plain, but not coarse—just enough for the utmost convenience, but nothing superfluous. The articles of furniture figured, and partially described in the late works on those subjects, are mostly of too elaborate and expensive a cast to be generally introduced into our country houses. There is too much *nabobery* about them to meet the wants, or suit the taste of the plain American farmer.

As to out-houses — the barn, stable, carriage and wagon-house, tool-house, piggery, poultry-house, concrib, and granary, (to say nothing of the "rabbit-warren" and "dovecote,")— are necessary appendages of the farm house. Now, as cheapness is one great desideratum with nearly all our new beginners in this western region, it seems to me, that such plans as will conveniently include the greatest number of these under the same roof, will be best suited to their necessities. I do not mean to be understood that, for the sake of the first cost, we should pay no regard to the appearance, or that we should slight our work, or suffer it to be constructed of flimsy or perishable materials: we should not only have an eye to taste and durability, but put in practice the most strict economy.

I hope, in the above matters, you may be able to furnish something better suited to the necessities and means of our plain farmers, than has been done by any of your predecessors.

I remain, &c., most respectfully yours,

———, ———.

Having completed the series of Designs for dwelling houses, which we had proposed for this work, and followed them out with such remarks as were thought fitting to attend them, we now pass on to the second part of our subject: the out-buildings of the farm, in which are to be accommodated the domestic animals which make up a large item of its economy and management; together with other buildings which are necessary to complete its requirements. We trust that they will be found to be such as the occasion, and the wants of the farmer may demand; and in economy, accommodation, and extent, be serviceable to those for whose benefit they are designed.

AN APIARY, OR BEE-HOUSE.

Every farmer should keep bees—provided he have pasturage for them, on his own land, or if a proper range for their food and stores lie in his immediate vicinity. Bees are, beyond any other domestic *stock*, economical in their keeping, to their owners. Still they require care, and that of no inconsiderable kind, and skill, in their management, not understood by every one who attempts to rear them. They ask no food, they require no assistance, in gathering their daily stores, beyond that of proper housing in the cheapest description of tenement, and with that they are entirely content. Yet, without these, they are a contingent, and sometimes a troublesome appendage to the domestic stock of the farm.

We call them *domestic*. In one sense they are so; in another, they are as wild and untamed as when buzzing and collecting their sweets in the vineyard of Timnath, where the mighty Sampson took their honey from the carcass of the dead lion; or, as when John the Baptist, clothed with camel's hair, ate "locusts and wild honey" in the arid wastes of Palestine. Although kept in partial bondage for six thousand years, the ruling propensity of the bee is to seek a home and shelter in the forest, when it emerges in a swarm from the parent hive; and no amount of domestic accommodation, or kindness of treatment, will induce it willingly to migrate from its nursery habitation to another by its side, although provided with the choicest comforts to invite its entrance. It will soon fly to the woods, enter a hollow and dilapidated tree, and carve out for itself its future fortunes, amid a world of labor and apparent discomfort. The bee, too, barring its industry, patience, and sweetened labors, is an arrant thief—robbing its nearest neighbors, with impunity, when the strongest, and mercilessly slaughtering its weaker brethren, when standing in the way of its rapacity. It has been extolled for its ingenuity, its patience, its industry, its perseverance, and its virtue. Patience, industry, and perseverance it has, beyond a doubt, and in a wonderful degree; but ingenuity, and virtue, it has none, more than the spider, who spins his worthless web, or the wasp, who stings you when disturbing his labors. Instinct, the bee has, like all animals; but of kind feeling, and gratitude, it has nothing; and with all our vivid nursery remembrance of good Doctor Watts' charming little hymn—

"How doth the little busy bee," &c. &c.,

we have long ago set it down as incorrigible to kind treatment, or charitable sympathy, and looked upon it simply as a thing to be treated kindly for the sake of its labors, and as composing one of that delightful family of domestic objects which make our homes attractive, pleasant, and profitable.

The active labors of the bee, in a bright May or June morning, as they fly, in their busy order, back and forth from their hives, or the soothing hum of their playful hours, in a summer's afternoon, are among the most delightful associations of rural life; and as a luxury to the sight, and the ear, they should be associated with every farmer's home, and with every laborer's cottage, when practicable. And as their due accommodation is to be the object of our present writing, a plan is presented for that object.

In many of the modern structures held out for imitation, the bee-house, or apiary, is an expensive, pretentious affair, got up in an ambitious way, with efforts at style, in the semblance of a temple, a pagoda, or other absurdity, the very appearance of which frightens the simple bee from its propriety, and in which we never yet knew a colony of them to become, and remain successful. The insect is, as we have observed, wild and untamable — a savage in its habits, and rude in its temper. It rejects all cultivated appearances, and seeks only its own temporary convenience, together with comfortable room for its stores, and the increase of its kind; and therefore, the more rustic and simple its habitation, the better is it pleased with its position.

The bee-house should front upon a sheltered and sunny aspect. It should be near the ground, in a clean and quiet spot, free from the intrusion of other creatures, either human or profane, and undisturbed by noisome smells, and uncouth sounds — for it loathes all these instinctively, and loves nothing so much as the wild beauty of nature itself. The plan here presented

APIARY.

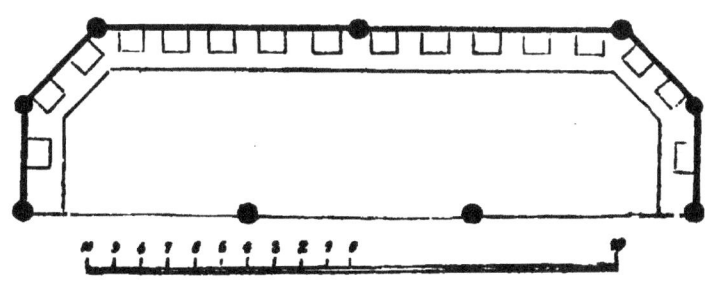

GROUND PLAN.

is of the plainest and least expensive kind. Nine posts, or crutches, are set into the ground sufficiently deep to hold them firm, and to secure them from heaving out by the frost. The distance of these posts apart may be according to the size of the building, and to give it strength enough to resist the action of the wind. The front posts should be 9 feet high, above the ground; the rear posts should be 7 feet—that a man, with his hat on, may stand upright under them—and 6 feet from the front line. The two end posts directly in the rear of the front corner posts, should be 3 feet back from them, and on a line to accommodate the pitch of the roof from the front to the rear. A light plate is to be fitted on the top line of the front posts; a plate at each end should run back to the posts in rear, and then another cross-plate, or girt, from each one of these middle posts, to the post in rear of all, to meet the plate which surmounts this rear line of posts; and a parallel plate, or rafter, should be laid from the two intermediate posts at the ends, to connect them, and for a central support to the roof. Intermediate central posts should also be placed opposite those in front, to support the central plate, and not exceeding 12 feet apart. A shed roof, of boards, or shingles, tightly laid, should cover the whole, sufficiently projecting over the front, rear, and sides, to give the house abundant shelter, and make it architecturally agreeable to the eye—say 12 to 18 inches, according to its extent. A corner board should drop two feet below the plate, with such finish, by way of ornament, as may be desirable. The ends should be tightly boarded up against the weather, from bottom to top. The rear should also be tightly boarded, from the bottom up to a level with the stand inside, for the hives, and from 15 to 18 inches above that to the roof. Fitted into the space thus left in the rear, should be a light, though substantial, swing door, hung from the upper boarding, made in sections, extending from one post to the other, as the size of the house may determine, and secured with hooks, or buttons, as may be convenient. The outside of the structure is thus completed.

The inside arrangement for the hives, may be made in two different ways, as the choice of the apiarian may govern in the mode in which his hives are secured. The most usual is the *stand* method, which may be made thus: At each angle, equidistant, say 18 to 24 inches, inside, from the rear side and ends of the building — as shown in the ground plan — and opposite to each rear and end post, suspend perpendicularly a line of stout pieces of two-inch plank, 4 inches wide, well spiked on to the rafters above, reaching down within two feet of the ground — which is to hold up the bottom of the stand on which the hives are to rest. From each bottom end of these suspended strips, secure another piece of like thickness and width, horizontally back to the post in rear of it, at the side and ends. Then, lengthwise the building, and turning the angles at the ends, and resting on these horizontal pieces just described, lay other strips, 3×2 inches, set edgewise — one in front, and another in rear, inside each post and suspended strip, and close to it, and secured by heavy nails, so that there shall be a double line of these strips on a level, extending entirely around the interior, from the front at each end. This forms the hanging frame-work for the planks or boards on which the hives are to rest.

Now for the hives. First, let as many pieces of sound one and a half, or two-inch plank as you have hives to set upon them, be cut long enough to reach from the boarding on the rear and ends of the building, to one inch beyond, and projecting over the front of the outer strip last described. Let these pieces of plank be well and smoothly planed, and laid lengthwise across the aforesaid strips, not less than four inches apart from each other—if a less number of hives be in the building than it will accommodate at four inches apart, no matter how far apart they may be—these pieces of plank are the *ferms* for the hives, on which they are to sit. And, as we have for many years adopted the plan now described, with entire success, a brief description is given of our mode of hive, and the process for obtaining the surplus honey. We say surplus, for destroying the bees to obtain their honey, is a mode not at all according to our notions of economy, or mercy; and we prefer to take that honey only which the swarm may make, after supplying their own wants, and the stores for their increasing family. This process is given in the report of a committee of gentlemen appointed by the New York State Agricultural Society, on a hive which we exhibited on that occasion, with the following note attached, at their show at Buffalo, in 1848:

"I have seen, examined, and used several different plans of *patent* hive, of which there are probably thirty invented, and used, more or less. I have found all which I have ever seen, unsatisfactory, not carrying out in full, the benefits claimed for them.

"The bee works, and lives, I believe, solely by instinct. I do not consider it an inventive, or very ingenious insect. To succeed well, its accommodations should be of the *simplest* and *securest* form. Therefore, instead of adopting the complicated plans of many of the patent hives, I have made, and used a simple box, like that now before you, containing a cube of one foot square *inside*—made of one and a quarter inch sound pine plank, well jointed and planed on all sides, and put together perfectly tight at the joints, with white lead ground in oil, and the inside of the hive at the bottom champered off to three-eighths of an inch thick, with a door for the bees in front, of four inches long by three-eighths of an inch high. I do this, that there may be a thin surface to come in contact with the shelf on which they rest, thus preventing a harbor for the bee-moth. (I have never used a patent hive which would exclude the bee-moth, nor any one which would so well do it as this, having never been troubled with that scourge since I used this tight hive.) On the top of the hive, an inch or two from the front, is made a passage for the bees, of an inch wide, and six to eight inches long, to admit the bees into an upper hive for surplus honey, (which passage is covered, when no vessel for that purpose is on the top.) For obtaining the honey, I use a common ten or twelve-quart water pail, inverted, with the bail turned over, in which the bees deposit their surplus, like the sample before you. The pail will hold about twenty pounds of honey. This is simple, cheap, and expeditious; the pail costing not exceeding twenty-five cents, is taken off in a moment, the bail replaced, and the honey ready for transportation, or market, and *always in place*. If there is time for more honey to be made, (my bees made two pails-full in succession this year,) another pail can be put on at once.

"Such, gentlemen, in short, is my method. I have kept bees about twenty years. I succeed better on this plan than with any other."

In addition to this, our hives are painted white, or other light color, on the outside, to protect them from warping, and as a further security against the bee-moth, or miller, which infests and destroys so many carelessly-made hives, as to discourage the efforts of equally careless people in keeping them. Inside the hive, on each end, we fasten, by shingle nails, about half-way between the bottom and top, a small piece of half-inch board, about the size of a common window button, and with a like notch in it, set upward, but stationary, on which, when the hive is to receive the swarm, a stick is laid across, to support the comb as is built, from falling in hot weather. At such time, also, when new, and used for the first time, the underside of the top is scratched with the tines of a table fork, or a nail, so as to make a rough surface, to which the new comb can be fastened. In addition to the pails on the top of the hives, to receive the surplus honey, we sometimes use a flat box, the size of the hive in diameter, and six or seven inches high *inside*, which will hold twenty-five to thirty pounds of honey. The pails we adopted as an article of greater convenience for transporting the honey.

The other plan of arranging the hives alluded to, is suspending them between the strips before described, by means of *cleats* secured on to the front and rear sides of the hive, say two-thirds the way up from the bottom. In such case, the strips running lengthwise the house must be brought near enough together to receive the hives as hung by the *cleats*, and the bottom boards, or forms, must be much smaller than those already described, and hung with wire hooks and staples to the sides, with a button on the rear, to close up, or let them down a sufficient distance to admit the air to pass freely across them, and up into the hive — Weeks' plan, in fact, for which he has a patent, together with some other fancied improvements, such as chambers to receive the boxes for the deposit of surplus honey. This, by the way, is the best "patent" we have seen; and Mr. Weeks having written an ingenious and excellent treatise on the treatment of the bee, we freely recommend his book to the attention of every apiarian who wishes to succeed in their management. As a rule, we have no confidence in *patent* hives. We have seen scores of them, of different kinds, have tried several of great pretension to sundry virtues — such as excluding moths, and other marvelous benefits — and, after becoming the victim of bee empirics to the tune of many a dollar, have thrown aside the gimcracks, and taken again to a common-sense method of keeping our bees, as here described. The bees themselves, we feel bound to say, seem to hold these patent-right habitations in quite as sovereign contempt as ourself, reluctantly going into them, and getting out of them at the first safe opportunity. But, as a treatise on bee-keeping is not a part of this present work, we must, for further information, commend the inquirer on that subject to some of the valuable treatises extant, on so prolific a subject, among which we name those of Bevan, Weeks, and Miner.

The bee-house should be thoroughly whitewashed *inside* every spring, and kept clean of cobwebs, wasp's nests, and vermin; and it may be painted outside, a soft and agreeable color, in keeping with the other buildings of the farm. Its premises should be clean, and sweet. The grass around should be kept mowed close. Low trees, or shrubbery, should stand within a few yards of it, that the new swarms may light upon them when coming out, and not, for want of such settling places, be liable to loss from flying away. It should, also, be within sight and hearing, and at no great distance from a continually-frequented room in the dwelling—perhaps the kitchen, if convenient, that, in their swarming season, they may be secured as they leave the parent hive. The apiary is a beautiful object, with its busy tenantry; and to the invalid, or one who loves to look upon God's tiny creatures, it may while away many an agreeable hour, in watching their labors — thus adding pleasure to profit.

The cost of a bee-house, on the plan given, may be from ten to fifty dollars, according to the price of material, and the amount of labor expended upon it. It should not be an expensive structure, in any event, as its purpose does not warrant it. If a gimcrack affair be wanted, for the purposes of ornament, or expense, any sum of money may be squandered upon it which the fancy of its builder may choose to spare.

AN ICE-HOUSE.

Among the useful and convenient appendages to the farm and country family establishment, is the ice-house. Different from the general opinion which prevailed in our country before ice became so important an article of commerce, and of home consumption, the building which contains it should stand above-ground, instead of below it. And the plainer and more simple it can be constructed, the better.

The position of the ice-house may be that which is most convenient to the dwelling, or to the wants of those who use it. If it can be placed beneath the shade of trees, it will so far be relieved from the influence of the sun; but it should be so constructed that sunshine will not affect the ice within it, even if it stand unsheltered; and as it has, by the ice-merchants of our eastern cities, who put up large quantities for exportation abroad, and others in the interior, who furnish ice in quantity for home consumption, been proved to be altogether the better plan to build the ice-house entirely above ground, we shall present no other mode of construction than this. It may be added, that five years' experience with one of our own building, has confirmed our opinion of the superiority of this over any other plan which may be adopted.

The design here presented is of the most economical kind, yet sufficiently ornamental to make it an agreeable appendage to any family establishment. The size may be 12 feet square—less than that would be too small for keeping ice well—and from that up to any required extent. The idea here given is simply the *principle* of construction. The posts should be full eight feet high above the ground, to where the plate of the roof is attached, and built thus:

Mark out your ground the size you require for the house; then, commencing at one corner, dig, opposite each other, a double set of holes, one foot deep, and two and a half feet apart, on each side of the intended building, say three feet equidistant, so that when the posts stand up they will present a double set, one and a half feet apart. Then set in your posts, which should be of oak, chestnut, or some lasting wood, and pack the earth firmly around them. If the posts are sawed, they may be 4×6 inches in size, set edgeways toward each other. If not sawed, they may be round sticks cut from the woods, or split from the body of a tree, quartered—but sizable, so as to appear decent—and the insides facing each other as they stand up, lined to a surface to receive the planking. Of course, when the posts are set in the ground, they are to show a square form, or skeleton of what the building is to be when completed. When this is done, square off the top of each post to a level, all round; then frame, or spike on to each line of posts a plate, say six inches

ICE-HOUSE.

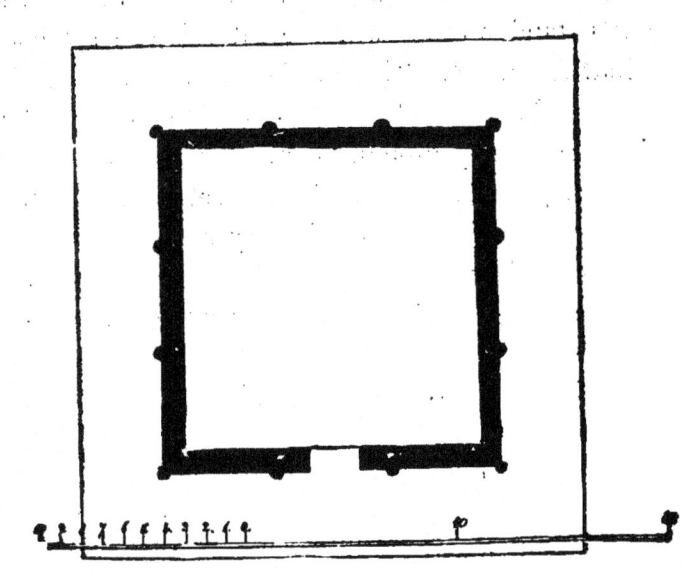

GROUND PLAN.

wide, and four to six inches deep, and stay the two plates together strongly, so as to form a double frame. Now, plank, or board up closely the *inside* of each line of posts, that the space between them shall be a fair surface. Cut out, or leave out a space for a door in the center of the side where you want it, two and a half or three feet wide, and six and a half feet high, and board up the inner partition sides of this opening, so as to form a door-casing on each side, that the space between the two lines of posts may be a continuous box all around. Then fill up this space between the posts with moist tan-bark, or saw-dust, well packed from the ground up to the plates; and the body of the house is inclosed, sun-proof, and air-proof, to guard the ice.

Now lay down, inside the building, some sticks—not much matter what, so that they be level—and on them lay loose planks or boards, for a floor. Cover this floor with a coating of straw, a foot thick, and it is ready to receive the ice.

For the roof, take common 3×4 joists, as rafters; or, in place of them, poles from the woods, long enough, in a pitch of full 35° from a horizontal line, to carry the roof at least four feet over the outside of the plates, and secure the rafters well, by pins or spikes, to them. Then board over and shingle it, leaving a small aperture at the top, through which run a small pipe, say eight inches in diameter—a stove-crock will do—for a ventilator. Then set in, 4 little posts, say two feet high—as in the design—throw a little four-sided, pointed cap on to the top of these posts, and the roof is done. If you want to ornament the under side of the roof, in a rude way—and we would advise it—take some pieces of 3×4 scantling, such as were used for the roof, if the posts are of sawed stuff—if not, rough limbs of trees from the woods, to match the rough posts of the same kind, and fasten them to the posts and the under side of the roof, by way of brackets, as shown in the design.

When the ice is put into the house, a close floor of boards should be laid on joists, which rest on the plates, loosely, so that this floor can be removed when putting in ice, and that covered five or six inches deep with tan, or saw-dust—straw will do, if the other can not be had—and the inside arrangement is complete. Two doors should be attached to the opening, where the ice is put in and taken out; one on the inner side of the lining, and the other on the outer side, both opening out. Tan, saw-dust, or straw should also be placed on the top of the ice, when put in, so as to keep the air from it as much as possible; and as the ice is removed, it will settle down upon, and still preserve it. Care must be taken to have a drain under the floor of the house, to pass off the water which melts from the ice, as it would, if standing there, injure its keeping.

It will be seen, that, by an error in the cut of the ground plan, the inside line of posts does not show, as in the outer line, which they should do; nor is the outside door inserted, as is shown in the elevation. These defects, however, will be rectified by the builder.

We have given considerable thought to this subject, and can devise no shape to the building more appropriate than this, nor one cheaper in construction. It may be built for fifty to a hundred dollars, according to the cost of material and labor, and the degree of finish given to it.

It is hardly worth while to expatiate upon the convenience and economy of an ice-house, to an American. Those who love well-kept meats, fruits, butter, milk, and various etceteras for the table, understand its utility well; to say nothing of the cooling draughts, in the way of drinks, in hot weather, to which it adds — when not taken to extremes — such positive luxury. We commend the ice-house, *well-filled*, most heartily, to every good country housekeeper, as a matter of convenience, economy, and luxury, adding next to nothing to the living expenses, and, as an appendage to the main buildings, an item of little cost, and a considerable degree of ornament.

If an under-ground ice-house be preferred to the plan here shown, a side hill, or bank, with a northerly exposure, is the best location for it; and the manner of building should be mainly like this, for the body of the house. The roof, however, should be only two-sided, and the door for putting in and taking out the ice may be in the gable, on the ground level. The drainage under the floor, and precautions for keeping the ice, should be quite as thorough as we have described; as, otherwise, the earth surrounding it on three sides, at least, of the house, will be a ready conductor of warmth, and melt the ice with great rapidity. If the under-ground plan is adopted, but little more than the roof will show, and of course, be of little ornament in the way of appearance.

THE ASH-HOUSE AND SMOKE-HOUSE.

These two objects may, both for convenience and economy, be well combined under one roof; and we have thus placed them in connection. The building is an exceedingly simple structure, made of stone, or brick; the body 10 feet high, and of such size as may be desirable, with a simple roof, and a plain, hooded chimney.

In the ground plan will be seen a brick, or stone partition—which may extend to such height as may be necessary to contain the bulk of ashes required for storage within it—on one side of the building, to which a door gives access. The opposite side, and overhead, is devoted to the smoke-house, in which the various girts and hooks may be placed, for sustaining the meats to be smoked. The building should be tied together by joists at the plates, properly anchored into the walls, to prevent their spreading. A stove, or pans, or neither, as the method of keeping the smoke alive may govern, can be placed inside, to which the chimney in the roof may serve as a partial escape, or not, as required. The whole process is so simple

ASH HOUSE AND SMOKE HOUSE.

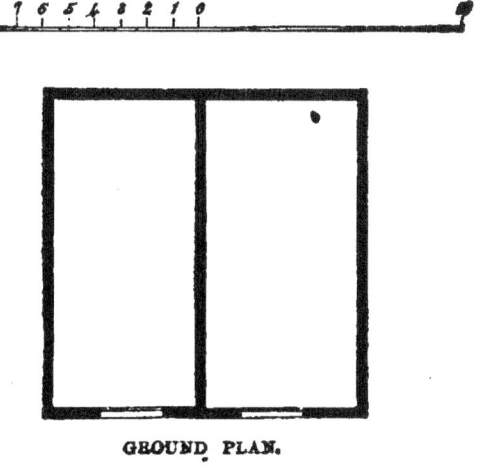

GROUND PLAN.

and so easily understood, that further explanation is unnecessary.

A great advantage that a house of this construction has, is the convenience of storing the smoked meats for an indefinite time, even through the whole season, keeping them dark, dry, and cool; and permitting, at any time, a smoke to be made, to drive out the flies, if they find their way into it.

The ashes can, of course, be removed at any time, by the door at which they are thrown in.

THE POULTRY-HOUSE.

As poultry is an indispensable appendage to the farm, in all cases, the poultry-house is equally indispensable, for their accommodation, and for the most profitable management of the fowls themselves, and most convenient for the production of their eggs and young. Indeed, without well-arranged quarters for the fowls of the farm, they are exceedingly troublesome, and of doubtful profit; but with the proper buildings devoted to them exclusively, they become one of the most interesting and agreeable objects with which either the farm or the country house is associated.

It is hardly worth while to eulogize poultry. Their merits and virtues are written in the hearts of all provident housekeepers; and their beauty and goodness are familiar to every son and daughter of the rural homestead. We shall, then, proceed at once to discuss their proper accommodation, in the cheapest and most familiar method with which we are acquainted.

The hen-house — for hens (barn-door fowls, we mean) are the first and chief stock, of the kind, to be provided for, and with them most of the other varieties can be associated — should be located in a warm, sheltered, and sunny place, with abundant grounds about it, where they can graze — hens eat grass — and scratch, and enjoy themselves to their heart's content, in all seasons, when the ground is open and they *can* scratch into, or range over its surface. Some people — indeed, a good many people — picket in their gardens, to keep hens *out;* but we prefer an enclosure to keep the hens *in*, at all seasons when they are troublesome, which, after all, is only during short seasons of the year, when seeds are planted, or sown, and grain and vegetables are ripening. Otherwise, they may range at will, on the farm, doing good in their destruction of insects, and deriving much enjoyment to themselves; for hens, on the whole, are happy things.

We here present the elevation of a poultry-house in perspective, to show the *principle* which we would adopt in its construction, and which may be extended to any required length, and to which may be added any given area of ground, or yard-room, which the circumstances of the proprietor may devote to it. It is, as will be seen, of a most rustic appearance, and built as cheaply, yet thoroughly, as the subject may require. Its length, we will say, is 20 feet, its breadth 16, and its height 10 feet, made of posts set into the ground — for we do not like sills, and floors of wood, because rats are apt to burrow under them, which are their worst enemies — and boarded up, either inside or outside, as in the case of the ice-house previously described, though not double. Plates are laid on these posts, to connect them firmly together; and the rafters

POULTRY LAWN.

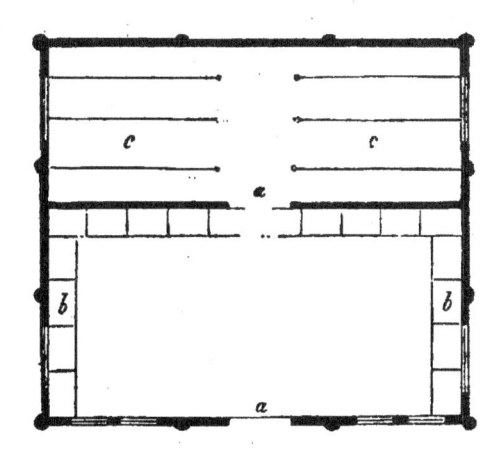

GROUND PLAN.

rest on the plates, as usual. The chamber floor is 9 feet high, above the ground, and may be used either for laying purposes by the fowls, or reserved as a storage-room for their feed. The roof is broadly drawn over the body of the building, to shelter it, and through the point of the roof, in the center, is a ventilator, with a covered top, and a vane significant of its purpose. It is also sufficiently lighted, with glass windows, into which our draughtsman has put the diamond-paned glass, contrary to our notions; but, as he had, no doubt, an eye to the "picturesque," we let it pass, only remarking, that if we were building the house on our own account, there should be no such nonsense about it. The front windows are large, to attract the warmth of the winter's sun. A section of picket fence is also attached, and trees in the rear — both of which are necessary to a complete establishment; the first, to secure the poultry in the contiguous yards, and the trees to give them shade, and even roosting-places, if they prefer such lodgings in warm weather — for which we consider them eminently wholesome.

The wooden floor is dispensed with, as was remarked, to keep rid of the vermin. If the ground be gravelly, or sandy, it will be sufficiently dry. If a heavy or damp soil be used, it should be under-drained, which will effectually dry it, and be better for the fowls than a floor of either wood, brick, or stone. Doors of sufficient size can be made on the yard sides of the house, near the ground, for the poultry to enter either the living or roosting apartments, at pleasure, and hung with butts on the upper side, to be closed when necessary.

INTERIOR ARRANGEMENT.

The front door opens into the main living room. At each end, and in the rear, are tiers of boxes, one foot wide, one and a half feet long, and one and a half feet high — the lowest tier elevated two feet above the ground — and built one tier above the other, and snugly partitioned between, with a hole at one corner of each, ten inches high, and eight inches wide, for passing in to them; and a shelf, or passage-board, nine inches wide, in front. These are the nesting boxes, and should be kept supplied with short, soft straw, or hay orts, for that purpose. Hens love secrecy in their domestic economy, and are wonderfully pleased with the opportunity to hide away, and conceal themselves while laying. Indeed, such concealment, or the supposition of it, we have no doubt promotes fecundity, as it is well known that a hen *can* stop laying, almost at pleasure, when disturbed in her regular habits and settled plans of life. Burns says —

"The best laid schemes of *mice* and *men*
Gang aft agley;"

and why not hen's? We think so. If turkeys be kept in the premises, the females can also be accommodated in these boxes, as they are fond of laying in company with the hens, and frequently in the same nests, only that they require larger entrances into them; or, a tier of boxes may be made on the ground, for their convenience.

A door leads from the rear of this room into the roosting apartment, through which is a passage to the back side of the building, and a door opposite, leading out into the yard. On each side of this passage are roosts, rising, each behind and above the other, 18 inches apart. The lowest roosts may be three feet from the ground, and the highest six feet, that they may easily fly from one to the other; and in this way they may all be approached, to catch the fowls, when required. For the roosts, slender poles, two to three inches in diameter—small trees, cut from the woods, with the bark on, are the best—may be used; and they should be secured through augur holes in board slats suspended from the floor joists overhead. This apartment should be cleaned out as often as once a fortnight, both for cleanliness and health—for fowls like to be clean, and to have pure air. A flight of stairs may be made in one corner of the front room, to go into the chamber, if preferred; but a swing ladder, hung by one end, with hinges, to the joists above, is, for such purpose, a more cleanly mode of access; which, when not in use, may be hooked up to the under side of the floor above; and a trap door, shutting into the chamber floor, and also hung on hinges, will accommodate the entrance.

For feeding troughs, we have seen many ingenious contrivances, and among them, possibly, a Yankee patent, or two; but all these we put aside, as of little account. A common segar box, or any other cast-off thing, that will hold their food, is just as good as the most complicated invention; and, in common feeding, there is no better mode than to scatter abroad their corn, and let them pick it up at their pleasure — when spread on a clean surface. We think, also, that, except for fattening poultry, stated hours of feeding are best for the birds themselves, and that they be fed' only such quantity as they will pick up clean. Water should, if possible, be kept constantly by them; and if a small running stream could pass through the yard, all the better.

If it be desirable to have fresh eggs during winter — and that is certainly a convenience — a box stove may be set in the living room, and properly protected by a grating around it, for warming the living apartment. It may be remarked, however, that this winter-laying of hens is usually a *forcing* business. A hen will lay but about a given number of eggs in a year; say a hundred — we believe this is about the number which the most observant of poultry-keepers allow them — and what she lays in winter must be substracted from the number she would otherwise lay in the spring, summer, or autumn. Yet a warm house will, laying, aside, keep the fowls with less food, and in greater comfort, than if cold, and left to their own natural warmth.

There is usually little difficulty in keeping hens, turkies, ducks, and geese together, in the same inclosure, during winter and early spring, before the grass grows. But geese and turkies require greater range during the warm season than the others, and should have it, both for convenience to themselves and profit to their owners. For winter quarters, low shelters may be made for the water-fowls in the yards, and the turkies will frequently prefer to share the shelter of the hens, on the roosts in the house. Guinea-hens—cruel, vindictive things, as they are—should never be allowed within a common poultry yard. Always quarrelsome, and never quiet, they should take to the farmyard, with the cattle, where they may range at will, and take their amusement in fisticuffs with each other, at pleasure. Neither should peacocks be allowed to come into the poultry inclosures, during the breeding season; they are anything but amiable in their manners to other birds.

With the care and management of the poultry department, after thus providing for their accommodation, it is not our province to interfere; that is a subject too generally understood, to require further remark. Nor need we discuss the many varieties of poultry which, at the present time, so arrest the attention of many of our good country people; and we will leave so important a subject to the meditations of the "New England Poultry Society," who have taken the gallinaceous, and other tribes under their special cognizance, and will, doubtless, in due time, illumine the world with various knowledge in this department of rural economy, not yet "dreamt of in our philosophy." The recently published poultry books, too, with an amplitude and particularity in the discussion of the different breeds and varieties, which shuts all suspicions of *self-interest* into the corner, have given such a fund of information on the subject, that any further inquiry may, with entire good will, be turned over to their pages.

THE DOVECOTE.

This is a department, in itself, not common among the farm buildings, in the United States; and for the reason, probably, that the domestic pigeon, or house-dove is usually kept more for amusement than for profit—there being little actual profit about them—and is readily accommodated in the spare lofts of sheds and out-buildings devoted to other purposes. Pigeons, however, add to the variety and interest of the poultry department; and as there are many different breeds of them, they are general favorites with the juveniles of the family.

Our present object is, not to propose any distinct building for pigeon accommodation; but to give them a location in other buildings, where they will be conveniently provided with room, and least annoying by their presence—for, be it known, they are oft-times a most serious annoyance to many crops of the farm, when kept in any considerable numbers, as well as in the waste and havoc they make in the stores of the barns and granaries. Although graceful and beautiful birds, generally clean and tidy in their personal habits out of doors, they are the filthiest housekeepers imaginable, and no building can be especially devoted to their use, if not often swept and cleaned, but what will soon become an intolerable nuisance within, and not much better without, and the ground immediately around the premises a dirty place. The common pigeon is a pugnacious cavalier, warring apparently upon mere punctilio, as we have often seen, in the distant strut-and-coo of a stranger bird to his mate, even if she be the very incarnation of "rejected addresses." On all these accounts, we would locate—unless a small and select family of fancy birds, perhaps—the pigeon stock at the principal farm-yard, and in the lofts of the cattle sheds, or the chambers of the stable.

Wherever the pigeon accommodations are designed to be, a close partition should separate their quarters from the room occupied for other purposes, with doors for admission to those who have to do with them, in cleaning their premises, or to take the birds, when needed. A line of holes, five inches high, and four inches wide—the top of the hole slightly arched—should be made, say 18 inches apart, for the distance of room they are to occupy in the building. A foot above the top of these, another line may be made; and so on, tiering them up to the height intended to devote to them. A line of shelves, or lighting-boards, six to eight inches wide, should then be placed one inch below the bottom of these holes, and firmly braced beneath, and nailed to the weather-boarding of the house. Inside, a range of box should be made, of corresponding length with the line of holes, to embrace every entrance from the outside, 18 inches wide, and partitioned equidistant between each entrance, so as to give a square box of 18 inches to each pair of birds. The bottom board of each ascending tier of boxes will, of course, be the top of the boxes below, and these must be made *perfectly tight*, to prevent the offal of the upper ones from falling through, to the annoyance of their neighbors below. The back of these boxes should have a line of swing doors, hung with butts, or hinges, from the top, and fastened with buttons, or hooks, at the bottom, to allow admission, or examination, at any time, to those who have the care of them. This plan of door is indispensable, to clean them out—which should be done as often as once a week, or fortnight, at farthest—and to secure the birds as they may be wanted for the table, or other purposes—for it will be recollected that squabs, just feathered out, are considered a delicious dish, at the most sumptuous tables. It will be understood, that these boxes above described, are within a partitioned room, with a floor, in their rear, with sufficient space for the person in charge of them to pass along, and to hold the baskets, or whatever is to receive the offal of their boxes, as it is taken out. This offal is valuable, as a highly stimulating manure, and is sought for by the morocco tanners, at a high price—frequently at twenty-five cents a bushel.

As pigeons are prolific breeders, laying and hatching six or seven times a year, and in warm climates oncr, they require a good supply of litter—short t, soft straw is the best—which should be freely supplied at every new incubation, and the old litter removed. The boxes, too, should be in a warm place, snugly made, and well sheltered from the wind and driving storms; for pigeons, although hardy birds when grown, should be well protected while young.

The common food of the pigeon is grain, of almost any kind, and worms, and other insects, which they pick up in the field. On the whole, they are a pleasant bird, when they can be conveniently kept, and are worth the trifling cost that their proper housing may demand.

If our opinion were asked, as to the best, and least troublesome kind of pigeon to be kept, we should say, the finest and most hardy of the common kind, which are usually found in the collections throughout the the country. But there are many *fancy* breeds — such as the fan-tail, the powter, the tumbler, the ruffler, and perhaps another variety or two — all pretty birds, and each distinct in their appearance, and in some of their domestic habits. The most beautiful of the pigeon kind, however, is the Carrier. They are the very perfection of grace, and symmetry, and beauty. Their colors are always brilliant and changing, and in their flight they cleave the air with a rapidity which no other variety — indeed, which scarce any other bird, of any kind, can equal. History is full of examples of their usefulness, in carrying tidings from one country to another, in letters, or tokens, fastened to their necks or legs, for which they are trained by those who have thus used them; but which, now, the well known telegraph wire has nearly superseded.

All these fancy breeds require great care in their management, to keep them pure in blood, as they will all mix, more or less, with the common pigeon, as they come in contact with them; and the selection of whatever kind is wanted to be kept, must be left to those who are willing to bestow the pains which their necessary care may demand.

A PIGGERY.

The hog is an animal for which we have no especial liking, be he either a tender suckling, nosing and tugging at the well-filled udder of his dam, or a well-proportioned porker, basking in all the plenitude of swinish luxury; albeit, in the use of his flesh, we affect not the Jew, but liking it moderately well, in its various preparations, as a substantial and savory article of diet. Still, the hog is an important item of our agricultural economy, and his production and proper treatment is a valuable study to all who rear him as a creature either of profit or convenience. In the western and southern states, a mild climate permits him to be easily reared and fed off for market, with little heed to shelter or protection; while in the north, he requires care and covering during winter. Not only this; in all places the hog is an unruly, mischievous creature, and has no business really in any other place than where he can be controlled, and kept at a moment's call.

But, as tastes and customs differ essentially, with regard to his training and destiny, to such as agree with us in opinion, that his proper place is in the sty, particularly when feeding for pork, a plan of piggery is given, such as may be economical in construction, and convenient in its arrangement, both for the swine itself, and him who has charge of him.

The design here given, is for a building, 36 feet long, and 24 feet wide, with twelve-feet posts; the lower, or living room for the swine, 9 feet high, and a storage chamber above, for the grain and other food required for his keeping. The roof has a pitch of 40° from a horizontal line, spreading over the sides and gables at least 20 inches, and coarsely bracketed. The entrance front projects 6 feet from the main building, by 12 feet in length. Over its main door, in the gable, is a door with a hoisting beam and tackle above it, to take in the grain, and a floor over the whole area receives it. A window is in each gable end. A ventilator passes up through this chamber and the roof, to let off the steam from the cooking vats below, and the foul air emitted by the swine, by the side of which is the furnace-chimney, giving it, on the whole, as respectable an appearance as a pigsty need pretend to.

PIGGERY.

GROUND PLAN.

INTERIOR ARRANGEMENT.

At the left of the entrance is a flight of stairs, (b,) leading to the chamber above. On the right is a small area, (a,) with a window to light it. A door from this leads into the main room, (c,) where stands a chimney, (d,) with a furnace to receive the fuel for cooking the food, for which are two kettles, or boilers, with wooden vats, on the top, if the extent of food demands them; these are secured with broad wooden covers, to keep in the steam when cooking. An iron valve is placed in the back flue of the furnace, which may fall upon either side, to shut off the fire from either of the kettles, around which the fire may revolve; or, the valve may stand in a perpendicular position, at will, if both kettles be heated at the same time. But, as the most economical mode is to cook one kettle while the other is in process of feeding out, and *vice versa*, scarcely more than one at a time will be required in use. Over each kettle is a sliding door, with a short spout to slide the food into them, when wanted. If necessary, and it can be conveniently done, a well may be sunk under this room, and a pump inserted at a convenient place; or if equally convenient, a pipe may bring the water in from a neighboring stream, or spring. On three sides of this room are feeding pens, (e_2) and sleeping partitions, (f,) for the swine. These several apartments are accommodated with doors, which open into separate yards on the sides and in rear, or a large one for the entire family, as may be desired.

CONSTRUCTION.

The frame of this building is of strong timber, and stout for its size. The sills should be 8 inches square, the corner posts of the same size, and the intermediate posts 8×6 inches in diameter. In the center of these posts, grooves should be made, 2 inches wide, and deep, to receive the *plank* sides, which should be 2 inches thick, and let in from the level of the chamber by a flush cutting for that purpose, out of the grooves inside, thus using no nails or spikes, and holding the planks tight in their place, that they may not be rooted out, or rubbed off by the hogs, and the inner projection of the main posts left to serve as rubbing posts for them — for no creature so loves to rub his sides, when fatting, as a hog, and this very natural and praiseworthy propensity should be indulged. These planks, like the posts, should, particularly the lower ones, be of *hard* wood, that they may not be eaten off. Above the chamber floor, thinner planks may be used, but all should be well jointed, that they may lie snug, and shut out the weather. The center post in the floor plan of the engraving is omitted, by mistake, but it should stand there, like the others. Inside posts at the corners, and in the sides of the partitions, like the outside ones, should be also placed and grooved to receive the planking, four and a half feet high, and their upper ends be secured by tenons into mortices in the beams overhead. The troughs should then, if possible, be made of *cast iron*, or, in default of that, the hardest of white oak plank, strongly spiked on to the floor and sides; and the apartment may then be called hog-proof—for a more unquiet, destructive creature, to a building in which he is confined, does not live, than the hog. The slide, or spout to conduct the swill and other feed from the feeding-room into the trough, should be inserted through the partition planks, with a steep *slant* the whole length of the trough, that the feed may be readily thrown into any or all parts of it. This slide should be of two-inch white-oak plank, and bound along the bottom by a strip of hoop-iron, to prevent the pigs from eating it off—a habit they are prone to; then, firmly spiked down to the partition planks, and through the ends, to the adjoining studs, and the affair is complete. With what experience we have had with the hog, and that by no means an agreeable one, we can devise no better method of accommodation than this here described, and it certainly is the cheapest. But the timber and lumber used must be sound and strong; and then, properly put together, it may defy their most destructive ingenuity. Of the separate uses to which the various apartments may be put, nothing need be said, as the circumstances of every farmer will best govern them.

One, to three hundred dollars, according to price of material and labor, will build this piggery, besides fitting it up with furnace and boilers. It may be contracted, or enlarged in size, as necessity may direct; but no one, with six to twenty porkers in his fatting pens, a year, will regret the expense of building a convenient appurtenance of this kind to his establishment.

A word may be pardoned, in relation to the too universal practice of permitting swine to prowl along the highways, and in the yards and lawns of the farm house. There is nothing so slovenly, wasteful, and destructive to one's thrift, and so demoralizing, in a small way, as is this practice. What so revolting to one, of the least tidy nature whatever, as a villainous brute, with a litter of filthy pigs at her heels, and the slimy ooze of a mud-puddle reeking and dripping from their sides? See the daubs of mud marking every fence-post, far and near, along the highway, or wherever they run! A burrow is rooted up at every shady point, a nuisance at every corner you turn, and their abominable snouts into everything that is filthy, or obscene — a living curse to all that is decent about them. An Ishmaelite among the farm stock, they are shunned and hated by every living thing, when at large. But, put the creature in his pen, with a ring in his nose, if permitted to go into the adjoining yard, and comfortably fed, your pig, if of a civilized breed, is a quiet, inoffensive — indeed, gentlemanly sort of animal; and as such, he is entitled to our toleration — regard, we cannot say; for in all the pages of our reading, we learn, by no creditable history, of any virtuous sympathies in a hog.

FARM BARNS.

The farm barn, next to the farm house, is the most important structure of the farm itself, in the Northern and Middle States; and even at the south and southwest, where less used, they are of more importance in the economy of farm management than is generally supposed. Indeed, to our own eyes, a farm, or a plantation appears incomplete, without a good barn accommodation, as much as without good household appointments — and without them, no agricultural establishment can be complete in all its proper economy.

The most *thorough* barn structures, perhaps, to be seen in the United States, are those of the state of Pennsylvania, built by the German farmers of the lower and central counties. They are large, and expensive in their construction; and, in a strictly economical view, perhaps more costly than required. Yet, there is a substance and durability in them, that is exceedingly satisfactory, and, where the pecuniary ability of the farmer will permit, may well be an example for imitation.

In the structure of the barn, and in its interior accommodation, much will depend upon the branches of agriculture to which the farm is devoted. A farm cultivated in grain chiefly, requires but little room for stabling purposes. Storage for grain in the sheaf, and granaries, will require its room; while a stock farm requires a barn with extensive hay storage, and stables for its cattle, horses, and sheep, in all climates not admitting such stock to live through the winter in the field, like the great grazing states west of the Alleghanies. Again, there are wide districts of country where a mixed husbandry of grain and stock is pursued, which require barns and out-buildings accommodating both; and to supply the exigencies of each, we shall present such plans as may be appropriate, and that may, possibly, by a slight variation, be equally adapted to either, or all of their requirements.

It may not be out of place here, to remark, that many *designers* of barns, sheds, and other out-buildings for the accommodation of farm stock, have indulged in fanciful arrangements for the convenience and comfort of animals, which are so complicated that when constructed, as they sometimes are, the practical, common-sense farmer will not use them; and, in the *learning* required in their use, are altogether unfit for the use and treatment they usually get from those who have the daily care of the stock which they are intended for, and for the rough usage they receive from the animals themselves. A very pretty, and a very plausible arrangement of stabling, and feeding, and all the etceteras of a barn establishment, may be thus got up by an ingenious theorist at the fireside, which will work to a charm, as he dilates upon its good qualities, untried; but, when subjected to experiment will be utterly worthless for practical use. All this we, in our practice, have gone through; and after many years experience, have come to the conclusion that the simplest plan of construction, consistent with an economical expenditure of the material of food for the consumption of stock, is by far the most preferable.

Another item to be considered in this connection, is the comparative value of the stock, the forage fed to them, and the *labor* expended in feeding and taking care of them. We will illustrate: Suppose a farm to lie in the vicinity of a large town, or city. Its value is, perhaps, a hundred dollars an acre. The hay cut upon it is worth fifteen dollars a ton, at the barn, and straw, and coarse grains in proportion, and hired labor ten or twelve dollars a month. Consequently, the manager of this farm should use all the economy in his power, by the aid of cutting-boxes, and other machinery, to make the least amount of forage supply the wants of his stock; and the internal economy of his barn arranged accordingly; because labor is his cheapest item, and food the dearest. Then, for any contrivance to work up his forage the closest — by way of machinery, or manual labor — by which it will serve the purposes of keeping his stock, is true economy; and the making, and saving of manures is an item of the first importance. His buildings, and their arrangements throughout, should, on these accounts, be constructed in accordance with his practice. If, on the other hand, lands are cheap and productive, and labor comparatively dear, a different practice will prevail.

He will feed his hay from the mow, without cutting. The straw will be either stacked out, and the cattle turned to it, to pick what they like of it, and make their beds on the remainder; or, if it is housed, he will throw it into racks, and the stock may eat what they choose. It is but one-third, or one-half the labor to do this, that the other mode requires, and the saving in this makes up, and perhaps more than makes up for the increased quantity of forage consumed. Again, climate may equally affect the mode of winter feeding the stock. The winters may be mild. The hay may be stacked in the fields, when gathered, or put into small barns built for hay storage alone; and the manure, scattered over the fields by the cattle, as they are fed from either of them, may be knocked to pieces with the dung-beetle, in the spring, or harrowed and bushed over the ground; and with the very small quantity of labor required in all this, such practice will be more economical than any other which can be adopted. It is, therefore, a subject of deliberate study with the farmer, in the construction of his out-buildings, what plans he shall adopt in regard to them, and their fitting up and arrangement.

With these considerations before us, we shall submit such plans of barn structures as may be adapted for general use, where shelters for the farm crops, and farm stock, are required; and which may, in their interior arrangement, be fitted for almost any locality of our country, as the judgment and the wants of the builder may require.

Design I.

This is a design of barn partially on the Pennsylvania plan, with under-ground stables, and a stone-walled basement on three sides, with a line of posts standing open on the yard front, and a wall, pierced by doors and windows, retreating 12 feet under the building, giving, in front, a shelter for stock. Two sheds, by way of wings, are run out to any desired length, on each side. The body of this barn, which is built of wood, above the basement, is 60×46 feet; the posts 18 feet high, above the sills; the roof is elevated at an angle of 40° from a horizontal line, and the gables hooded, or truncated, 14 feet wide at the verge, so as to cover the large doors at the ends. The main roof spreads 3 to 4 feet over the body of the barn, and runs from the side eaves in a *straight* line, different from what is shown in the engraving, which appears of a gambrel or hipped fashion. The sides are covered with boards laid vertically, and battened with narrow strips, 3 inches wide. The large doors in the ends are 14 feet wide, and 14 feet high. A slatted blind window is in each gable, for ventilation, and a door, 9×6 feet, on the yard side.

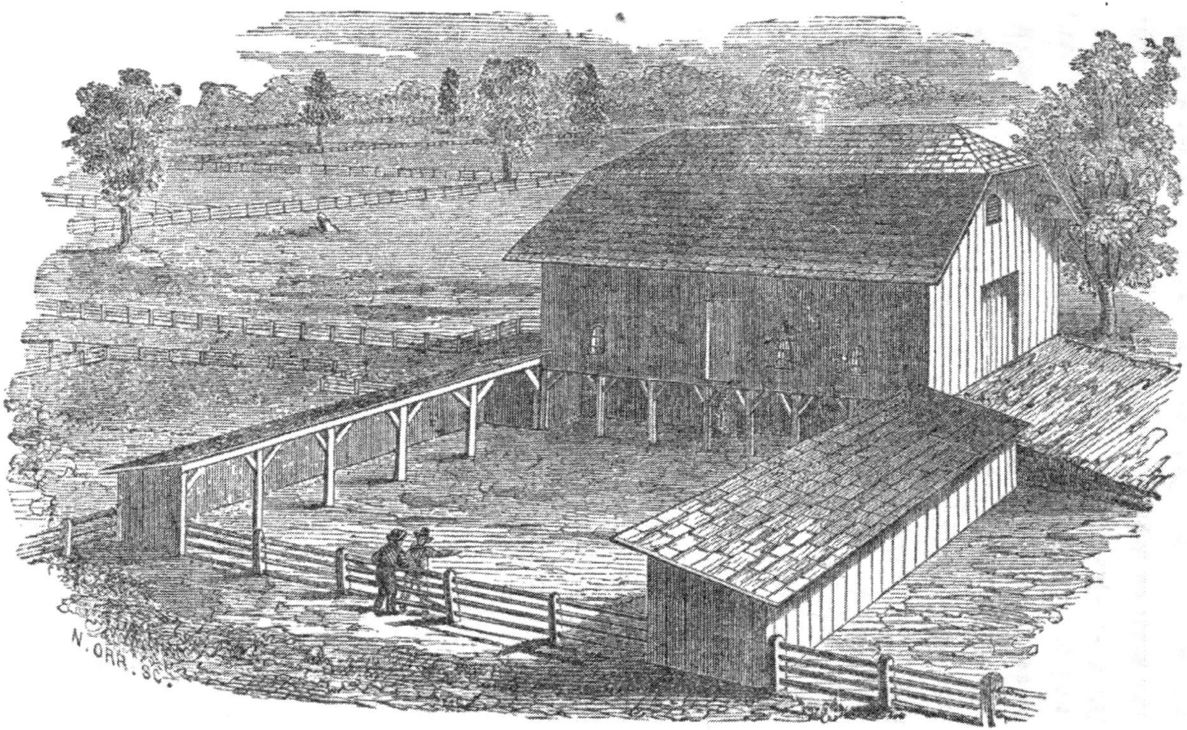
N. ORR. SC.

INTERIOR ARRANGEMENT.

A main floor, *A*, 12 feet wide, runs the whole length through the center of the barn. *S, S,* are the large doors. *H, H,* are trap doors, to let hay or straw down to the alleys of the stables beneath. *B,* is the principal bay for hay storage, 16 feet wide, and runs up to the roof. *C,* is the bay, 26×16 feet, for the grain mow,

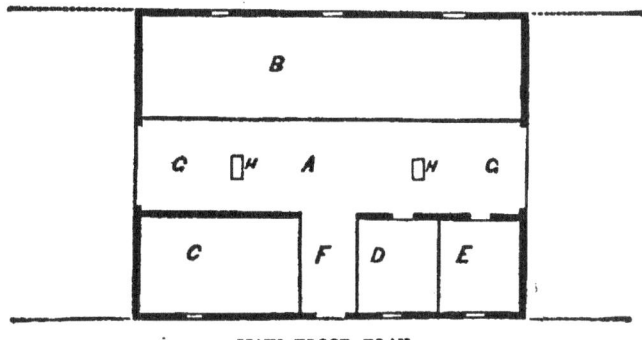

MAIN FLOOR PLAN.

if required for that purpose. *D,* is a granary, 13×16 feet, and 8 feet high. *E,* a storage room for fanning mill, cutting-box, or other machinery, or implements, of same size and height as the granary. *F,* is a passage, 8 feet wide, leading from the main floor to the yard door, through which to throw out litter. Over this passage, and the granary, and store-room, may be stored grain in the sheaf, or hay. The main floor will accommodate the thrashing-machine, horse-power, cutting box, &c., &c., when at work. A line of movable sleepers, or poles, may be laid across the floor, 10 feet above it, on a line of girts framed into the main posts, for that purpose, over which, when the sides of the barn are full, either hay or grain may be deposited, up to the ridge of the roof, and thus afford large storage. And if the demands of the crops require it, after the sides and over the floor is thus filled, the floor itself may, a part of it, be used for packing away either hay or grain, by taking off the team after the load is in, and passing them out by a retreating process, on the side of the cart or wagon; and the vehicle, when unloaded, backed out by hand. We have occasionally adopted this method, when crowded for room for increased crops, to great advantage. It requires somewhat more labor, to be sure, but it is much better than stacking out; and a well-filled barn is a good sight to look upon.

Underneath the body of the barn are the stables, root cellar, calf houses, or any other accommodation which the farm stock may require; but, for the most economical objects, is here cut up into stables. At the ends, *l, l,* are passages for the stock to go into their stalls; and also, on the sides, for the men who attend to them. The main passage through the center double line of stalls is 8 feet wide; and on each side are double stalls, 6½ feet wide. From the two end walls, the cattle passages are 5 feet wide, the partition between the stalls running back in a *slant,* from 5 feet high at the mangers to the floor, at that distance from the walls. The mangers, *j, j,* are 2 feet wide, or may be 2½ feet, by taking an additional six inches out of the rear passage. The passage is, between the mangers, 3 feet wide, to receive the hay from the trap doors in the floor above.

UNDER-GROUND PLAN AND YARD.

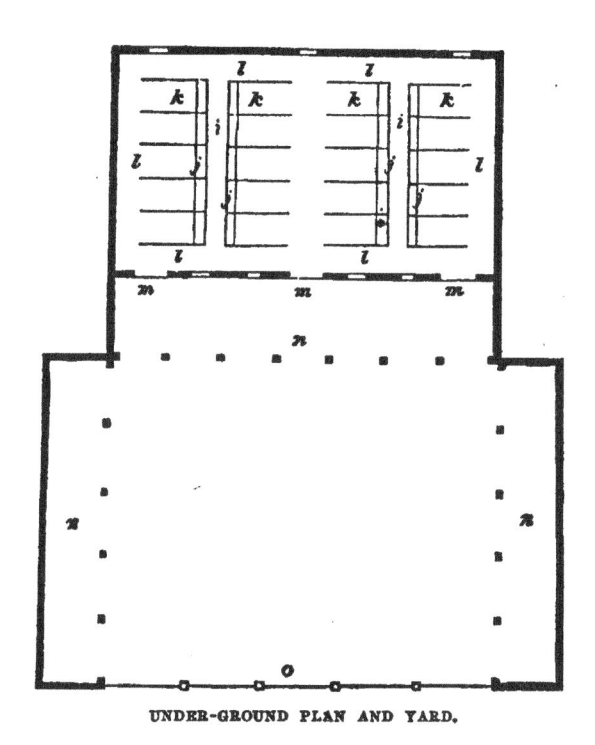

The most economical plan, for room in tying cattle in their stalls, is to fasten the rope, or chain, whichever is used, (the wooden stanchion, or *stanchel*, as it is called, to open and shut, enclosing the animal by the neck, we do not like,) into a ring, which is secured by a strong staple into the post which sustains the partition, just at the top of the manger, on each side of the stall. This prevents the cattle in the same stall from interfering with each other, while the partition effectually prevents any contact from the animals on each side of it, in the separate stalls. The bottom of the mangers, for grown cattle, should be a foot above the floor, and the top two and a half feet, which makes it deep enough to hold their food; and the whole, both sides and bottom, should be made of two-inch, sound, strong plank, that they may not be broken down. The back sides of the stalls, next the feeding alleys, should be full 3½ feet high; and if the cattle are large, and disposed to climb into their mangers with their forefeet, as they sometimes do, a pole, of 2½ or 3 inches in diameter, should be secured across the front of the stall, next the cattle, and over the mangers — say 4½ feet above the floor, to keep them out of the manger, and still give them sufficient room for putting their heads between that and the top of the manger, to get their food. Cattle thus secured in double stalls, take up less room, and lie much warmer, than when in single stalls; besides, the expense of fitting them up being much less — an experience of many years has convinced us on this point. The doors for the passage of the cattle in and out of the stables, should be five feet wide, that they may have plenty of room.

In front of these stables, on the outside, is a line of posts, the feet of which rest on large flat stones, and support the outer sill of the barn, and form a recess, before named, of 12 feet in width, under which may be placed a line of racks, or mangers for outside cattle, to consume the orts, or leavings of hay rejected by the in-door stock; or, the manure may be housed under it, which is removed from the stables by wheel-barrows. The low line of sheds which extend from the barn on each side of the yard, may be used for the carts, and wagons of the place; or, racks and mangers may be fitted up in them, for outside cattle to consume the straw and coarse forage; or, they may be carried higher than in our plan, and floored overhead, and hay, or other food stored in them for the stock. They are so placed merely to give the idea.

There may be no more fitting occasion than this, perhaps, to make a remark or two on the subject of managing stock in stables of any kind, when kept in any considerable numbers; and a word may not be impertinent to the subject in hand, as connected with the construction of stables.

There is no greater benefit to cattle, after coming into winter quarters, than a straight-forward regularity in everything appertaining to them. Every animal should have its own particular stall in the stable, where it should *always be kept, and in no other*. The cattle should be fed and watered at certain hours of the day, as near as may be. When let out of the stables for water, unless the weather is very pleasant, when they may be permitted to lie out an hour or two, they should be immediately put back, and not allowed to range about with the outside cattle. They are more quiet and contented in their stables than elsewhere, and eat less food, than if permitted to run out; and are every way more comfortable, if properly bedded and attended to, as every one will find, on trying it. The habit of many people, in turning their cattle out of the stables in the morning, in all weathers — letting them range about in a cold yard, hooking and thorning each other — is of no possible benefit, unless to rid themselves of the trouble of cleaning the stables, which pays twice its cost in the saving of manure. The outside cattle, which occupy the yard, are all the better, that the stabled ones do not interfere with them. They become habituated to their own quarters, as the others do to their's, and all are better for being each in their own proper place. It may appear a small matter to notice this; but it is a subject of importance, which every one may know who tries it.

It will be seen that a driving way is built up to the barn doors at the ends; this need not be expensive, and will add greatly to the ease and convenience of its approach. It is needless to remark, that this barn is designed to stand on a shelving piece of ground, or on a slope, which will admit of its cellar stables without much excavation of the earth; and in such a position it may be economically built. No estimate is given of its cost, which must depend upon the price of materials, and the convenience of stone on the farm. The size is not arbitrary, but may be either contracted or extended, according to the requirements of the builder.

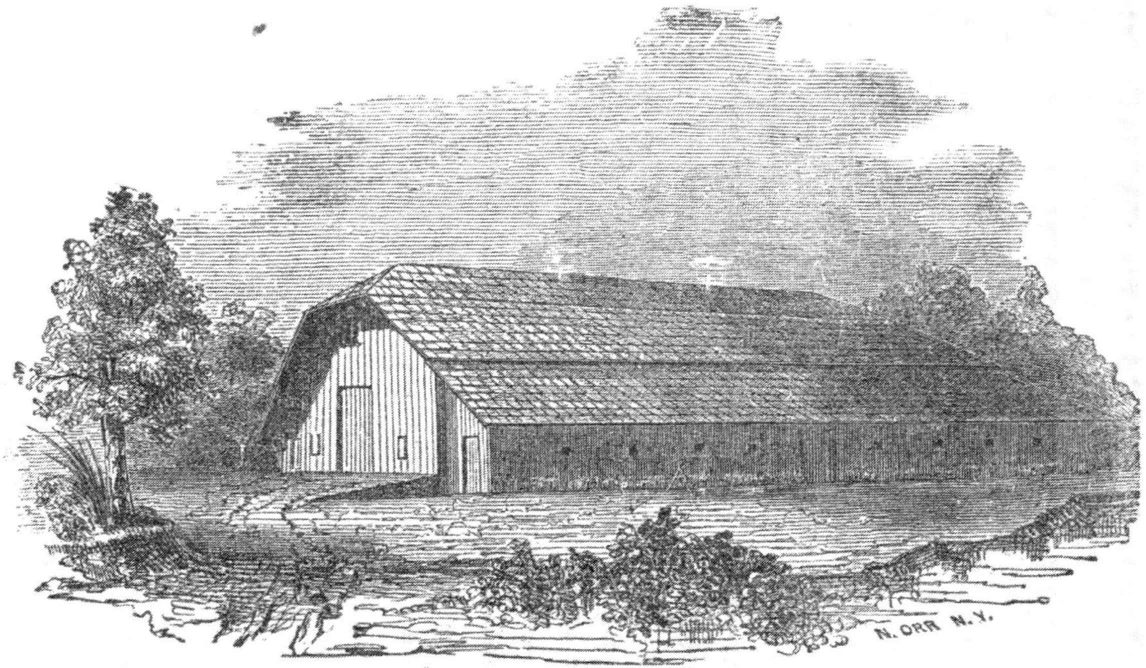
N. ORR N.Y.

Design II.

Here is presented the design of a barn built by ourself, about sixteen years since, and standing on the farm we own and occupy; and which has proved so satisfactory in its use, that, save in one or two small particulars, which are here amended, we would not, for a stock barn, alter it in any degree, nor exchange it for one of any description whatever.

For the farmer who needs one of but half the size, or greater, or less, it may be remarked that the extent of this need be no hindrance to the building of one of any size—as the general *design* may be adopted, and carried out, either in whole or in part, according to his wants, and the economy of its accommodation preserved throughout. The *principle* of the structure is what is intended to be shown.

The *main* body of this barn stands on the ground, 100×50 feet, with eighteen-feet posts, and a broad, sheltering roof, of 40° pitch from a horizontal line, and truncated at the gables to the width of the main doors below. The sills stand 4 feet above the ground, and a raised driving way to the doors admits the loads of grain and forage into it. The manner of building the whole structure would be, to frame and put up the main building as if it was to have no attachment whatever, and put on the roof, and board up the gable ends. Then frame, and raise adjoining it, on the long sides, and on the rear end — for the opposite gable end to that, is the entrance front to the barn — a continuous lean-to, 16 feet wide, attaching it to the posts of the barn, strongly, by girts. These ranges of lean-to stand on the ground level, nearly — high enough, however, to let a terrier dog under the floors, to keep out the rats — but quite 3 feet below the sills of the barn. The outer posts of the lean-to's should be 12 feet high, and 12½ feet apart, from center to center, except at the extreme corners, which would be 16 feet. One foot below the roof-plates of the main building, and across the rear gable end, a line of girts should be framed into the posts, as a *rest* for the upper ends of the lean-to rafters, that they may pass under, and a foot below the lower ends of the main roof rafters, to make a break in the roof of one foot, and allow a line of eave gutters under it, if needed, and to show the lean-to line of roof as distinct from the other. The stables are 7 feet high, from the lower floor to the girts overhead, which connect them with the main line of barn posts; thus giving a loft of 4 feet in height at the eaves, and of 12 feet at the junction with the barn. In this loft is large storage for hay, and coarse forage, and bedding for the cattle, which is put in by side windows, level with the loft floor — as seen in the plate. In the center of the rear, *end* lean-to, is a large door, corresponding with the front entrance to the barn, as shown in the design, 12 feet high, and 14 feet wide.

to pass out the wagons and carts which have discharged their loads in the barn, having entered at the main front door. A line of board, one foot wide, between the line of the main and lean-to roofs, is then nailed on, to shut up the space; and the rear gable end boarded down to the roof of the lean-to attached to it. The front end, and the stables on them vertically boarded, and battened, as directed in the last design; the proper doors and windows inserted, and the outside is finished.

INTERIOR ARRANGEMENT.

Entering the large door, (a,) at the front end, 14 feet wide, and 14 feet high, the main floor (g,) passes through the entire length of the barn, and rear lean-to, 116 feet — the last 16 feet through the lean-to — and sloping 3 feet to the outer sill, and door, (a,) of that appendage. On the left of the entrance is a recess, (e,) of 20×18 feet, to be used as a thrashing floor, and for machinery, cutting feed, &c., &c.— 5 feet next the end being cut off for a passage to the stable. Beyond this is a bay, (b,) 18×70 feet, for the storage of hay, or grain, leaving a passage at the further end, of 5 feet wide, to go into the further stables. This bay is bounded on the extreme left, by the line of outside posts of the barn. On the right of the main door is a granary, (d,) 10×18 feet, two stories high, and a flight of steps leading from the lower into the upper room. Beyond this is another bay, (b,) corresponding with the one just described on the opposite side. The passages at the ends of the bays, (c, e,) have steps of 3 feet descent, to bring them down on to a level with the stable floors of the lean-to. A passage in each of the two long side lean-to's, (*e, e,*) 3 feet wide, receives the hay forage for cattle, or other stock, thrown into

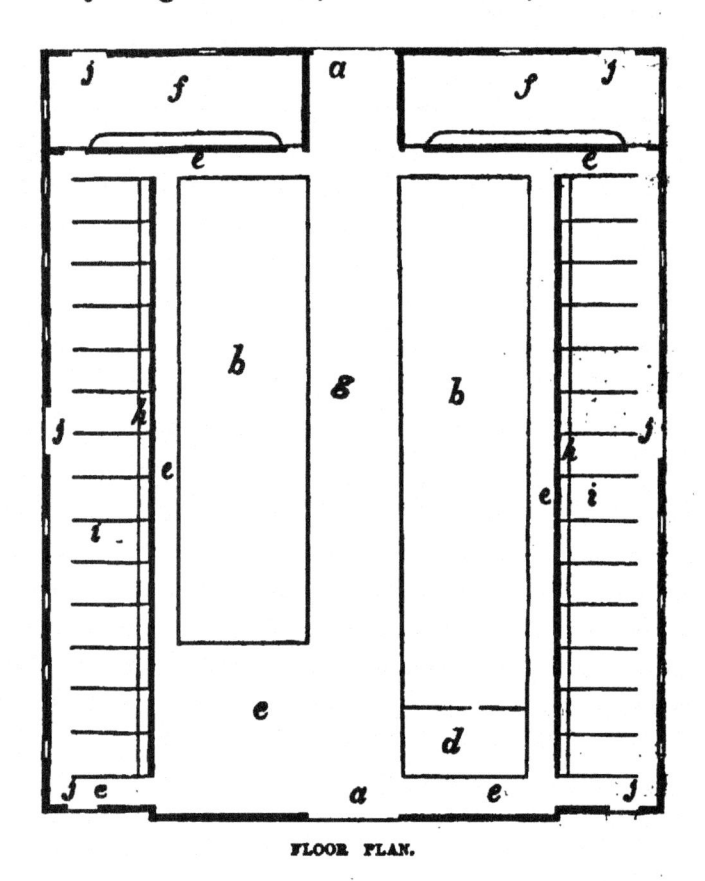

FLOOR PLAN.

them from the bays, and the lofts over the stables; and from them is thrown into the mangers, (*h, h.*) The two apartments in the extreme end lean-to, (*f, f,*) 34×16 feet each, may be occupied as a hospital for invalid cattle, or partitioned off for calves, or any other purpose. A calving house for the cows which come in during the winter, is always convenient, and one of these may be used for such purpose. The stalls, ($i, i,$) are the same as described in Design I, and back of them is the passage for the cattle, as they pass in and out of their stalls. The stable doors, ($j, j,$) are six in number. Small windows, for ventilation, should be cut in the rear of the stalls, as marked, and for throwing out the manure, with sliding board shutters. This completes the barn accommodation — giving twenty-eight double stalls, where fifty-six grown cattle may be tied up, with rooms for twenty to thirty calves in the end stables. If a larger stock is kept, young cattle may be tied up, with their heads to the bays, on the main floor, beyond the thrashing floor, which we practice. This will hold forty young cattle. The manure is taken out on a wheel-barrow, and no injury done to the floor. They will soon eat out a place where their forage can be put, and do no injury beyond that to the hay in the bays, as it is too closely packed for them to draw it out any farther. In this way we can accommodate more than a hundred head of cattle, of assorted ages.

The hay in the bays may drop three feet below the level of the main floor, by placing a tier of rough timbers and poles across them, to keep it from the ground, and many tons of additional storage be thus provided. We have often stored one hundred and fifty tons of hay in this barn; and it will hold even more, if thoroughly packed, and the movable girts over the main floor be used, as described in Design I.

The chief advantages in a barn of this plan are, the exceeding convenience of getting the forage to the stock. When the barn is full, and feeding is first commenced, with a hay knife, we commence on each side next the stables, on the top of the bays, cut a *well* down to the alley way in front of the mangers, which is left open up to the stable roof. This opens a passage for the hay to be thrown into the alleys, and in a short time it is so fed out on each side, that, the sides of the main barn being open to them, the hay can be thrown along their whole distance, and fed to the cattle as wanted; and so at the rear end stables, in the five-foot alley adjoining them. If a root cellar be required, it may be made under the front part of the main floor, and a trap-door lead to it. For a milk dairy, this arrangement is an admirable one—we so used it for four years; or for stall-feeding, it is equally convenient. One man will do more work, so far as feeding is concerned, in this barn, than two can do in one of almost any other arrangement; and the yards outside may be divided into five separate inclosures, with but little expense, and still be large enough for the cattle that may want to use them. It matters not what kind of stock may be kept in this barn; it is convenient for all alike. Even sheep may be accommodated in it with convenience. But low, open sheds, inclosed by a yard, are better for them; with storage for hay overhead, and racks and troughs beneath.

This barn is built of wood. It may be well constructed, with stone underpinning, without mortar, for $1,000 to $1,500, as the price of materials may govern.

And if the collection of the water from the roofs be an object, cheap gutters to carry it into one or more cisterns may be added, at an expense of $200 to $300.

As before observed, a barn may be built on this principle, of any size, and the stables, or lean-to's may only attach to one side or end; or they may be built as mere sheds, with no storage room over the cattle. The chief objection to stabling cattle in the *body* of the barn is, the continual decay of the most important timbers, such as sills, sleepers, &c., &c., by the leakage of the stale, and manure of the cattle on to them, and the loss of so much valuable storage as they would occupy, for hay and grain. By the plan described, the stables have no attachment to the sills, and other durable barn timbers below; and if the stable sills and sleepers decay, they are easily and cheaply replaced with others. Taking it altogether, we can recommend no better, nor, as we think, so good, and so cheap a plan for a *stock* barn, as this.

We deem it unnecessary to discuss the subject of water to cattle yards, as every farm has its own particular accommodations, or inconveniences in that regard; and the subject of leading water by pipes into different premises, is too well understood to require remark. Where these can not be had, and springs or streams are not at hand, wells and pumps must be provided, in as much convenience as the circumstances of the case will admit. Water is absolutely necessary, and that in quantity, for stock uses; and every good manager will exercise his best judgment to obtain it.

BARN ATTACHMENTS.

It may be expected, perhaps, that in treating so fully as we have of the several kinds of farm building, a full cluster of out-buildings should be drawn and exhibited, showing their relative positions and accommodation. This can not be done, however, except as a matter of "fancy;" and if attempted, might not be suited to the purposes of a single individual, by reason of the particular location where they would be situated, and the accommodation which the buildings might require. Convenience of access to the barns, from the fields where the crops are grown, a like convenience to get out manures upon those fields, and a ready communication with the dwelling house, are a part of the considerations which are to govern their position, or locality. Economy in labor, in the various avocations at the barn, and its necessary attachments; and the greatest convenience in storage, and the housing of the various stock, grains, implements, and whatever else may demand accommodation, are other considerations to be taken into the account, all to have a bearing upon them. Compactness is always an object in such buildings, when not obtained at a sacrifice of some greater advantage, and should be one of the items considered in placing them; and in their construction, next to the arrangement of them in the most convenient possible manner for their various objects, a due regard to their architectural appearance should be studied. Such appearance, where their objects are apparent, can easily be secured. *Utility* should be their chief point of expression; and no style of architecture, or finish, can be really *bad*, where this expression is duly consulted, and carried out, even in the humblest way of cheapness, or rusticity.

We have heretofore sufficiently remarked on the folly of unnecessary pretension in the farm buildings, of any kind; and nothing can appear, and really be more out of place, than ambitious structures intended only for the stock, and crops. Extravagant expenditure on these, any more than an extravagant expenditure on the dwelling and its attachments, does not add to the *selling* value of the farm, nor to its economical management, in a productive capacity; and he who is about to build, should make his proposed buildings a study for months, in all their different requirements and conveniences, before he commences their erection. Mistakes in their design, and location, have cost men a whole after life of wear-and-tear of temper, patience, and labor, to themselves, and to all who were about them; and it is better to wait even two or three years, to fully mature the best plans of building, than by hurrying, to mis-locate, mis-arrange, and miss, in fact, the very best application in their structure of which such buildings are capable.

A word might also be added about barn-*yards*. The planning and management of these, also, depends much upon the course the farmer has to pursue in the keeping of his stock, the amount of waste litter, such as straw, &c., which he has to dispose of, and the demands of the farm for animal and composted manures. There are different methods of constructing barn-yards, in different parts of the country, according to climate and soils, and the farmer must best consult his own experience, the most successful examples about him, and the publications which treat of that subject, in its connection with farm husbandry, to which last subject this item more properly belongs.

RABBITS.

It may appear that we are extending our "Rural Architecture" to an undue length, in noticing a subject so little attended to in this country as Rabbit accommodations. But, as with other small matters which we have noticed, this may create a new source of interest and attachment to country life, we conclude to give it a place.

It is a matter of surprise to an American first visiting England, to see the quantities of game which abound at certain seasons of the year in the London and other markets of that country, in contrast with the scanty supply, or rather no supply at all, existing in the markets of American cities. The reason for such difference is, that in England, Scotland, Wales, and Ireland, every acre of the soil is appropriated to some profitable use, while we, from the abundance of land in America, select only the best for agricultural purposes, and let the remainder go barren and uncared for. Lands appropriated to the rearing of game, when fit for farm pasturage or tillage, is unprofitable, generally, with us; but there are thousands of acres barren for other purposes, that might be devoted to the breeding and pasturage of rabbits, and which, by thus appropriating them, might be turned to profitable account. All the preparation required is, to enclose the ground with a high and nearly close paling fence, and the erection of a few rude hutches inside, for winter shelter and the storage of their food. They will burrow into the ground, and breed with great rapidity; and in the fall and winter seasons, they will be fat for market with the food they gather from the otherwise worthless soil over which they run. Rocky, bushy, and evergreen grounds, either hill, dale, or plain, are good for them, wherever the soils are dry and friable. The rabbit is a gross feeder, living well on what many grazing animals reject, and gnawing down all kinds of bushes, briars, and noxious weeds.

The common domestic rabbits are probably the best for market purposes, and were they to be made an object of attention, immense tracts of mountain land in New Jersey, Pennsylvania, and the New York and New England highlands could be made available for this object.

Some may think this a small business. So is making pins, and rearing chickens, and bees. But there are an abundance of people, whose age and capacity are just fitted for it, and for want of other employment are a charge upon their friends or the public; and now, when our cities and large towns are so readily reached by railroads from all parts of the country, our farmers should study to apply their land to the production of everything that will find a profitable market. Things unthought of, a few years ago, now find a large consumption in our large cities and towns, by the aid of railroads; and we know of no good reason, why this production and traffic should not continue to an indefinite extent. When the breeding of rabbits is commenced, get a good treatise on the breeding and rearing of them, which may be found at many of the bookstores.

As the rearing of rabbits, and their necessary accommodation, is not a subject to which we have given much personal attention, we applied to Francis Rotch, Esq., of Morris, Otsego county, New York, who is probably the most accomplished rabbit "fancier" in the United States, for information, with which he has kindly furnished us. His beautiful and high-bred animals have won the highest premiums, at the shows of the New York State Agricultural Society. He thus answers:

"I now forward you the promised plan from Mr. Alfred Rodman, of Dedham, Massachusetts, which, I think, will give you the information you wish upon these subjects.

"Rabbits kept for profit in the vicinity of a city, and where there are mills, may be raised at a very small cost; and when once known as an article of food, will be liberally paid for by the epicure, for their meat is as delicate as a chicken's, and their fat mild, and very rich.

"I am surprised they are not more generally kept, as a source of amusement, and for the purposes of experiment.

"There is, I think, in many, a natural fondness for animals, but not easily indulged without more room than is often to be found in city residences. Fowls, and pigeons, trespass on our neighbors, and are a frequent cause of trouble. This objection does not hold good against the rabbit, which occupies so small a space, that where there is an outhouse there may be a rabbitry. *English* children are encouraged in their fondness for animals, as tending to good morals and good feelings, and as offering a *home* amusement, in contradistinction to *street* associations."

Mr. Rotch continues:

"I have just finished the enclosed drawing of a 'fancy rabbit,' which I hope will answer your purpose, as an illustration of what the little animal should be in form, color, marking, and carriage, according to the decisions of the various societies in and out of London, who are its greatest admirers and patrons. These amateurs hold frequent meetings for its exhibition, at which premiums are awarded, and large prizes paid for such specimens as come up to their standard of excellence. This standard is, of course, conventional; and, as might be expected, is a combination of form and color very difficult to obtain — based, it is true, on the most correct principles of general breeding; but much of *fancy* and beauty is added to complete the requisites of a prize rabbit. For instance, the head must be small and clean; the shoulders wide and full; the chest broad and deep; the back wide, and the loin large. Thus far, these are the

Drawn from life, by Mr. FRANCIS BATON.

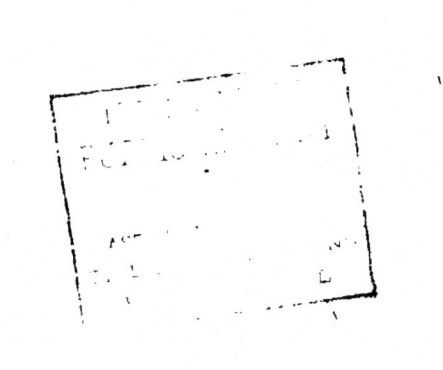

characteristics of all really *good* and *improved* animals; to which are to be added, on the score of 'fancy,' an eye round, full, and bright; an ear *long*, broad, and pendant, of a soft, delicate texture, dropping nearly perpendicularly by the side of the head — this is termed its 'carriage.' The color must be in rich, unmixed *masses* on the body, spreading itself over the back, side, and haunch, but breaking into spots and patches on the shoulder, called the 'chain;' while that on the back is known as the 'saddle.' The head must be full of color, broken with white on the forehead and cheeks; the marking over the bridge of the nose and down on both sides into the lips, should be dark, and in shape somewhat resembling a butterfly, from which this mark takes its name; the ear, however, must be uniform in color. Add to all this, a large, full dewlap, and you will have a rabbit fit to '*go in and win.*'

"The most esteemed colors are black and white; yellow and white; tortoise-shell and white; blue and white, and gray and white. These are called 'broken colors,' while those of *one* uniform color are called selfs.'"

It will be observed that Mr. Rotch here describes a beautiful "fancy" variety of "lop-eared" rabbits, which he brought from England a few years since. They were, originally, natives of Madagascar. He continues:

"The domestic rabbit, in all its varieties, has always been, and still is, a great favorite, in many parts of the European continent:

"In Holland, it is bred with reference to color only, which must be a pure white, with dark ears, feet, legs, and tail; this distribution has a singular effect, but, withal, it is a pretty little creature. The French breed a long, rangy animal, of great *apparent* size, but deficient in depth and breadth, and of course, wanting in constitution; no attention is paid to color, and its marking is matter of accident. The White Angola, with its beautiful long fur and red eyes, is also a great favorite in France.

"In England, the rabbit formerly held the rank of 'farm stock!' and thousands of acres were exclusively devoted to its production; families were supported, and rents, rates, and taxes were paid from its increase and sale. The '*gray-skins*' went to the hatter, the '*silver-skins*' were shipped to China, and were dressed as furs; while the flesh was a favorite dish at home. This was the course pursued in Yorkshire, Lincolnshire, and many other counties, with their light sandy soils, before the more general introduction of root culture, and the rotation of crops, gave an increased value to such land. Since then, however, I remember visiting a farm of Lord Onslow's, in Surrey, containing about 1,400 acres. It was in the occupation of an eminent flock-master and agriculturist, who kept some hundreds of hutched rabbits for the sake of their manure, which he applied to his turnep crop; added to this, their skins and carcasses were quite an item of profit, notwithstanding the care of them required an old man and boy, with a donkey and cart. The food used was chiefly brewer's grains, miller's waste, bran and hay, with clover and roots, the cost of keeping not exceeding two pence a week. The hutches stood under a long shed, open on all sides, for the greater convenience of cleaning and feeding. I was told that the manure was much valued by the market gardeners round London, who readily paid 2s. 6d. a bushel at the rabbitries. These rabbitries are very numerous in all the towns and cities of England, and form a source of amusement or profit to all classes, from the man of fortune to the day laborer. Nor is it unfrequent that this latter produces a rabbit from an old tea-chest, or dry-goods box, that wins the prize from its competitor of the mahogany hutch or ornamental rabbitry.

"The food of the rabbit embraces great variety, including grain of all kinds, bran, pea-chaff, miller's waste, brewer's grains, clover and other hay, and the various weeds known as plantain, dock, mallow, dandelion, purslain, thistles, &c., &c.

"The rabbit thus easily conforms itself to the means, condition, and circumstances of its owner; occupies but little space, breeds often, comes early to maturity, and is withal, a healthy animal, requiring however, to be kept clean, and to be *cautiously* fed with *succulent* food, which must always be free from dew or rain — water is unnecessary to them when fed with 'greens.' My own course of feeding is, one gill of oats in the morning, with a medium-sized cabbage leaf, or what I may consider its *equivalent* in any other vegetable food, for the rabbit in confinement must be, as already stated, cautiously fed with what is succulent. At noon, I feed a handful' of cut hay or clover chaff, and in the evening the same as in the morning To does, when suckling, I give what they will eat of both green and dry food. The cost to me is about three cents per week, per head.

"I by no means recommend this as the best, or the most economical mode of feeding, but it happens to suit my convenience. Were I in a town, or near mills I should make use of other and cheaper substitutes. My young rabbits, when taken from the doe, say at eight, ten, or twelve weeks old, are turned out together till about six months old, when it becomes necessary to take them up, and put them in separate hutches, to prevent their fighting and destroying each other. The doe at that age is ready to breed; her period of gestation is about thirty-one or two days, and she produces from three or four to a dozen young at a 'litter.' It is not well to let her raise more than six, or even four at once—the fewer, the larger and finer the produce.

"Young rabbits are killed for the table at any age, from twelve weeks to twelve months old, and are a very acceptable addition to the country larder. The male is not allowed to remain with the doe, lest he should destroy the young ones.

"Hutches are made singly, or in stacks, to suit the apartment, which should be capable of thorough ventilation. The best size is about three feet long, two feet deep, and fourteen inches high, with a small apartment partitioned off from one end, nearly a foot wide, as a breeding place for the doe. A wire door forms the front, and an opening is left behind for cleaning; the floor should have a descent to the back of the hutch of two inches. All edges should be tinned, to save them 'rom being gnawed.

"Having now given the leading characteristics and qualities which constitute a good 'fancy lop-eared rabbit,' and its general management, allow me to remark on the striking difference observable between Americans and the people of many other countries, as to a fondness for animals, or what are termed 'fancy pets,' of and for which we, as a people, know and care very little. Indeed, we scarcely admit more than a selfish fellowship with the dog, and but too seldom does our attachment even for this faithful companion, place him beyond the reach of the *omnipotent dollar*.

"The operatives, mechanics, and laborers, in other countries, seem to have a perfect passion for such pursuits, and take the greatest interest and pride in breeding and perfecting the lesser animals, though often obliged to toil for the very food they feed to them. Here, too, home influences are perceived to be good, and are encouraged by the employer, as supplying the place of other and much more questionable pursuits and tastes."

We here present the elevation, and floor plan of Mr. Rodman's rabbitry, together with the front and rear views of the hutches within them:

NO. I.—ELEVATION.

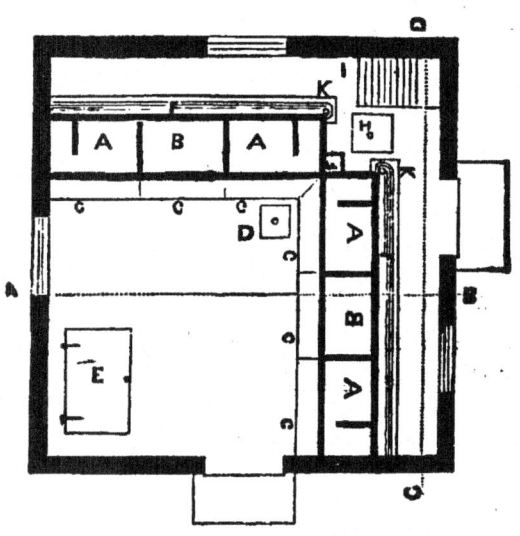

NO. II.—MAIN FLOOR PLAN.

No. 1 is the gable end elevation of the building, with a door and window.

No. 2 is the main-floor plan, or living room for the rabbits.

EXPLANATION.

A, the doe's hutches, with nest boxes attached. B, hutches three feet long, with movable partitions for the young rabbits; the two lower hutches are used for the stock bucks. C, a tier of grain boxes on the floor for feeding the rabbits — the covers sloping out toward the room. D, small trapdoor, leading into the manure cellar beneath. E, large trapdoor leading into root cellar. F, troughs for leading off urine from rear of hutches into the manure cellar at K, K. G, wooden trunk leading from chamber above No. 3, through this into manure cellar. H, trap opening into manure cellar. I, stairs leading into loft No. 3, with hinged trapdoor overhead; when open, it will turn up against the wall, and leave a passage to clear out the hutches.

NOTE.—The grain boxes are one foot high in front, and fifteen inches at the back, with sloping bottoms, and sloping covers. The floors of the hutches have a slope of two inches back. The hutches are furnished, at the back of the floor, with pieces of zinc, to keep them free from the drippings from above. The hutches are 16 inches high, 3 feet long, and 2 feet deep.

The foregoing plans and explanations might perhaps be sufficient for the guidance of such as wish to construct a rabbitry for their own use; but as a complete arrangement of all the rooms which may be conveniently appropriated to this object, to make it a complete thing, may be acceptable to the reader, we conclude, even at the risk of prolixity, to insert the upper loft, and cellar apartments, with which we have been furnished; hoping that our youthful friends will set themselves about the construction of a branch of rural employment so home-attaching in its associations.

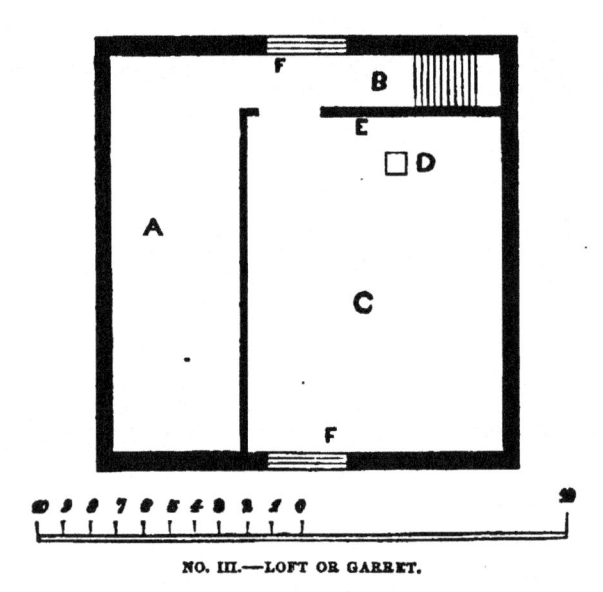

NO. III.—LOFT OR GARRET.

No. 3 is the loft or chamber story, next above the main floor.

EXPLANATION.

A, place for storing hay. B, stairs leading from below. C, room for young rabbits. D, trapdoor into trunk leading to manure cellar. E, partition four feet high. This allows of ventilation between the two windows, in summer, which would be cut off, were the partition carried all the way up.

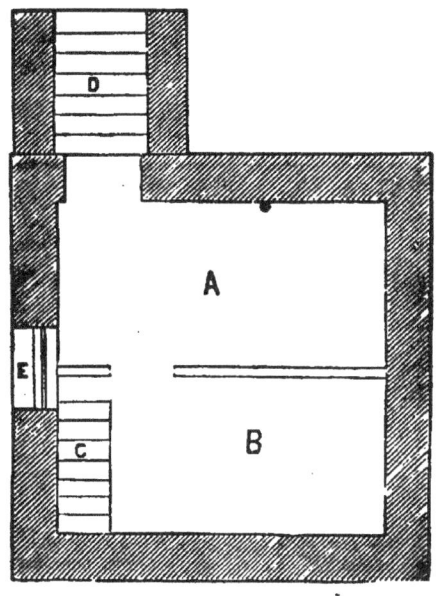

NO. IV.—CELLAR.

No. 4 is the cellar under the rabbitry.

EXPLANATION.

A, manure cellar. B, root cellar. C, stairs leading to first, or main floor. D, stairs leading outside. E, window — lighting both rooms of cellar.

No. 5 is a front section of rabbit hutches, eight in number, two in a line, four tiers high, one above another, with wire-screened doors, hinges, and buttons for fastening. A, the grain trough, is at the bottom

No. 6 is the floor section of the hutches, falling, as before mentioned, two inches from front to rear.

A, is the door to lift up, for cleaning out the floors. B, is the zinc plate, to carry off the urine and *running*

NO. V. NO. VI.

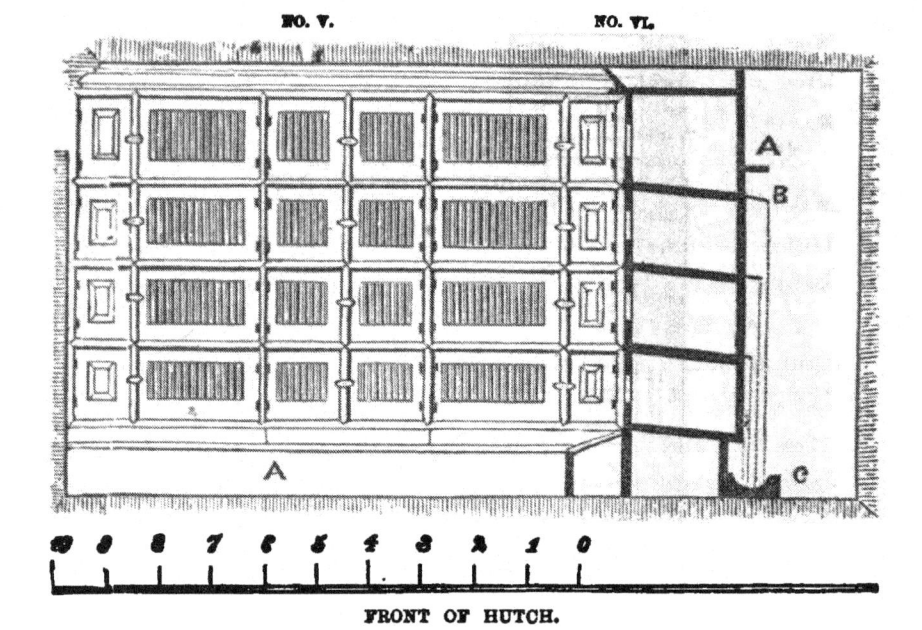

FRONT OF HUTCH.

NO. VII. NO. VIII.

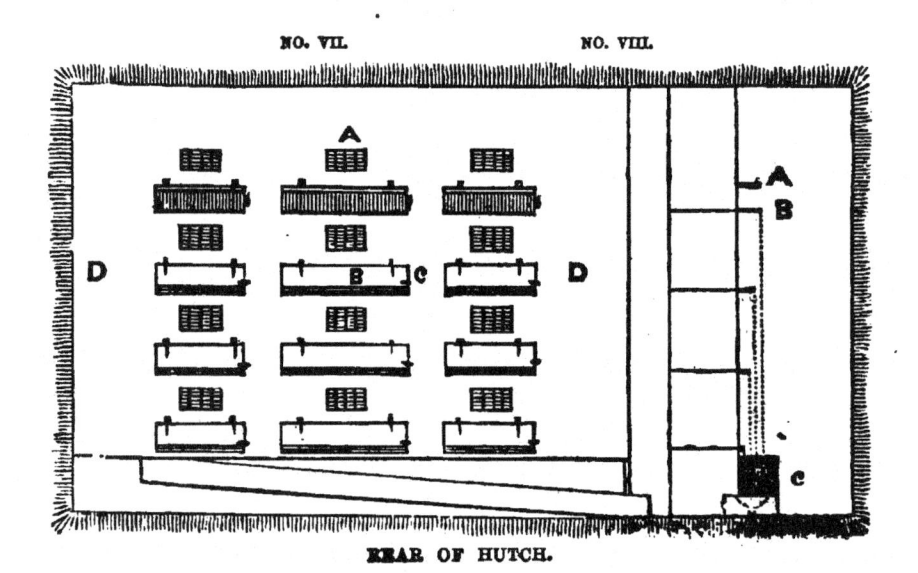

REAR OF HUTCH.

wash of the floors. C, is the trough for carrying off this offal into the manure cellars, through the trunk, as seen in No. 2.

No. 7 is a rear section of hutches, same as in No. 5, with the waste trough at the bottom leading into the trench before described, with the cross section, No. 8, before described in No. 6.

A, a grated door at the back of the hutch, for ventilation in summer, and covered with a thin board in winter. B, a flap-door, four inches wide, which is raised for cleaning out the floor; under this door is a space of one inch, for passing out the urine of the rabbits. C, are buttons for fastening the doors. D, the backs of the bedrooms, without any passage out on back side.

This matter of the rabbitry, and its various explanations, may be considered by the plain, matter-of-fact man, as below the dignity of people pursuing the *useful and money-making* business of life. Very possible. But many boys—for whose benefit they are chiefly introduced—and *men*, even, may do worse than to spend their time in such apparent trifles. It is better than going to a horse-race. It is better even than going to a trotting match, where *fast men*, as well as *fast* horses congregate. It is better, too, than a thousand other places where boys *want* to go, when they have nothing to interest them at home.

One half of the farmer's boys, who, discontented at home, leave it for something more congenial to their feelings and tastes, do so simply because of the excessive dullness, and want of interest in objects to attract them there, and keep them contented. Boys, in

America at least, are apt to be *smart*. So their parents think, at all events; and too smart they prove, to stay at home, and follow the beaten track of their fathers, as their continual migration from the paternal roof too plainly testifies. This, in many cases, is the fault of the parents themselves, because they neglect those little objects of interest to which the minds and tastes of their sons are inclined, and for want of which they *imagine* more attractive objects abroad, although in the search they often fail in finding them. We are a progressive people. Our children are not always content to be what their fathers are; and parents must yield a little to "the spirit of the age" in which they live. And boys *pay* too, as they go along, if properly treated. They should be made companions, not servants. Many a joyous, hearty spirit, who, when properly encouraged, comes out a whole man at one-and-twenty, if kept in curb, and harnessed down by a hard parent, leaves the homestead, with a curse and a kick, determined, whether in weal or in woe, never to return. Under a different course of treatment, he would have fixed his home either at his birthplace, or in its immediate vicinity, and in a life of frugality, usefulness, and comparative ease, blessed his parents, his neighborhood, and possibly the world, with a useful example — all, perhaps, grown out of his youthful indulgence in the possession of a rabbit-warren, or some like trifling matter.

This may appear to be small morals, as well as small business. We admit it. But those who have been well, and indulgently, as well as methodically trained, may look back and see the influence which all such little things had upon their early thoughts and inclinations; and thus realize the importance of providing for the amusements and pleasures of children in their early years. The dovecote, the rabbitry, the poultry-yard, the sheep-fold, the calf-pen, the piggery, the young colt of a favorite mare, the yoke of yearling steers, or a fruit tree which they have planted, and nursed, and called it, or the fruit it bears, *their own*,—anything, in fact, which they can call *theirs*—are so many objects to bind boys to their homes, and hallow it with a thousand nameless blessings and associations, known only to those who have been its recipients. Heaven's blessings be on the family homestead!

"Be it ever so humble, there's no place like home!"

sung the imaginary maid of Milan, the beautiful creation of John Howard Payne, when returning from the glare and pomp of the world, to her native cottage in the mountains of Switzerland. And, although all out of date, and conventionally vulgar this sentiment may be *now* considered, such is, or should be the subdued, unsophisticated feeling of all natives of the farm house, and the country cottage. We may leave the quiet roof of our childhood; we may mix in the bustling contentions of the open world; we may gain its treasures; we may enjoy its greatness, its honors, and its applause; but there are times when they will all fade into nothing, in comparison with the peace, and quietude, and tranquil happiness of a few acres of land, **a comfortable roof, and contentment therewith!**

DAIRY BUILDINGS.

Wherever the dairy is made an important branch of farm production, buildings for its distinct accommodation are indispensable. The dairy is as much a *manufactory* as a cotton mill, and requires as much conveniences in its own peculiar line. We therefore set apart a building, on purpose for its objects; and either for cheese, or butter, separate conveniences are alike required. We commence with the

CHEESE DAIRY HOUSE.

This building is one and a half stories high, with a broad, spreading roof of 45° pitch; the ground plan is 10 feet between joists, and the posts 16 feet high. An ice-house, made on the plan already described, is at one end, and a wood-shed at the opposite end, of the same size. This building is supposed to be erected near the milking sheds of the farm, and in contiguity to the feeding troughs of the cows, or the piggery, and adapted to the convenience of feeding the whey to

CHEESE DAIRY HOUSE.

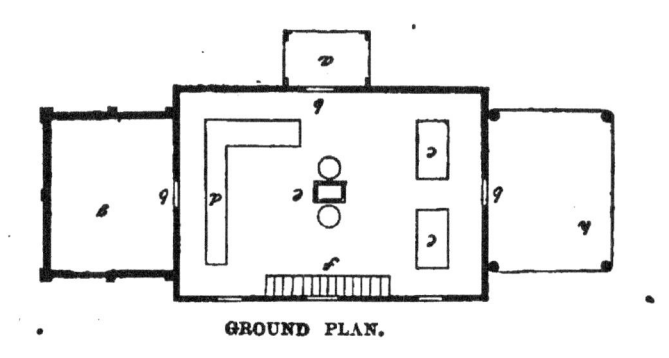

GROUND PLAN.

whichever of these animals the dairyman may select, as both, or either are required to consume it; and to which it may be conveyed in spouts from the dairy-room.

INTERIOR ARRANGEMENT.

The front door is protected by a light porch, (*a*,) entering by a door, (*b*,) the main dairy room. The cheese presses, (*c, c,*) occupy the left end of the room, between which a passage leads through a door, (*l*,) into the wood-shed, (*h*,) open on all sides, with its roof resting on four posts set in the ground. The large cheese-table, (*d*,) stands on the opposite end, and is 3 feet wide. In the center of the room is a chimney, (*e*,) with a whey and water boiler, and vats on each side. A flight of stairs, (*f*,) leading into the storage room above, is in the rear. A door, (*b*,) on the extreme right, leads into the ice-house, (*g*.) There are four windows to the room—two on each side, front and rear. In the loft are placed the shelves for storing the cheese, as soon as sufficiently prepared on the temporary table below. This loft is thoroughly ventilated by windows, and the heat of the sun upon it ripens the cheese rapidly for market. A trapdoor, through the floors, over which is hung a tackle, admits the cheese from below, or passes it down, when prepared for market.

The cheese house should, if possible, be placed on a sloping bank, when it is designed to feed the whey to pigs; and even when it is fed to cows, it s more convenient to pass it to them on a lower level, than to carry it out in buckets. It may, however, if on level ground, be discharged into vats, in a cellar below, and pumped out as wanted. A cellar is convenient—indeed, almost indispensable—under the cheese dairy; and water should be so near as to be easily pumped, or drawn, into the vats and kettles used in running up the curd, or for washing the utensils used in the work. When the milk is kept over night, for the next morning's curd, temporary tables may be placed near the ice-room, to hold the pans or tubs in which it may be set, and the ice used to temper the milk to the proper degree for raising the cream. If the dairy be of such extent as to require larger accommodation than the plan here suggested, a room or two may be partitioned off from the main milk and pressing-room, for washing the vessels and other articles employed, and for setting the milk. Every facility should be made for neatness in all the operations connected with the work.

Different accommodations are required, for making the different kinds of cheese which our varied markets demand, and in the fitting up of the dairy-house, no *positive* plan of arrangement can be laid down, suited alike to all the work which may be demanded. The dairyman, therefore, will best arrange all these for the particular convenience which he requires. The main plan, and style of building however, we think will be generally approved, as being in an agreeable architectural style, and of convenient construction and shape for the objects intended.

THE BUTTER DAIRY.

This, if pursued on the same farm with the cheese dairy, and at different seasons of the year, may be carried on in the lower parts of the same building But as it is usually a distinct branch of business, when prosecuted as the chief object on a farm, it should have accommodations of its own kind, which should be fitted up specially for that purpose.

We cannot, perhaps, suggest a better model of a building for the butter dairy, than the one just submitted for the cheese-house, only that there is no necessity for the upper story; and the posts of the main building should not stand more than nine feet above the sills. A good, walled cellar, well lighted, as a room for setting the milk, is indispensable, with a broad, open flight of steps, from the main floor above, into it. Here, too, should stand the stone slabs, where the butter is worked, and the churns, to be driven by hand, or water, or animal power, as the two latter may be provided, and introduced into the building by belt, shaft, or crank. If running water can be brought on to the milk-shelves, from a higher level, which, fo this purpose, should have curbs two or three inches high on their sides, it can flow in a constant gentle current over them, among the pans, from a receiving vat, in which ice is deposited, to keep the milk at the proper temperature—about 55° Fahrenheit—for raising the cream; and, if the quantity of milk be large, the shelves can be so arranged, by placing each tier of shelf lower than the last, like steps, that the water may pass among them all before it escapes from the room. Such a mode of applying water and ice, renders the entire process of cream-rising almost certain in all weathers, and is highly approved wherever it has been practiced. The low temperature of the room, by the aid of water and ice, is also beneficial to the butter packed in kegs, keeping it cool and sweet—as much like a spring-house as possible, in its operation.

The washing and drying of pans, buckets, churns, and the heating of water, should all be done in the room above, where the necessary kettles are set, and kept from contact with the cool atmosphere of the lower room. The latter apartment should have a well-laid stone or brick floor, filled and covered with a strong cement of water lime, and sloping gradually to the outer side, where all the water may pass off by a drain, and everything kept sweet and clean. The buttermilk may, as in the case of the whey, in the cheese dairy, be passed off in spouts to the pigsty, which should not be far distant.

As all this process of arrangement, however, must conform somewhat to the shape of the ground, t_ locality, and the facilities at hand where it may be constructed; it is hardly possible to give any one system of detail which is applicable to an uniform mode of structure; and much will be left to the demands and the skill of the dairyman himself, in the plan he may finally adopt.

THE WATER RAM.

As water, and that of a good quality, and in abundant quantity, is indispensable to the various demands of the farm, it is worth some pains to provide it in the most economical manner, and at the most convenient points for use. In level grounds, wells are generally dug, and the water drawn up by buckets or pumps. In a hilly country, springs, and streams from higher grounds, may be brought in by the aid of pipes, the water flowing naturally, under its own head, wherever it may be wanted, away from its natural stream.

But, of all contrivances to elevate water from a *lower* fountain, or current, to a *higher* level, by its *own action*, the Water Ram is the most complete in its operation, and perfect in its construction, of anything within our knowledge. And as it may not be generally known to our readers, at our request, Messrs. A. B. ALLEN & Co., of New York—who keep them of all sizes for sale, at their agricultural warehouse, No'.

189 and 191, Water-street—have kindly furnished us with the following description of the machine, given by W. & B. Douglass, of Middletown, Connecticut, manufacturers of the article:

WATER RAM.

"H, spring or brook. C, drive, or supply-pipe from brook to ram. G, discharge pipe, conveying water to house or other point required for use. B, D, A, E, I, the Ram. J, the plank or other foundation to which the machine is secured for use.

"The various uses of the ram are at once obvious, viz., for the purposes of irrigating lands, and supplying dwellings, barnyards, gardens, factories, villages, engines, railroad stations, &c., with running water.

"The simplicity of the operation of this machine, together with its effectiveness, and very apparent durability, renders it decidedly the most important and valuable apparatus yet developed in hydraulics, for forcing a portion of a running stream of water to any elevation, proportionate to the fall obtained. It is perfectly applicable where no more than eighteen inches fall can be had; yet, the greater the fall applied, the more powerful the operation of the machine, and the higher the water may be conveyed. The relative proportions between the water raised, and wasted, is dependent entirely upon the relative height of the spring or source of supply above the ram, and the elevation to which it is required to be raised. The quantity raised varying in proportion to the height to which it is conveyed, with a given fall; also, the distance which the water has to be conveyed, and consequent length of pipe, has some bearing on the quantity of water raised and discharged by the ram; as, the longer the pipe through which the water has to be forced by the machine, the greater the friction to be overcome, and the more the power consumed in the operation; yet, it is common to apply the ram for conveying the water distances of one and two hundred rods, and up elevations of one and two hundred feet. Ten feet fall from the spring, or brook, to the ram, is abundantly sufficient for forcing up the water to any elevation under say one hundred and fifty feet in height, above the level of the point where the ram is located; and the same ten feet fall will raise the water to a much higher point than above last named, although in a *diminished* quantity, in proportion as the height is increased. When a sufficient quantity of water is raised with a given fall, it is not advisable to increase said fall, as in so doing the force with which the ram works is increased, and tne amount of labor which it has to perform greatly augmented, the wear and tear of the machine proportionably increased, and the durability of the same lessened; so that economy, in the expense of keeping the ram in repair, would dictate that no greater fall should be applied, for propelling the ram, than is sufficient tc raise a requisite supply of water to the place of use To enable any person to make the calculation, as to what fall would be sufficient to apply to the ram, to raise a sufficient supply of water to his premises, we would say, that in conveying it any ordinary distance, of say fifty or sixty rods, it may be safely calculated that about one-seventh part of the water can be raised and discharged at an elevation above the ram five times as high as the fall which is applied to the ram, or one-fourteenth part can be raised and discharged, say ten times as high as the fall applied; and so in that proportion, as the fall or rise is varied. Thus, if the ram be placed under a head or fall of five feet, of every seven gallons drawn from the spring, one may be raised twenty-five feet, or half a gallon fifty feet. Or with ten feet fall applied to the machine, of every fourteen gallons drawn from the spring, one gallon may be raised to the height of one hundred feet above the machine; and so in like proportion, as the fall or rise is increased or diminished.

"It is presumed that the above illustrations of what the machine will do under certain heads and rise, will be sufficient for all practical purposes, to enable purchasers of the article to determine, with a sufficient degree of nicety, as to the head or fall to apply to the ram for a given rise and distance, which they may wish to overcome in raising water from springs or brooks to their premises, or other places where water is required. Yet, we have the pleasure of copying the following article, which we find in the 'American Agriculturist,' a very valuable journal published by C. M. Saxton, 152 Fulton-street, New York, which may serve to corroborate our statements as to what our ram will accomplish under given circumstances:

"'The following is a correct statement of a water ram I have had in successful operation for the last six months:

"'1. The fall from the surface of the water in the spring is four feet. 2. The quantity of water delivered per ten minutes, at my house, is three and a quarter gallons, and that discharged at the ram twenty-five gallons. Thus, nearly one-seventh part of the water is saved. 3. The perpendicular height of the place of delivery above the ram is nineteen feet—say fifteen feet above the surface of the spring. 4. The length of the pipe leading from the ram to the house is one hundred and ninety feet. 5. The pipe leading from the ram to the house has three right angles, rounded by curves. 6. The ram is of Douglass' make, of a small size. 7. The length of the drive or supply-pipe is sixty feet. Its inner diameter one inch. 8. The depth of water in the spring, over the drive pipe, is six inches. 9. The inner diameter of the pipe, conducting the water from the ram to the house, is three-eighths of an inch.

"'I consider it very essential that the drive or supply-pipe should be laid as straight as possible, as in the motion of the water in this pipe consists the power of the ram.
V. H. HALLOCK.
NORTH-EAST CENTER, N. Y., April 2d, 1849.'"

We have seen several of these rams at work; and in any place where the required amount of fall can be had, with sufficient water to supply the demand, we are entirely satisfied that no plan so cheap and efficient can be adopted, by which to throw it to a higher level, and at a distance from the point of its flow. We heartily commend it to all who need a thing of the kind, and have at hand the facilities in the way of a stream for its use.

It is hardly worth while to add, that by the aid of the ram, water can be thrown into every room in the dwelling house, as well as into the various buildings, and yards, and fields of the farm, wherever it may be required.

RAT-PROOF GRANARY.

This plan, and description, we take from an agricultural periodical published in New York — "The Plow." We can recommend no plan of a better kind for the objects required. It is an old-fashioned structure, which many of our readers will recognize — only, that it is improved in some of its details.

GRANARY

The illustration above needs but little description. The posts should be stone, if procurable, one foot square, and four feet long, set one-third in the ground, and capped with smooth flat stones, four to six inches thick, and two feet, at least, across. If wooden posts are used, make them sixteen inches square, and set them in a hole previously filled, six inches deep, with charcoal, or rubble stone and lime grouting, and fill around the posts with the same. Four inches from the top, nail on a flange of tin or sheet iron, six inches wide, the projecting edge of which may be serrated, as a further preventive against the depredating rascals creeping around. The steps are hinged to the door-sill, and should have a cord and weight attached to the door, so that whenever it is shut, the steps should be up also; this would prevent the possibility of carelessness in leaving them down for the rats to walk up. The sides should be made of slats, with large cracks between, and the floor under the corn-crib, with numerous open joints; no matter if shattered corn falls through, let the pigs and chickens have it; the circulation of the air through the pile of corn, will more than pay for all you will lose through the floor. If you intend to have sweet grain, be sure to have a ventilator in the roof, and you may see by the vane on the top of it, how the wind will always blow favorably for you.

IMPROVED DOMESTIC ANIMALS.

Having completed the series of subjects which we had designed for this work, we are hardly content to send it out to the public, without inviting the attention of our farmers, and others who dwell in the country and occupy land, to the importance of surrounding themselves with the best breeds of domestic animals, as an item of increased profit in their farm management, and as a subject of interest and satisfaction to themselves in the embellishment of their grounds.

We have addressed ourselves through these pages to the good sense of men who, in their general character and pursuits, comprise the most stable class of our population. We have endeavored to impress upon them the importance of providing all the conveniences and comforts to themselves, in their dwellings, as well as the due provision for their animals and crops, in the rougher farm buildings, which their circumstances will admit; and we trust they have been shown that it is proper economy so to do. We have, in addition to these, somewhat dilated upon objects of embellishment, in the way of grounds to surround them, and trees to beautify them, which will in no way interfere with a just economy, and add greatly to the pleasure and interest of their occupation. We now want them to introduce into those grounds such domestic animals as shall add to their ornament, and be far more profitable to themselves, than the inferior things which are called the common, or native stock of the country. Without this last lesson, half our object would be lost. Of what avail will be the best provision for the conveniences of a family, and the labors of the farm, if the farm be badly cultivated, and a worthless or inferior stock be kept upon it? The work is but half done at best; and the inferiority of the last will only become more conspicuous and contemptible, in contrast with the superior condition of the first.

It is not intended to go into an examination of the farm-stock of our country at large, nor into their modes of treatment; but, to recommend such varieties of animals as are profitable in their breeding and keeping, both to the professional farmer in his vocation, and to such as, beyond this, find them an object of convenience, or of pleasure.

We, in America, are comparatively a young people. Yet, we have surmounted *necessity*. We have arrived at the period when we enjoy the fruits of competence — some of us, the luxuries of wealth. A taste for superior domestic animals has been increasing, and spreading over the United States for many years past; so that now, a portion of our farmers and country people understand somewhat of the subject. It has been thoroughly demonstrated, that good farm stock is better, and more profitable than poor stock. Still, a taste for good stock, and the advantages of keeping them, over the common stock of the country, is not *generally* understood; and that taste has to be cultivated. It is not altogether a thing of nature, any more than other faculties which require the aid of education to develope. We have known many people who had a fine perception in many things: an eye for a fine house, pleasant grounds, beautiful trees, and all the surroundings which such a place might command; and when these were complete, would place about it the veriest brutes, in the way of domestic animals, imaginable. The resident of the city, who lives at his country-house in summer, and selects a picture of mean or inferior quality, to hang up in his house by way of ornament, would be laughed at by his friends; yet he may drive into his grounds the meanest possible creature, in the shape of a cow, a pig, or a sheep, and it is all very well—for neither he nor they know any better; yet, the one is quite as much out of place as the other. The man, too, who, in good circumstances, will keep and drive a miserable horse, is the ridicule of his neighbors, because everybody knows what a good horse is, and that he should be well kept. Yet, the other stock on his farm may be the meanest trash in existence, and it creates no remark. On the contrary, one who at any *extra* cost has supplied himself with stock of the choicer kinds, let their superiority be ever so apparent, has often been the subject of ribaldry, by his unthinking associates. And such, we are sorry to say, is still the case in too many sections of our country. But, on the whole, both our public spirit, and our intelligence, is increasing, in such things.

Now, we hold it to be a *practical* fact, that no farm, or country place, can be complete in its appointments, without good stock upon it; and it is useless for any one to suppose that his farm, or his place, is *finished*, without it. The man who has a fine lawn, of any extent, about his house, or a park adjoining, should have something to graze it—for he cannot afford to let it lie idle; nor is it worth while, even if he can afford it, to be mowing the grass in it every fortnight during the summer, to make it sightly. Besides this, grass will grow under the trees, and that too thin, and short, for cutting. This ground must, of course, be pastured. Now, will he go and get a parcel of mean scrubs of cattle, or sheep, to graze it, surrounding his very door, and disgracing him by their vulgar, plebeian looks, and yielding him no return, in either milk, beef, mutton, or wool? Of course not, if he be a wise, or a provident man, or one who has any true taste in such matters. He will rather go and obtain the best stock he can get, of breeds suited to the climate, and soil, which will give him a profitable return, either in milk, or flesh, or their increase, for his outlay; and which will also embellish his grounds, and create an interest in his family for their care, and arrest the attention of those who visit him, or pass by his grounds. Of the proper selection of this branch of his stock, we shall now discourse.

In cattle, if your grounds be rich, and your grass abundant, the short-horns are the stock for them. They are "the head and front," in appearance, size, and combination of good qualities—the very aristocracy of all neat cattle. A well-bred, and well developed short-horn cow, full in the qualities which belong to ner character, is the very perfection of her kind. Her large, square form; fine orange, russet, or nut-colored muzzle; bright, prominent, yet mild, expressive eye, small, light horn; thin ears; clean neck; projecting brisket; deep, and broad chest; level back, and loin; broad hips; large, and well-spread udder, with its silky covering of hair, and clean, taper, wide-standing teats, giving twenty to thirty quarts of rich milk in a day; deep thigh, and twist; light tail; small, short legs; and, added to this, her brilliant and ever-varying colors of all, and every-intermingling shades of red, and white, or either of them alone; such, singly, or in groups, standing quietly under the shade of trees, grazing in the open field, or quietly resting upon the grass, are the very perfection of a cattle picture, and give a grace and beauty to the grounds which no living thing can equal.

Nor, in this laudation of the short-horns, are we at all mistaken. Go into the luxuriant blue-grass pastures of Kentucky; the rich, and wide-spread grazing regions of central and lower Ohio; the prairies of Indiana, and Illinois, just now beginning to receive them; the sweet, and succulent pastures of central and western New York, or on the Hudson river; and now and then, a finely-cultivated farm in other sections of the United States, where their worth has become established; and they present pictures of thrift, of excellence, of beauty, and of profit, that no other neat cattle can pretend to equal.

As a family cow, nothing can excel the short-horn in the abundance and richness of her milk, and in the profit she will yield to her owner; and, on every place where she can be supplied with abundance of food, she stands without a rival. From the short-horns, spring those magnificent fat oxen and steers, which attract so much admiration, and carry off the prizes, at our great cattle shows. Thousands of them, of less or higher grade in blood, are fed every year, in the Scioto, the Miami, and the other great feeding valleys of the west, and in the fertile corn regions of Kentucky, and taken to the New York and Philadelphia markets. As a profitable beast to the grazier, and the feeder, nothing can equal them in early maturity and excellence. For this purpose, the short horns are steadily working their way all over the vast cattle-breeding regions of the west; and, for the richness and abundance of her milk, the cow is eagerly introduced into the dairy, and milk-producing sections of the other states, where she will finally take rank, and maintain her superiority over all others, on rich and productive soils.

On lighter soils, with shorter pastures; or on hilly and stony grounds, another race of cattle may be kept, better adapted to such localities, than those just described. They are the Devons—also an English breed, and claimed there as an aboriginal race in England; and if any variety of cattle, exhibiting the blood-like beauty, and fineness of limb, the deep uniformity of color, and the gazelle-like brilliancy of their eye, can claim a remote ancestry, and a pure descent, the Devons can make such claim, beyond almost any other. They were introduced—save now and then an isolated animal at an earlier day—into the United States some thirty-two or three years ago, about the same time with the short-horns; and like them, have been added to, and improved by frequent importations since; until now, probably our country will show some specimens equal in quality to their high general character in the land of their nativity. Unlike the short-horn, the Devon is a much lighter animal, with a like fine expression of countenance; an elevated horn; more agile in form; yet finer in limb and bone; a deep mahogany-red in color; and of a grace, and beauty in figure excelled by no other breed whatever. The Devon cow is usually a good milker, for her size; of quiet temper; docile in her habits; a quick feeder; and a most satisfactory animal in all particulars. From the Devons, spring those beautifully-matched red working-oxen, so much admired in our eastern states; the superiors to which, in kindness, docility, endurance, quickness, and honesty of labor, no country can produce. In the *quality* of their beef, they are unrivaled by any breed of cattle in the United States; but in their early maturity for that purpose, are not equal to the short-horns.

Several beautiful herds of Devons are to be found in New York, in Maryland, in Connecticut, and in Massachusetts; and some few in other states, where they can be obtained by those who wish to purchase.

Another branch of domestic stock should also excite the attention of those who wish to embellish their grounds, as well as to improve the quality of their mutton—obtaining, withal, a fleece of valuable wool. These are the Southdown, and the Cotswold, Leicester, or other improved breeds of long-wooled sheep. There is no more peaceful, or beautiful small animal to be seen in an open park, or pleasure ground, or in the paddock of a farm, than these.

The Southdown, is a fine, compact, and solid sheep, with dark face and legs; quiet in its habits, mild in disposition, of a medium quality, and medium weight of fleece; and yielding a kind of mutton unsurpassed in flavor and delicacy—equal, in the estimation of many, to the finest venison. The carcass of a Southdown wether, when well fatted, is large, weighing, at two to three years old, a hundred to a hundred and twenty pounds. The ewe is a prolific breeder, and a good nurse. They are exceedingly hardy, and will thrive equally well in all climates, and on all our soils, where they can live. There is no other variety of sheep which has been bred to that high degree of perfection, in England. The great Southdown breeder, Mr. Webb, of Batraham, has often received as high as fifty, to one hundred guineas, in a season, for the *use* of a single ram. Such prices show the estimation in which the best Southdowns are held there, as well as their great popularity among the English farmers.

The Cotswold, New Oxford, and Leicester sheep, of the long-wooled variety, are also highly esteemed, in the same capacity as the Southdowns.

They are large; not so compactly built as the Southdowns; producing a heavy fleece of long wool, mostly used for combing, and making into worsted stuffs. They are scarcely so hardy, either, as the Southdowns, nor are they so prolific. Still, they have many excellent qualities; and although their mutton has not the fine grain, nor delicacy, of the other, it is of enormous weight, when well fattened, and a most profitable carcass. It has sometimes reached a weight of two hundred pounds, when dressed. They are gentle, and quiet in their habits; white in the face and legs; and show a fine and stately contrast to the Southdowns, in their increased size, and breadth of figure. They require, also, a somewhat richer pasture; but will thrive on any good soil, yielding sweet grasses.

That the keeping of choice breeds of animals, and the cultivation of a high taste for them, is no *vulgar* matter, with even the most exalted intellects, and of men occupying the most honorable stations in the state, and in society; and that they concern the retired gentleman, as well as the practical farmer, it is only necessary to refer to the many prominent examples in Great Britain, and our own country, within the last fifty years.

The most distinguished noblemen of England, and Scotland, have long bred the finest of cattle, and embellished their home parks with them. The late Earl Spencer, one of the great patrons of agricultural improvement in England, at his death owned a herd of two hundred of the highest bred short-horns, which he kept on his home farm, at Wiseton. The Dukes of Bedford, for the last century and a half, have made extraordinary exertions to improve their several breeds of cattle. The late Earl of Leicester, better known, perhaps, as Mr. Coke, of Holkham, and the most celebrated farmer of his time, has been long identified with his large and select herds of Devons, and his flocks of Southdowns. The Duke of Richmond has his great park at Goodwood stocked with the finest Southdowns, Short-horns, and Devons. Prince Albert, even, has caught the infection of such liberal and useful example, and the royal park at Windsor is tenanted with the finest farm stock, of many kinds; and he is a constant competitor at the great Smithfield cattle shows, annually held in London. Besides these, hundreds of the nobility, and wealthy country gentlemen of Great Britain, every year compete with the intelligent farmers, in their exhibitions of cattle, at the royal and provincial shows, in England, Scotland and Ireland.

In the United States, Washington was a great promoter of improvement in farm stock, and introduced on to his broad estate, at Mount Vernon, many foreign animals, which he had sent out to him at great expense; and it was his pride to show his numerous and distinguished guests, his horses, cattle, sheep, and pigs. Henry Clay, of Kentucky, was among the first promoters of the improvement of domestic animals in the fertile region, of which his own favorite Ashland is the center; and to his continued efforts in the breeding of the finest short-horns, and mules, is the state of Kentucky greatly indebted for its reputation in these descriptions of stock. Daniel Webster has introduced on to his estate, at Marshfield, the finest cattle, and sheep suited to its soil and climate, and takes much pride in showing their good qualities. Indeed, we have never heard either of these two last remarkable men more eloquent, than when discoursing of their cattle, and of their pleasure in ranging over their pastures, and examining their herds and flocks. They have both been importers of stock, and liberal in their dissemination among their agricultural friends and neighbors. Public-spirited, patriotic men, in almost every one of our states, have either imported from Europe, or drawn from a distance in their own country, choice animals, to stock their own estates, and bred them for the improvement of their several neighborhoods. Merchants, and generous men of other professions, have shown great liberality, and the finest taste, in importing, rearing, and distributing over the country the best breeds of horses, cattle, sheep, and pigs. Their own beautiful home grounds are embellished with them, in a style that all the dumb statuary in existence can not equal in interest — models of grace, and beauty, and utility, which are in vain sought among the sculpture, or paintings of ancient time. And many a plain and unpretending farmer of our country, emulating such laudable examples, now shows in his luxuriant pastures, and well-filled barns and stables, the choicest specimens of imported stock; and their prizes, won at the cattle shows, are the laudable pride of themselves, and their families.

Nor is this laudable taste, confined to *men* alone. Females of the highest worth, and domestic example, both abroad and at home, cultivate a love for such objects, and take much interest in the welfare of their farm stock. We were at the annual state cattle show, in one of our large states, but a short time since, and in loitering about the cattle quarter of the grounds, met a lady of our acquaintance, with a party of her female friends, on a tour of inspection among the beautiful short-horns, and Devons, and the select varieties of sheep. She was the daughter of a distinguished statesman, who was also a large farmer, and a patron of great liberality, in the promotion of fine stock in his own state. She was bred upon the farm, and, to rare accomplishments in education, was possessed of a deep love for all rural objects; and in the stock of the farm she took a peculiar interest. Her husband was an extensive farmer, and a noted breeder of fine animals.

She had her own farm, too, and cattle upon it, equally as choice as his, in her own right; and they were both competitors at the annual exhibitions. Introduced to her friends, at her request, we accompanied them in their round of inspection. There were the beautiful cows, and the younger cattle, and the sheep—all noticed, criticised, and remarked upon; and with a judgment, too, in their various properties, which convinced us of her sound knowledge of their physiology, and good qualities, which she explained to her associates with all the familiarity that she would a tambouring frame, or a piece of embroidery. There was no squeamish fastidiousness; no affectation of prudery, in this; but all natural as the pure flow of admiration in a well-bred lady could be. At her most comfortable, and hospitable residence, afterward, she showed us, with pride, the several cups, and other articles of plate, which her family had won as prizes, at the agricultural exhibitions; and which she intended to preserve, as heir-looms to her children. This is not a solitary example; yet, a too rare one, among our fair countrywomen. Such a spirit is contagious, and we witness with real satisfaction, their growing taste in such laudable sources of enjoyment: contrary to the *parvenue* affectation of a vast many otherwise sensible and accomplished females of our cities and towns—comprising even the wives and daughters of farmers, too—who can saunter among the not over select, and equivocal representations, among the paintings and statuary of our public galleries; and descant with entire freedom, on the various attitudes, and artistical merits of the works before them; or gaze with apparent admiration upon the brazen pirouettes of a public dancing girl, amid al' the equivoque of a crowded theater; and yet, whose delicacy is shocked at the exhibitions of a cattle show! Such females as we have noticed, can admire the living, moving beauty of animal life, with the natural and easy grace of purity itself, and without the slightest suspicion of a stain of vulgarity. From the bottom of our heart, we trust that a reformation is at work among our American women, in the promotion of a taste, and not only a taste, but a genuine *love* of things connected with country life. It was not so, with the mothers, and the wives, of the stern and earnest men, who laid the foundations of their country's freedom and greatness. They were women of soul, character, and stamina; who grappled with the *realities* of life, in their labors; and enjoyed its pleasures with truth and honesty. This over-nice, mincing delicacy, and sentimentality, in which their grand-daughters indulge, is but the off-throw of the boarding-school, the novelist, and the prude — mere "leather and prunella." Such remarks may be thought to lie beyond the line of our immediate labor. But in the discussion of the collateral subjects which have a bearing upon country life and residence, we incline to make a clean breast of it, and drop such incidental remark as may tend to promote the enjoyment, as well as instruction, of those whose sphere of action, and whose choice in life is amid the pure atmosphere, and the pure pleasures of the country.

WATER-FOWLS.

If a stream flow through the grounds, in the vicinity of the house; or a pond, or a small lake be near, a few varieties of choice water-fowls may be kept, adding much to the interest and amusement of the family. Many of the English nobility, and gentry, keep swans for such purpose. They are esteemed a bird of much grace and beauty, although silent, and of shy, unsocial habits, and not prolific in the production of their young. For such purposes as they are kept in England, the great African goose, resembling the China, but nearly double in size, is a preferable substitute in this country. It is a more beautiful bird in its plumage; equally graceful in the water; social, and gentle in its habits; breeding with facility, and agreeable in its voice, particularly at a little distance. The African goose will attain a weight of twenty to twenty-five pounds. Its body is finely formed, heavily feathered, and its flesh is of delicate flavor. The top of the head, and the back of its neck, which is long, high, and beautifully arched, is a dark brown; its bill black, with a high protuberance, or knob, at its junction with the head; a dark hazel eye, with a golden ring around it; the under part of the head and neck, a soft ash-color; and a heavy dewlap at the throat. Its legs and feet are orange-colored; and its belly white. Taken altogether, a noble and majestic bird.

CHINA GOOSE.

The small brown China goose is another variety which may be introduced. She is nearly the color of the African, but darker; has the same black bill, and high protuberance on it, but without the dewlap under the throat; and has black legs and feet. She is only half the size of the other; is a more prolific layer,— frequently laying three or four clutches of eggs in a year; has the same character of voice; an equally high, arched neck, and is quite as graceful in the water. The neck of the goose in the cut should be one-third longer, to be an accurate likeness.

The White China is another variety, in size and shape like the last, but perfectly white, with an orange colored bill and legs. Indeed, no swan can be more beautiful than this, which is of the same pure, clean plumage, and, in its habits and docility, equally a favorite with the others we have described.

The Bremen goose is still another variety, of about the same size as the African, but in shape and appearance, not unlike the common goose, except in color, which is pure white. Young geese of this breed, at nine months old, frequently weigh twenty pounds, alive. We have had them of that weight, and for the table, none can be finer. They are equally prolific as the common goose, but, as a thing of ornament, are far behind the African and the China. Still, they are a stately bird, and an acquisition to any grounds where water-fowls are a subject of interest, convenience, or profit.

All these birds are more domestic, if possible, than the common goose, and we have found them less troublesome, not inclined to wander abroad, and, in all the qualities of such a bird, far more agreeable. We have long kept them, and without their presence, should consider our grounds as incomplete, in one of the most attractive features of animated life.

It is too much a fault of our farming population, that they do not pay sufficient attention to many little things which would render their homes more interesting, both to themselves, if they would only think so, and to their families, most certainly. If parents have no taste for such objects as we have recommended, or even others more common, they should encourage their children in the love of them, and furnish them for their amusement. The very soul of a farmer's home is to cluster every thing about it which shall make it attractive, and speak out the character of the country, and of his occupation, in its full extent. Herds and flocks upon the farm are a matter of course; and so are the horses, and the pigs. But there are other things, quite as indicative of household abundance, and domestic enjoyment. The pigeons, and the poultry of all kinds, and perhaps the rabbit warren, which are chiefly in charge of the good housewife, and her daughters, and the younger boys, show out the domestic feeling and benevolence of character in the family, not to be mistaken. It is a sign of enjoyment, of domestic contentment, and of mental cultivation, even, that will lead to something higher, and more valuable in after life; and it is in such light that it becomes an absolute *duty* of the farmer who seeks the improvement and education of his children, to provide them with all these little objects, to engage their leisure hours and promote their happiness. How different a home like this from one —which is, really, not a home—where no attention is paid to such minor attractions; where a few starveling things, by way of geese, perhaps, picked half a dozen times a year, to within an inch of their lives, mope about the dirty premises, making their nightly sittings in the door yard, if the house has one; a stray turkey, or two, running, from fear of the untutored dogs, into the nearest wood, in the spring, to make their rude nests, and bring out half a clutch of young, and creeping about the fields through the summer with a chicken or two, which the foxes, or other vermin, have spared, and then dogged down in the winter, to provide a half got-up Christmas-dinner; and the hens about the open buildings all the year, committing their nuisances in every possible way! There need be no surer indication than this, of the utter hopelessness of progress for good, in such a family.

A WORD ABOUT DOGS.

We always loved a dog; and it almost broke our little heart, when but a trudging schoolboy, in our first jacket-and-trowsers, our kind mother made us take back the young puppy that had hardly got its eyes open, which we one day brought home, to be kept until it was fit to be taken from its natural nurse. We are now among the boys, John, Tom, and Harry; and intend to give them the benefit of our own experience in this line, as well as to say a few words to the elder brothers,— and fathers, even,— if they do not turn up their noses in contempt of our instruction, on a subject so much beneath their notice.

We say that we love dogs: not *all* dogs, however. But we love some dogs — of the right breeds. There is probably no other civilized country so dog-ridden as this, both in

> "Mongrel, puppy, whelp, and hound,
> And curs of *low* degree."

Goldsmith, kind man that he was, must have been a capital judge of dogs, like many other poetical gentlemen. Still, other men than poets are sometimes good judges, and great lovers of dogs; but the mass of people are quite as well satisfied with one kind of dog as with another, so that it be a dog; and they too often indulge in their companionship, much to the annoyance of good neighborhood, good morals, and, indeed, of propriety, thrift, and common justice. Of all these we have nothing to say—here, at least. Ours is a "free country"—for dogs, if for nothing else. Nor shall we discuss the various qualities, or the different breeds of dogs for sporting purposes. We never go out shooting; nor do we take a hunt — having no taste that way. Perhaps in this we are to be pitied; but we are content as it is. Therefore we shall let the hounds, and pointers, and setters, the springers, and the land and the water spaniels, all alone. The mastiffs, and the bull dogs, too, we shall leave to those who like them. The poodle, and the little lap-dog of other kinds, also, we shall turn over to the kindness of those who—we are sorry for them, in having nothing better to interest themselves about—take a pleasure in keeping and tending them.

We want to mix in a little *usefulness*, as well as amusement, in the way of a dog; and after a whole life, thus far, of dog companionship, and the trial of pretty much every thing in the line of a dog—from the great Newfoundland, of a hundred pounds weight, down to the squeaking little whiffet, of six—we have, for many years past, settled down into the practical belief that the small ratting terrier is the only one, except the shepherd dog, we care to keep; and of these, chiefly, we shall speak.

There are many varieties of the Terrier. Some are large, weighing forty or fifty pounds, rough-haired, and savage looking. There is the bull-terrier, of less size, not a kindly, well-disposed creature to strangers; but irrascibly inclined, and unamiable in his deportment; still useful as a watch-dog, and a determined enemy to all vermin, whatever. Then, again, are the small rat-terriers, as they are termed, weighing from a dozen to twenty pounds; some with rough, long, wiry hair; a fierce, whiskered muzzle; of prodigious strength for their size; wonderful instinct and sagacity; kind in temper; and possessing valuable qualities, bating a lack of beauty in appearance. They are of all colors, but are generally uniform in their color, whatever it be. Another kind, still, is the smooth terrier, of the same sizes as the last; a very pretty dog indeed; with a kinder disposition to mankind; yet equally destructive to vermin, and watchful to the premises which they inhabit, or of whatever else is put under their charge. The fidelity of the terrier to his master is wonderful; equal, if not superior to any other dog whatever. In courage and perseverance, in hardihood, and feats of daring, he has hardly an equal; and in general *usefulness*, no dog can compare with him.

THE SMOOTH TERRIER.

Sir Walter Scott, who was a great friend to dogs, as well as a nice and critical judge of their qualities, used to tell this story:—When a young man, first attending, as an advocate, the Jedburgh assizes, a notorious burglar engaged Sir Walter to defend him on his trial for housebreaking in the neighborhood. The case was a hard one; the proof direct and conclusive; and no ingenuity of the defence could avoid the conviction of the culprit. The matter was settled beyond redemption; and before he left for his imprisonment, or transportation, the thief requested Sir Walter to come into his cell. On meeting, the fellow frankly told his counsel that he felt very grateful to him for his efforts to clear him; that he had done the best he could; but the proof was too palpable against him. He would gladly reward Sir Walter for his services; but he had no money, and could only give him a piece of advice, which might, perhaps, be serviceable hereafter. Sir Walter heard him, no doubt, with some regret at losing his fee; but concluding to hear what he had to say. "You are a housekeeper, Mr. Scott. For security to your doors, use nothing but a common lock—if rusty and old, no matter; they are quite as hard to pick as any others. (Neither Chubbs' nor Hobbs' *non-pickable* locks were then invented.) Then provide yourself with a small rat terrier, and keep him in your house at night. There is no safety in a mastiff, or bull-dog, or in a large dog of any breed. They can always be appeased and quieted, and burglars understand them; but a terrier can neither be terrified nor silenced; nor do we attempt to break in where one is known to be kept." Sir Walter heeded the advice, and, in his housekeeping experience, afterward, confirmed the good qualities of the terrier, as related to him by the burglar. He also commemorated the conversation by the following not exceedingly poetical couplet:

> "A terrier dog and a rusty key,
> Was Walter Scott's first Jedburgh fee."

The terrier has a perfect, thorough, unappeasable instinct for, and hatred to all kinds of vermin. He takes to rats and mice as naturally as a cat. He will scent out their haunts and burrows. He will lie for hours by their places of passage, and point them with the sagacity of a pointer at a bird. He is as quick as lightning, in pouncing upon them, when in sight, and rarely misses them when he springs. A single bite settles the matter; and where there are several rats found together, a dog will frequently dispatch half a dozen of them, before they can get twenty feet from him. A dog of our own has killed that number, before they could get across the stable floor. In the grain field, with the harvesters, a terrier will catch hundreds of field-mice in a day; or, in the hay field, he is equally destructive. With a woodchuck, a raccoon, or anything of their size — even a skunk, which many dogs avoid — he engages, with the same readiness that he will a rat. The night is no bar to his vigils. He has the sight of an owl, in the dark. Minks, and weasels, are his aversion, as much as other vermin. He will follow the first into the water, till he exhausts him with diving, and overtakes him in swimming. He is a hunter, too. He will tree a squirrel, or a raccoon, as readily as the best of sporting dogs. He will catch, and hold a pig, or anything not too large or heavy for him. He will lie down on your garment, and watch it for hours; or by anything else left in his charge. He will play with the children, and share their sports as joyfully as a dumb creature can do; and nothing can be more affectionate, kind, and gentle among them. He is cleanly, honest, and seldom addicted to tricks of any kind.

We prefer the high-bred, smooth, English terrier, to any other variety. They are rather more gentle in temper, and very much handsomer in appearance, than the rough-haired kind; but perhaps no better in their useful qualities. We have kept them for years; we keep them now; and no reasonable inducement would let us part with them. A year or two ago, having accidentally lost our farm terrier, and nothing remaining on the place but our shepherd dog, the buildings soon swarmed with rats. They were in, and about everything. During the winter, the men who tended the horses, and cattle, at their nightly rounds of inspection, before going to bed, would kill, with their clubs, three or four, in the barns and stables, every evening. But still the rats increased, and they became unendurable. They got into the grain-mows, where they burrowed, and brought forth with a fecundity second only to the frogs of Egypt. They gnawed into the granaries. They dug into the dairy. They entered the meat barrels. They carried off the eggs from the hen-nests. They stole away, and devoured, the young ducks, and chickens. They literally came into the "kneading troughs" of the kitchen. Oh! the rats were intolerable! Traps were no use. Arsenic was innocuous — they would n't touch it. Opportunity favored us, and we got two high-bred, smooth, English terriers — a dog, and a slut. Then commenced such a slaughter as we seldom see. The rats had got bold. The dogs caught them daily by dozens, as they came out from their haunts, fearless of evil, as before. As they grew more shy, their holes were watched, and every morning dead rats were found about the premises. The dogs, during the day, pointed out their holes. Planks were removed, nests were found, and the rats, young and old, killed, *instanter*. Hundreds on hundreds were slaughtered, in the first few weeks; and in a short time, the place was mostly rid of them, until enough only are left to keep the dogs "in play," and to show that in spite of all precaution, they will harbor wherever there is a thing to eat, and a possible place of covert for them to burrow.

To have the terrier in full perfection, it is important that the breed be *pure*. We are so prone to mix up everything we get, in this country, that it is sometimes difficult to get anything exactly as it should be; but a little care will provide us, in this particular. He should be properly trained, too, when young. That is, to mind what is said to him. His intelligence will be equal to all your wants in the *dog*-line; but he should not be *fooled* with. His instincts are *sure*. And, with a good education, the terrier will prove all you need in a farm, and a watch-dog. We speak from long experience, and observation.

The shepherd dog is another useful — almost indispensable — creature, on the sheep, or dairy farm. This cut is an accurate representation of the finest of the breed. To the flock-master, he saves a world of labor, in driving and gathering the flocks together, or from one field, or place, to another. To the sheep-drover, also, he is worth a man, at least; and in many cases, can do with a flock what a man can not do. But for this labor, he requires training, and a strict, thorough education, by those who know how to do it. He is a peaceable, quiet creature; good for little else than driving, and on a stock farm will save fifty times his cost and keeping, every year. He is a reasonably good watch-dog, also; but he has neither the instinct, nor sagacity of the terrier, in that duty. To keep him

THE SHEPHERD DOG.

in his best estate, for his own peculiar work, he should not be troubled with other labors, as it distracts his attention from his peculiar duties. We had a remarkably good dog, of this kind, a few years since. He was worth the services of a stout boy, in bringing up the cattle, and sheep, until an idle boy or two, in the neighborhood, decoyed him out in "*cooning,*" a few nights during one autumn — in which he proved a most capital hunter; and after that, he became worthless, as a cattle dog. He was always rummaging around among the trees, barking at birds, squirrels, or any live thing that he could find; and no man could coax him back to the dull routine of his duty. A shepherd dog should never go a-hunting.

We would not be understood as condemning everything else, excepting the dogs we have named, for farm use. The Newfoundland, and the mastiff, are enormously large dogs, and possessed of some noble qualities. They have performed feats of sagacity and fidelity which have attracted universal admiration; but, three to one, if you have them on your farm, they will kill every sheep upon it; and their watchfulness is no greater than that of the shepherd dog, or the terrier. We have spoken of such as we have entire confidence in, and such as we consider the best for useful service. There are some kinds of cur dog that are useful. They are of no *breed* at all, to be sure; but have, now and then, good qualities; and when nothing better can be got, they will do for a make-shift. But as a rule, we would be equally particular in the *breed* of our dog, as we would in the breed of our cattle, or sheep. There are altogether too many dogs kept, in the country, and most usually by a class of people who have no need of them, and which prove only a nuisance to the neighborhood, and a destruction to the goods of others. Thousands of useful sheep are annually destroyed by them; and in some regions of the country, they can not be kept, by reason of their destruction by worthless dogs, which are owned by the disorderly people about them. In a western state, some time ago, in conversing with a large farmer, who had a flock of perhaps a hundred sheep running in one of his pastures, and who also kept a dozen hounds, for hunting, we asked him whether the dogs did not kill his sheep? "To be sure they do," was his reply; "but the dogs are worth more than the sheep, for they give us great sport in hunting deer, and foxes; and the sheep only give us a little mutton, now and then, and some wool for the women to make into stockings!" This is a mere matter of taste, thought we, and the conversation on that subject dropped. Yet, this man had a thousand acres of the richest land in the world; raised three or four hundred acres of corn, a year; fed off a hundred head of cattle, annually; and sold three hundred hogs every year, for slaughtering!

FISH-PONDS.

Wherever water in sufficient quantity can be introduced by a side-cut from a stream, by damming the stream itself or by drawing it from a large spring, and the face of the ground in the vicinity of the house can afford a suitable place, either by inclosing a natural hollow or ravine by a dam, or by excavation, a fishpond is well worthy the attention of a country resident, even if he be but a small farmer. As an ornamental feature of the place, it is of the most agreeable character; its utility will be unquestioned. The size of the pond is immaterial, beyond half an acre in area—less it should not be—and if it embrace even twenty, thirty, or fifty acres, provided the proprietor can afford to devote so much land to that object, it will be all the better for the fish, both in numbers and in quality.

The depth of water may vary—no matter how deep —but the deepest part should not be less than ten feet, that there may be a cool retreat for the fish in summer, and a warm resting-place in winter; and if a depth to that extent can be made close to the margin on a part of the boundary, it will be all the better, as the fish may then enjoy the overhanging shade of the bank. The shore should be undulating if possible; irregular in its outline, and a part of it shaded by trees and shrubbery, as fish love shade as well as sunshine. A part of the shore should be shallow, and shelve off gradually into the deep water, and if partially grown up with rushes, or lying on a smooth, clean sand or gravel, it will accommodate the different varieties of fish to bed and spawn upon; some preferring the shady and muddy bottom of the rush beds, and others the pebbly, clear and sunny floor of the pond for that object. The temperature of the water will vary, according to its depth and proximity to the shore, from ten to twenty degrees at any given time, thus affording accommodation to different varieties of the fish which may inhabit it in the various conditions of breeding, growth, and feeding, as they are enabled to treat themselves in their natural haunts in wild waters.

According to the clearness, temperature, and purity of the water, will depend the selection of the kinds of fish which are to inhabit it. If the soil forming the bed of the pond be light, and clean, and stony, and the water be let in from a spring, or a spring brook of a low temperature, the Speckled Trout, and the cold-water fishes which are found in the same natural waters with them, may be introduced. Yet for trout, the water should have some current. They are a playful and active fish, and nothing delights them more than the bubbling water of a spring, or the rapid shooting of a stream over a rugged bed. Still in cool and clear water, a pond will satisfy them if the circulation be such as to avoid stagnation. The trout, too, love a deep hole, under a shaded bank, by the side of a projecting rock, or beneath the roots of a huge tree. There the larger ones love to gather, and from such haunts are the finest specimens to be drawn with the hook. They love to spawn in clear eddies, in sunny spots, over a stony or sandy bed, where their young fry can feed upon the animalculi and insects which play about the margin.

The Yellow Perch, a beautiful and delicious fish, may also be introduced into clear and cool water. It is quick and active in its movements, bites readily at the hook, and is exceedingly prolific. In the spring and summer season it loves to lie among rushes on the margin of a gently-flowing stream or a still pond, when it spawns and breeds. The perch will thrive in water too warm and sluggish for the trout, but like the trout, it loves to retreat and hide itself under a bank in the deep shadow during the day.

If the pond be sufficiently extensive, the Bass, in its varieties may be introduced; but as they are a much larger fish than the trout or the perch, they require a greater depth of water and a wider range for their food. The bass is an excellent table fish, and prolific in the propagation of its kind.

The Pike might also be added, in clear and cool waters. But it is a voracious, heartless wretch preying upon every other fish of lesser size within its reach, and by its rapid movements enabled to dart and seize upon everything inhabiting the same waters from which it cannot escape. A single pike or two, introduced into a close pond, has been known within a few months to entirely depopulate it of all other sizeable fish. Although, in its natural haunts, a fish of excellent quality of flesh, they should hardly be introduced into the domestic pond.

The Yellow Carp (the gold fish) is a beautiful creature to throw into the pond. They are not a fish of prey upon its fellows, but live chiefly on insects and worms. They may be domesticated like the perch, and fed from the hand, and called by a bell to their accustomed feeding places in the pond. When turned out at large, their progeny will change into silver and brown varieties of color, while some of them will retain the deep orange of the originals. On the whole they are a beautiful and interesting fish, and should always be introduced into the pond.

In dark waters, resting on an oozy or muddy bottom, the European Carp is a capital and appropriate fish for propagation. It feeds like the yellow carp, chiefly on water-worms, and has a "sucker" mouth, and grows to the weight of five, to ten or twelve pounds.

The Mullet is also a good fish and of equal size to the carp, and when the waters are cold, of the finest flavor for the table. In warm weather, its flesh is apt to become soft and flavorless. The mullet also takes its food by suction. It is a fish of exceeding beauty, having large scales of most brilliant varying shades of silver, purple and yellow, which give it an uncommon richness in appearance. These "sucker-mouthed" fish do not take the hook like the trout, the perch, or the bass, but may be caught by the net, or spear, as they lie in the shallow water near the shore, either in the day-time, or by torch-light at night.

The Silver Eel may also be put into the muddy bottom pond, but when confined, they make sad havoc with the other fish, as well as with young ducks or goslings, if they are permitted to swim in it. Although a migratory fish, they will remain in confined waters; but they have too many disagreeable qualities in their social relations to be the companions of the better fish that we have named.

In all waters where edible fish are kept, smaller varieties should be introduced, as the Chub, the Sun Fish or Roach, the Dace, the Shiner, the Smelt, and the Minnow; they are prolific in breeding, and furnish abundant food for the Bass, the Trout, and the Perch, which fatten upon them. The larger of these yield the finest of sport to the children, with their pin hooks and thread lines if they have no better. They are a nice pan fish also, bating the multitude of their little bones; but fried to a crisp, they are seldom in the way. In stocking a new pond, a sufficient variety of both the smaller and the larger kinds should be introduced, so that a fair trial may be had with each, and such as the waters best suit will ultimately become the chief tenants of the domain; but if Pike and Eels be introduced, let them by all means be put in together, and alone, to feed upon the frogs and lizards, or each other as chance and might may govern. As a rule however, the small fry should have possession of the waters for at least one year in advance, that they may multiply to a sufficient extent to supply partial food to the larger ones; and as they spawn, and keep in the shallowest waters, they will thus propagate in sufficient abundance to prevent a future scarcity when their more voracious fellow-lodgers are introduced.

In ponds of sufficient extent, fish may be kept and

propagated to profit, aside from supplying the family with so great a luxury in food as fresh fish are usually esteemed. They may be fed with the offal meats of the slaughter-house or the farm, or with balls of flour or meal, boiled or baked. They may be called to a particular point of the pond to feed at regular hours, if they become accustomed to it. Such extra feeding will give them an earlier and increased growth, and having less need to prey upon the smaller fish, the stock of course will be largely increased.

The feeding and care of fish will also be a source of pleasure and amusement to the members of the family; and while away many an hour of leisure or idleness that might otherwise tempt away the younger ones to resorts of dissipation or vice. In short, aside from its useful objects, we would have the fish-pond, as we would the dove-cote or the rabbitry, to give pleasure and variety to the farm, and to cluster around it all the endearments with which life in the country should be surrounded.

To give the fish-pond its most ornamental features as an object of interest or beauty, it should be partially clothed with trees and shrubs. In trees we would select the soft or water maples, the willows, the water, or black ash, the birch, and the lowland poplar. In the way of shrubbery, the black alder, the wild rose, and the osier willow, make a beautiful fringe to a water margin. A certain expression of wildness should be given to the pond, where it is of any size, and if it have some hidden nooks and recesses difficult to approach from the shore, it will be all the better. Fish love seclusion. Indeed, a pond haunted on every side by the foot of man, or the tread of animals, is but an indifferent spot for their welfare, and the more it can resemble, in outward appearance and keeping, the wild water of the river, the lake, or the natural pond, the more congenial will it be to the tastes and habits of the fish, and of course more profitable to the proprietor.

It is scarcely necessary to add that the pond should have an outlet of sufficient capacity to let off its surplus water, and be thoroughly secured against accident in bursting away, as an occurrence of this kind might in a few hours, destroy the labor and solicitude o years.